SCREENING THE CITY

EDITED BY **MARK SHIEL**
AND **TONY FITZMAURICE**

VERSO

London · New York

First published by Verso 2003
This collection © Mark Shiel and Tony Fitzmaurice 2003
Individual chapters © the authors
The moral rights of the authors have been asserted

Verso
UK: 6 Meard Street, London W1F 0EG
USA: 180 Varick Street, New York, NY 10014–4606
www.versobooks.com

Verso is the imprint of New Left Books

ISBN 1–85984–690–4
ISBN 1–85984–476–6 (pbk)

British Library Cataloguing in Publication Data
A catalogue record for this book is available from the British Library

Library of Congress Cataloging-in-Publication Data
A catalog record for this book is available from the Library of Congress

Typeset in Garamond 3 and Gill Sans by The Running Head Limited, Cambridge
www.therunninghead.com

Printed and bound in Great Britain by
Bath Press

CONTENTS

ACKNOWLEDGMENTS

We would like to thank the Faculty of Arts and the Board of Studies of the Centre for Film Studies at University College Dublin for hosting the international, interdisciplinary *Cinema and the City* conference in March 1999 which was organized by us and in which this book has its origins. Our special thanks go to Professor Fergus D'Arcy, Dean of the Faculty of Arts.

We are particularly grateful to Mike Davis for his early support and encouragement in developing the book, and for sharing his ideas on many of the issues which underpin it. At Verso, Jane Hindle has been an enthusiastic and endlessly helpful editor, guiding the book through its various stages with patience and dedication throughout.

We are very grateful to have received research funding during the preparation of the book from two sources: for Mark Shiel, a Small Research Grant from the British Academy; for Tony Fitzmaurice, financial support from the Centre for Film Studies/UCD School of Film.

For practical assistance in the preparation of the final manuscript, we would particularly like to thank Margaret Brindley of the Centre for Film Studies/UCD School of Film.

Finally, as always, our warm gratitude goes to our respective families and friends for their support and inspiration.

Mark Shiel and Tony Fitzmaurice
Dublin, October 2002

INTRODUCTION

This book examines the relationship between the cinema and the city within the terms of the modernism/postmodernism debate which has animated critical discussion and analysis of culture and society since the 1960s. With regard to the cinema–city relationship, there has been for some time now a growing body of interest and research in the ways in which cinema has impacted upon the formation of cities, both physically and as cultural constructs, and the ways in which the city has impacted upon cinema in providing, for over a century, a particularly dynamic space of representational interest. The important work of such figures as Mike Davis, James Donald, and James Hay is only the most visible manifestation of a two-way process which has fundamentally changed the ways in which we think about motion pictures.[1] Recent years have witnessed the increasing interpollination of film studies with such diverse fields as architecture, urban studies, geography, sociology, and social theory, all of which have been newly invigorated by a distinctive "spatial turn."[2] At the same time there has been an intensified recognition within film studies of the city (and the city-film) as the archetypal ground for examination of visual and sensory experience, form and style, perception, cognition, and the meaning of the filmic image and filmic text.[3]

The work we present here seeks to extend this set of concerns by close examination of two crucial tendencies in twentieth-century cinematic and urban history. Part I of the book investigates the avant-garde and experimental film in

Central and Eastern European cities of the first half of the twentieth century and beyond, particularly as these have dealt with the experience of social collapse and totalitarian control. Part II considers realist or narrative cinema in North American cities since World War Two, particularly as these have envisioned or implied the possibility of revolutionary change in Western capitalist democracies. Another way of expressing this dichotomy is through the now established (though still contested) distinction between the "modern" and the "postmodern." The two-part construction of this book is intended to set up a dialectical argument over the usefulness and viability of such periodizing terminology as it may be applied to the history of film and urban society, while avoiding the schematic over-simplification which sometimes accompanies these categories.

Part I focuses upon cities from Moscow, Leningrad, and Berlin in the 1920s and 1930s, to Prague and Warsaw in the 1970s and 1980s. All of these were united in the twentieth century not only by the experience of acute social and political upheaval but by the emergence of film cultures which critiqued but also celebrated this experience in terms of a distinctively avant-gardist filmic practice. An aggressive strain of modernization in Central and Eastern Europe throughout the first half of the twentieth century produced both a peculiarly deep rift between a new urban–industrial capitalist society and feudal rural life, and a bitter antagonism between the bourgeois and proletarian classes which naturally established Moscow, Berlin, and other cities as the crucibles of socialist and communist revolutionary theory and practice. Accompanying these social and political conditions, such avant-garde movements in film as Russian Constructivism, German Expressionism, and the New Objectivity sought, through formal reflexivity, self-consciousness, and stylistic excess, to articulate the dynamism and contradictions of societies which seemed to exist in a state of perpetual crisis.

In his "Uncanny Spaces," Carsten Strathausen offers a close reading of Ruttmann's *Berlin, The Symphony of a Great City* (1927) and Vertov's *Man with a Movie Camera* (1929) as two archetypal "city films" which deployed a combination of everyday images and complex montage to articulate the new intensity of activity and sensation which defined life in the modern city. Strathausen draws on Siegfried Kracauer to argue that such avant-garde films were characterized by a profound "schizophrenia" between the desire to celebrate the "perceptual revolution" of urban modernity and an anxious (though unacknowledged) recognition of the actual emptiness and alienation of the metropolitan experience.[4]

Martin Gaughan uses *Berlin, The Symphony of a Great City* to examine the heated discourse which grew up around the film on its release and the associated phenomenon of the New Objectivity—that is, the dominant visual aesthetic which informed the film, art, architecture, and popular culture of the day, and which generally endorsed the rise of consumer-oriented urban modernity in Weimar Germany. Gaughan analyses in detail the writings of such seminal critics of Weimar culture as Walter Benjamin, Ernst Bloch, and Siegfried Kracauer in order to draw out the various and complex attitudes to avant-garde and mass culture which the film precipitated.[5] As Gaughan's chapter demonstrates, Weimar Germany was a paradigmatic moment in the history of the cinema–city relationship, not only in the films which it produced but in terms of the theoretical discourse and cultural analysis to which they gave rise.

This rich filmic and critical culture of Weimar Germany was, of course, shortly to be overrun by the rise of the Nazi regime. Strathausen and Gaughan stress the degree to which the abstract formalism of the city film, whatever its ideological good intentions, left avant-garde aesthetics open to appropriation by the newly emergent fascist regimes of Europe as well as to retrospective accusations of ideological weakness or complicity. If Vertov's *Man with a Movie Camera* was among the last experiments in Soviet montage to be tolerated by the Russian authorities before the Stalinist clampdown on artistic innovation in the 1930s, a parallel fate befell the German literary avant garde in the screen adaptation of Alfred Döblin's novel *Berlin Alexanderplatz* by Piel Jutzi in 1931.[6] As Peter Jelavich explains in "The City Vanishes," Jutzi's adaptation entailed an unhappy dilution of the formal and political radicalism of the source novel under the entertainment and profit imperatives of the mainstream German film industry within which it was produced, and in the increasingly hostile filmmaking and censorship environment which characterized Weimar Germany in the final two years before the establishment of Hitler's regime.

After World War Two, cinematic engagement with the Central and Eastern European city continued to be preoccupied with the common experience of the weak or dysfunctional state and its crisis of legitimation. Despite their obvious formal differences, the films of the Quay Brothers, Jan Švankmajer, and Krzysztof

Kieślowski are united by an interest in the creation of cinematic spaces of resistance to totalitarianism, the remembering and forgetting of Nazism and Stalinism, and their tragic implications. In contrast to the utopian contemporaneity of Weimar cinema their use of the later-twentieth-century form of avant-garde animation involves a turning away from the social reality and documentation of the city.

As Tyrus Miller explains, in their film *The Street of Crocodiles* (1986) the Brothers Quay present a Freudian landscape as an antidote to the material world of urban modernity. Invoking the fairytale imagery of Central European folklore, they invent an unstable urban terrain whose fragility allegorizes the traumatic history of occupation and domination of wartime Polish towns and cities and the larger history of deterritorialization and reterritorialization to which much of Central and Eastern Europe was subject throughout the twentieth century, from the dissolution of the Ottoman and Austro-Hungarian empires to the end of the Cold War. Miller examines the Quay Brothers' use of the fragile mechanical body of the puppet as a metaphor of the instability and destruction of urban and national spaces and identities.

But where the Quay Brothers examine the past of Polish cities, looking back, as it were, from "postmodernity" to "modernity," David Sorfa's essay "Architorture" explores Jan Švankmajer's combination of animation and Czech Surrealism as an agit-prop avant-garde rejection of the illegitimate Soviet state in post-1968 Prague. Characteristically, in his short film *Flora* (1989), Švankmajer's animated images of the gradually decomposing body in the private and restricted space of the downtown apartment, in combination with a soundtrack of the everyday noise of the city outside, project a nightmare of invasion, isolation, displacement, and oppressive control. Sorfa proposes that Švankmajer's films may be considered as explorations of what he calls a "secret map" of Prague, as a means of resistance to its totalitarian domination. Švankmajer's mobilization of the paradigmatic imagery of the body as a soft machine, which was so central to the work of the Paris Surrealists, identifies his work from the 1960s to the 1980s as an example of late-modernist avant-gardism in resistance to the specific oppressiveness of the Soviet system, long after the notion of the modernist avant garde had withered away elsewhere, particularly in the Western world of "postmodern global capitalism."

Jessie Labov's essay investigates Krzysztof Kieślowski's development of an entirely different strategy in order to combat the unbearable oppression and impoverishment of social conditions in the latter stages of the Soviet era in Poland. Working within the mainstream of realist narrative film and television, Kieślowski effects a liberal humanist undermining of the monolithic State in his depictions of Warsaw, particularly in *Dekalog* (1988). In his selective focusing on particular urban environments—especially the Soviet-era housing *blok*—Kieślowski refuses to cooperate with official projections of the city, rejecting its Stalinist landmarks and, by implication, the very existence of the Communist regime itself. Drawing particularly upon the theories of Henri Lefebvre, Labov demonstrates that the selective use of the city in *Dekalog* extended the larger, ultimately successful, strategy of the Solidarity movement in 1980s Poland to undermine the Soviet state by ignoring it, withdrawing from the realm of the political into the resistant practice of "everyday life" at the level of the personal.[7]

As Labov points out, the end of the Soviet era in Poland, in which Kieślowski's work may be claimed to have played an important role, has opened the possibility of the incorporation of Poland today in the global capitalist order. Correspondingly, where Part I of the book presents Central and Eastern Europe as a region characterized by intense internal contestation and historical layering, Part II turns to the North American paradigm which, ostensibly, is destined to supersede it. If the practice of everyday life and the realm of the personal provided key modes of resistance to totalitarianism in Poland, many of the chapters in this second part question the viability of just these categories—everyday life and the personal—as means of resistance to the ongoing expansion and incorporation of consumer capitalism in the United States and Canada. The essays here, therefore, are equally, though differently, concerned with the issues of individual and social self-preservation within the context of contemporary Western capitalist democracy.

Part II focuses on the cities of New York, Los Angeles, and Toronto since World War Two, but especially since the emergence of what many social and cultural historians characterize as "postmodernity" in the 1960s. Since 1945, the United States in particular has experienced the phenomenal rise of an unprecedentedly affluent and globally powerful society based upon amplified intensities of urban expansion, technological sophistication, new industrial divisions of labor, and the growth of capital (particularly corporate capital). All of these, while leading many commentators to recommend the development of additional vocabularies appropriate to the new realities of "postmodernism" or "post-industrialism," have nonetheless failed to eradicate massive levels of social inequality, disempowerment, and conflict, albeit not articulated as clearly in terms of the dialogics of class as in earlier moments in history or other parts of the world.

Corresponding to this new post-1960s dispensation, the chapters in Part II examine a diverse range of films and filmic practices which have attempted to respond to this changing economic and social landscape, less through formal reflexivity and self-consciousness than was the case with the films in Part I but certainly with at least as much social and political engagement. For the most part, this new balance of formal innovation and thematic relevance has manifested itself in a realist examination of contemporary urban environments, especially through location filming. Strategies range widely, from the radical documentary of the 1960s such as Newsreel, through sophisticated social commentaries from 1970s Hollywood such as *Annie Hall* and *Network*, to the so-called New Black Realism of 1990s US cinema, or the more recent phenomenon of "indie" film. The essays in Part II attempt to make new connections between these diverse types of filmmaking and a variety of conditions of urban experience determined not only by class but also by race and gender in late-twentieth-century North America.

In his essay, Allan Siegel identifies the 1960s as a defining moment of structural crisis in the hegemony of Western capitalism and its cinematic representations, in which filmmakers in a wide range of cities—from London and Paris to New York, Chicago, and Los Angeles—recognized the urgent integral relationship between radical social transformation, formal experimentation with the representation of the city as a highly political space, and fundamental change in the ownership and control of cinematic production and distribution. Siegel argues that the historical development of the representation of the city in European and American film from World War Two to the 1960s is best understood in terms of the ever-greater restructuring of urban space by global capital and information technology. In contrast to the radical energy of 1960s filmmaking itself, Siegel alleges that critical discourse (including film studies) has since retreated from praxis to academe, and continues to be insufficiently attentive to social and political engagement with film and media. The possibility of such re-engagement, in continuity with the radicalism of the 1960s, lies for Siegel in the democratic and empowering potential of new digital video technologies and their alternative modes of production, distribution, and exhibition.

Like Siegel, Mark Shiel in his essay, "A Nostalgia for Modernity," sees the 1960s as a crucial moment in which a fundamental paradigm shift was effected from modernity to postmodernity. Drawing upon a historical materialist mode of analysis, Shiel proposes modernity and postmodernity as defining stages in the development of Western capitalism, emblematized in key mid-1970s Hollywood representations of New York and Los Angeles, respectively. Focusing on Lumet's *Network* (1976) and Allen's *Annie Hall* (1977), Shiel examines the ways in which the shifting representations of urban space in the two films maps the historical development of global capitalism. The post-1960s loss of optimism evident in both films is nowhere clearer than in what Shiel calls their shared "nostalgia for modernity," a modernity which they tend to identify with the specific cultural meanings and landscapes—what Marshall Berman has called the "forest of symbols"—of New York City.[8]

The essays by Paul Gormley and Paula J. Massood point to the significance of New Black Realism as a re-emergence of political cinema within the US mainstream since the late 1980s. Gormley critiques what he sees as white cultural appropriation of black American culture—specifically blaxploitation and New Black Realism films such as *Boyz N the Hood*—through the work of the celebrated (white) filmmaker Quentin Tarantino. Through an analysis of processes of spectatorship and the action of the image upon the viewer, Gormley argues that the popularity of Tarantino's *Pulp Fiction* depends upon a voyeuristic appetite among white American audiences for the perceived depth and authenticity of black urban experience and lifestyle, an appetite which he dissects by reference to the racial theories of Frantz Fanon and the postcolonial analysis of cinema by Ella Shohat and Robert Stam.[9]

Describing New Black Realism as a powerful and meaningful expression of political difference and resistance in the 1990s, Massood's essay notes the desire for historical and geographical authenticity and detail as one of the most important characteristics of New Black Realism films such as *New Jack City*, *Clockers*, and *Menace II Society*. For Massood, the space of the "hood" presented in these films is a distillation of complex sets of historically and geographically specifiable social conditions concentrated in one space and time—the hood—which Massood examines by invoking Mikhail Bakhtin's concept of the "chronotope."[10] However, while Bakhtin's concept usefully highlights the specificity of the hood, it also serves to remind us that New Black Realism is only one highly visible type of African-American city film among many others. Massood traces the complex and often forgotten history of representations of black urban life in twentieth-century film and literature, from Oscar Micheaux's 1920s films of Harlem life to the literary social commentary of such seminal figures as W. E. B. DuBois.

In his essay "Against the Los Angeles Symbolic," Jude Davies examines three recent films which deal with race in contemporary Los Angeles but which cannot be described as New Black Realism: *Colors* (1988), *Falling Down* (1993), and *Devil in a Blue Dress* (1995). For Davies these films provide interesting and complex examinations of race in contemporary LA without participating in the commodification of black LA culture which the 1990s success of hip-hop and New Black Realism entailed. In particular, Davies analyzes the complex significations of race and power in the representation and narrative function of the automobile in these films. This analysis serves, for Davies, as a means to problematize what he sees as the over-simplification of the "LA symbolic" by such critics as Fredric Jameson, Edward Soja, and Jean Baudrillard—an "LA symbolic" first defined in relation to 1940s *film noir*, and which has been largely constructed in terms of a white, male, heterosexual subjectivity not only in cinema but also in critical discourse.[11] For Davies, this insufficiency in critical discourse brings into question the usefulness of the concept of "postmodernism" itself.

Matthew Gandy's essay on the film *[Safe]* (1995) shifts attention away from the racially conflicted and socially underprivileged setting of New Black Realism's South Central LA to the materially affluent LA "suburb" of the San Fernando Valley. In its story of the "environmental estrangement" of a typical suburban housewife, the film presents a strong critique of the self-absorption of the white middle class and its collective retreat from a political understanding of the world to New Age spiritualism, gurus, and group therapy since the 1970s. Extending Mike Davis' discussion of the "gated community" phenomenon in *City of Quartz*, Gandy proposes that the gradual isolation of the film's protagonist in a remote health clinic in the desert provides a double allegory: on the one hand, of the "white flight" which has plagued American cities since the 1960s; and, on the other, of the decline of the American left over the past thirty years.[12]

While the innovative cinematography and editing of *[Safe]* distinguish it from New Black Realism in terms of form, the crisis of white society in the film shares with that of the black community in New Black Realism a common origin in the conservative backlash of the Reagan era. As Darrell Varga's essay demonstrates, however, Cronenberg's inverted road movie *Crash* and Wenders' surveillance thriller *The End of Violence* provide striking indictments of postmodern urbanism but in much less historically or geographically defined terms. Drawing upon the work of Gilles Deleuze and Félix Guattari, Varga proposes the pseudo-pornographic aesthetic of *Crash* as a problematic, and perhaps defeatist, "indie film" response to "post-industrialism."[13] In what Varga describes as its redemptive modernism, however, the narrative of individual escape from the panoptic society in *The End of Violence* provides an antidote to the dispiriting triumph in *Crash* of high-tech communications and media-driven image culture over genuine human social interaction.

Of course, it is surely not incidental that, in the case of *The End of Violence*, Wenders is a European director working as a visitor in the United States. John Orr's Coda essay, "The City Reborn," takes the tension between the utopian and dystopian noted by Varga as its central focus, examining it in relation to a wide range of contemporary international cinema, such as *J'ai pas sommeil* (1994), *Cyclo* (1995), and *Felicia's Journey* (1999), and world cities such as Paris, Ho Chi Minh City, and Birmingham. Orr argues that the relationship between real city locations and their onscreen re-creation as urban settings is a reciprocal one to such an extent that it can be said that the city is seen *through the cinema*. For Orr, such films as these testify to an exciting recent "revival of the cinematic city," especially in films beyond the formal and thematic confines of the Hollywood mainstream. The films which interest Orr both reflect and produce what he calls a profoundly ambivalent "socio-pathology" in the contemporary cinematic city. Just as urban disconnection can result in the negative pathologies of violence and destruction which characterize films such as *Crash* (1995) and *Naked* (1993), so the "erotic moment" of desire between lovers can also function as an antidote to the failings of the cinematic city in such films as *Happy Together* (1997) and

Three Colors: Red (1994). The vibrant, mobile, diverse, and multi-cultural urban society which these various films present allows us, in a utopian sense, to conceive of improved social, political, and cultural futures beyond the present world system.

Many other multi-faceted connections can be drawn between the various essays. An interesting parallel might be developed, for example, between the coincidence of cinematic and critical–theoretical investigation which flourished in Weimar Berlin and that which has developed around contemporary Los Angeles in recent years.[14] This volume draws attention to both the continuities and discontinuities which may be detected between urban experience and its cinematic projections in each of those historical and geographical contexts. The motif of the articulated human body in the city, for example, recurs again and again throughout—from the shop-window mannequins of *Man with a Movie Camera* to Jan Švankmajer's decaying vegetable form, and David Cronenberg's damaged and prosthetic limbs—while the motif of perception extends from Ruttmann's totalizing and abstracting view in *Berlin, The Symphony of a Great City*, to the monotonous voyeurism of Kieślowski's *Dekalog* and the heavy authority of patrolling police helicopters in Singleton's *Boyz N the Hood*. On the other hand, one might equally identify a fundamental shift in the ontological status of the body in the cinematic city—from the de-individuated abstract forms of Vertov and Ruttmann to the palpable and textured flesh which marks the films of Wong Kar-wai and Spike Lee, and the physical–sensational impact of New Black Realism—or, in the realm of perception, in the gulf between the modernist faith in the power of the visible to produce reliable knowledge epitomized by Vertov's "kino-eye" and the disillusion and dislocation of the postmodern filmic image in Wenders or Atom Egoyan.[15] That such continuities and discontinuities exist, however, should not lead us to doubt strong distinctions between past and present—Weimar Berlin and contemporary Los Angeles—but should remind us more of the fact that, as Fredric Jameson counsels, postmodernism does not entail the eclipse of modernism so much as its logical extension and expansion.[16]

NOTES

1. See, for example, Mike Davis, *City of Quartz: Excavating the Future in Los Angeles*, London and New York: Verso, 1990; James Donald, *Imagining the Modern City*, London: Athlone Press, 1999; James Hay, "Piecing Together What Remains of the Cinematic City," in David Clarke, ed., *The Cinematic City*, London: Routledge, 1997, pp. 209–29; and James Hay, "Shamrock: Houston's Green Promise," in Mark Shiel and Tony Fitzmaurice, eds, *Cinema and the City: Film and Urban Societies in a Global Context*, Oxford and Malden, MA: Blackwell Publishing, 2001, pp. 75–87.

2. For more on this "spatial turn," see Shiel, "Cinema and the City in History and Theory," in Shiel and Fitzmaurice, *Cinema and the City*, pp. 1–18; and Edward Soja, *Postmodern Geographies: The Reassertion of Space in Critical Social Theory*, Verso: London and New York, 1994 (1989).

3. In addition to the above, see also Maria Balshaw and Liam Kennedy, *Urban Space and Representation*, London: Pluto Press, 2000; François Penz, *Cinema and Architecture*, London: BFI Publishing, 1997; Michael J. Dear, "Film, Architecture and Filmspace," in *The Postmodern Urban Condition*, Oxford and Malden, MA: Blackwell Publishing, 2000, pp. 176–98.

4. See Siegfried Kracauer, *From Caligari to Hitler*, Princeton, NJ: Princeton University Press, 1947.

5. Walter Benjamin, "The Work of Art in the Age of Mechanical Reproduction," in *Illuminations*, trans. Harry Zohn, London: Fontana/Collins, 1982, p. 244; Ernst Bloch, *Heritage of Our Times*, trans. Neville and Stephen Plaice, London: Polity Press, 1991; and Kracauer, *From Caligari to Hitler*.

6. On the relative decline of artistic freedom of expression and innovation in Soviet film of the 1930s, see Denise J. Youngblood, *Movies for the Masses: Popular Cinema and Soviet Society in the 1920s*, Cambridge: Cambridge University Press, 1992, pp. 28–34, 171–9; Richard Taylor and Ian Christie, eds, *The Film Factory: Russian and Soviet Cinema in Documents*, London: Routledge and Kegan Paul, 1988, pp. 1–17; Richard Taylor, *The Politics of the Soviet Cinema*, Cambridge: Cambridge University Press, 1979, pp. 102–23, 152–7.

7. See Henri Lefebvre, *Everyday Life in the Modern World*, trans. Sacha Rabinovitch, New Brunswick, NJ and London: Transaction, 1994.

8. Marshall Berman, *All That Is Solid Melts Into Air: The Experience of Modernity*, London: Verso, 1983, pp. 287–348.

9. Frantz Fanon, *Black Skins, White Masks*, New York: Grove Press, 1967; Ella Shohat and Robert Stam, *Unthinking Eurocentrism: Multiculturalism and the Media*, New York: Routledge, 1994.

10. M. M. Bakhtin, in Michael Holquist, ed., *The Dialogic Imagination*, trans. Caryl Emerson and Michael Holquist, Austin: University of Texas Press, 1981.

11. Fredric Jameson, *Postmodernism, or The Cultural Logic of Late Capitalism*, London and New York: Verso, 1993; Edward W. Soja, *Postmodern Geographies*; and Jean Baudrillard, *America*, trans. Chris Turner, London: Verso, 1988.

12. Davis, *City of Quartz*, pp. 185, 246–8; and *Ecology of Fear: Los Angeles and the Imagination of Disaster*, New York: Metropolitan Books, 1998, pp. 88–90, 326, 387–93.

13. Gilles Deleuze and Félix Guattari, *Anti-Oedipus: Capitalism and Schizophrenia*, trans. Robert Hurley, Mark Seem, and Helen R. Lane, Minneapolis: University of Minnesota Press, 1983.

14. In relation to Los Angeles, one thinks here of the work not only of Mike Davis and Edward Soja, but also, for example, of Norman M. Klein, *The History of Forgetting: Los Angeles and the Erasure of Memory*, London: Verso, 1997; Michael Dear, *The Postmodern Urban Condition*, Oxford and Malden, MA: Blackwell, 2000; Michael Dear, ed., *From Chicago to LA: Making Sense of Urban Theory*, Thousand Oaks, CA, and London: Sage Publications, 2002; and Allen J. Scott and Edward J. Soja, eds, *The City: Los Angeles and Urban Theory at the End of the Twentieth Century*, Berkeley and Los Angeles, CA: University of California Press, 1996. The relationship between these two tidal waves of combined urban growth and social theory—Weimar Berlin in the 1920s, and Los Angeles since the late 1980s—has not yet been fully explored in a synthetic way, although recently progress has been made in this direction by Janet Ward in the Introduction to her *Weimar Surfaces: Urban Visual Culture in 1920s Germany*, Berkeley and Los Angeles, CA: University of California Press, 2001.

15. On the status of perception in modernity and postmodernity, see Scott Bukatman, "The Artificial Infinite: On Special Effects and the Sublime," in Lynne Cooke and Peter Wollen, *Visual Display: Culture Beyond Appearances*, Seattle: Bay Press, 1995, pp. 255–89. This disillusion and dislocation of the postmodern filmic image in relation to the city is arguably nowhere more strikingly deployed than by Wenders in the fake grand masters of *The American Friend* (1977) and the fading photograph of "Paris" in *Paris, Texas* (1984).

16. Fredric Jameson, *Postmodernism, or The Cultural Logic of Late Capitalism*, London and New York: Verso, 1991, pp. 55–66; and *Signatures of the Visible*, New York and London: Routledge, 1992, pp. 155–230.

PART I

THE MODERN CITY:
CENTRAL AND EASTERN EUROPE

I

UNCANNY SPACES: THE CITY IN RUTTMANN AND VERTOV

CARSTEN STRATHAUSEN

In his discussion of the industrialization of light during the nineteenth century, Wolfgang Schivelbusch mentions the visionary idea of the prominent French architect Jules Bourdais to erect a gigantic tower in the center of Paris equipped with arc lights strong enough to illuminate the entire city at night.[1] In spite of the project never being realized, the very idea bespeaks the powerful legacy of the Enlightenment for cultural modernism, their shared preoccupation with an elucidating visibility rendering the dark spaces of the outside utterly transparent. "A fear haunted the latter half of the eighteenth century," stated Michel Foucault during one of his interviews, "the fear of darkened spaces, of the pall of gloom which prevents the full visibility of things, men and truths."[2] Foucault's formulation is reminiscent of Max Horkheimer and Theodor Adorno's earlier definition of the Enlightenment as "mythic fear turned radical," a fear they conceptualized in spatial terms: "Nothing at all may remain outside, because the mere idea of outsideness is the very source of fear."[3]

Modernity's oscillation between exposure and repression, between location and displacement, is strikingly captured by Freud's notion of the "uncanny," defined as "something which is familiar and old-established in the mind and which has become alienated from it only through the process of repression."[4] Freud's somewhat unsystematic remarks on the uncanny have given rise to various attempts at reinterpretation, most of which regard the uncanny as a kind of structural disturbance that "emerges with modernity and . . . constantly haunts it from the inside," as Mladen Dolar contends.[5] Arguing from a Lacanian perspective, Dolar identifies the uncanny with the "petit objet a" as the symptom of the *real* shattering the *apparent* wholeness and controllability of social reality. In contrast to Freud, who tries to muster and seize the uncanny as if it were an objective referent, the Lacanian interpretation insists on its formal (that is, structural) nature which prevents it from ever being fully present or completely visible. Uncanniness, Robin Lydenberg concludes with reference to the history and theory of narration, "stems from a reader's encounter with a story's linguistic structures and rhetorical effects, not just from its contents and context."[6] Shifting from the linguistic to the visual register, one might say that the uncanny can only be detected by looking at it from the side. Much like the phenomenon of anamorphosis, which Lacan discusses with reference to Holbein's painting *The Ambassadors*, the uncanny always distorts an otherwise perfect picture.[7] It literally functions as the blind-spot of modernity's pre-occupation with visual transparency in so far as it must necessarily remain obscure in order to enable vision. The Lacanian uncanny is a void signifying the implicit limits of interpretation, the lack of meaning necessary to sustain it.

It follows that any attempt to disclose the uncanny or to exorcise it by making it visible is bound to reproduce it.[8] One can easily detect the founding paradox of this explanation: the uncanny is understood as both the cause and the result of the perceptual crisis it represents, for it emerges as the irrecuperable blind-spot only after it has already caused the denial that supposedly engenders it.[9] Recent French theory has insisted that these paradoxes are not to be feared, but to be embraced as indicative of the self-limiting and even self-destructive tendencies constitutive of the modern period at large, an era ambiguously suspended in between order and chaos, and light and darkness, change and resistance. As Gilles Deleuze and Félix Guattari argue, the progress of modernity exhibits schizophrenic qualities such that their successful promulgation simultaneously gives rise to its own undoing: "What we are trying to say is that capitalism, through the process of production, produces an awesome schizophrenic accumulation of energy or charge, against which it brings all its vast powers of repressions to bear, but which nonetheless continues to act as capitalism's limit."[10]

In this chapter, I will locate the cinema and the city at the center of the schizophrenia that haunts modernity and finds its symptomatic expression in and through the uncanny. In the first part, I examine the ways in which the uncanny is literally built into both the metropolis and the cinematic apparatus. Anthony Vidler, for example, regards the widespread anxieties attached to urban landscapes as indicative of the impossibility of rendering modern cities transparent and "homely."[11] If the architectural uncanny marks the continued existence of city-labyrinths underneath the city of light, the history of cinema is similarly haunted by the myth of shock and fear that accompanies anecdotes of its "birth" in Paris in 1895.[12] As Noël Burch has argued with reference to scientific discourse at the turn of the twentieth century, the invention of cinema harbors a Frankensteinian project, since one of the explicit goals of cinema was to reanimate the dead and literally to grant "life" to the mere shadows of photographic images:

> How many people would be happy if they could only see once again the features of someone now dead. The future will see the replacement of motionless photographs, frozen in their frames, with animated portraits that can be brought to life with the turn of a handle . . . We shall do more than analyze, we shall bring back to life.[13]

In both cinema and the modern city something presumably dead is brought back to life and begins to haunt the living. Given this structural affinity, the cinema can be seen not only as a battleground for the new laws of urban perception discussed first by early critics of modernism around 1900 and again later, during the Weimar period, by members of the Frankfurt School. A darkened chamber typically located at the heart of the big city, the cinema provided the space where modernity negotiated and tried to come to terms with its contradictory impulses of repression and revelation, transparency and obscurity. Transgressing the boundary between life and death as well as between absence and presence, the imaginary signifier of film is nothing if not a symptom of uncanniness itself.

The second part of this chapter situates Walter Ruttmann's *Berlin, The Symphony of a Great City* (1927) and Dziga Vertov's *Man with a Movie Camera* (1929) within this context of modernity's failed attempt to exorcise the uncanny. Released in the late 1920s, these two films add a specific historical and political dimension to the cinematic exploration of city space. In particular, they point to the intertwined cultural dynamics between the cinematic avant garde and the

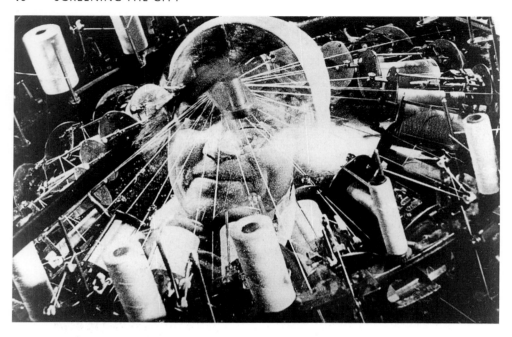

1 Dziga Vertov's *Man with a Movie Camera* (1929) (BFI Collections)

rise of totalitarianism in Europe, since both phenomena are primarily concerned with the ideological power of vision in the realm of mass culture. Unlike Nazi aesthetics, Ruttmann's and Vertov's films do not try to suppress modern fragmentation, but instead seek to express it aesthetically on the screen (**1, 2**). The goal, however, remains the same—namely to eradicate the fear of darkness and multiplicity that haunts the history of modernity. Vertov and Ruttmann fail in their efforts because they unwittingly end up projecting this fear onto technology and city life itself. Glorifying the omnipresence of the camera as a means for modern man to experience and feel at home in the big city, these city films unwittingly expose the increasing irrelevance of the human individual as it becomes *subjected to*, rather than the *subject of*, modern life. The modernist ideal of absolute vision shifts power from the "I" of man to the "eye" of the camera so that cinematic vision as such gains control in and of these films. Once in charge,

2 Walter Ruttmann's *Berlin, The Symphony of a Great City* (1927) (BFI Collections)

ra literally enables the modern uncanny to come to life in the form of a
rg-like being—the metropolis—which threatens to absorb and ulti-
lace the very humanity whom it was meant to benefit. In this sense,
...d Ruttmann's films give rise to the return of the repressed: they
implicitly acknowledge the frailty of the individual which the modernist ideal
of visual transparency and the films themselves seek to deny.

From Bentham's "Panopticon" to Le Corbusier's architecture and Foucault's
analysis of modern systems of surveillance, modernity's ideal of visual transparency found its most adequate expression in the concept of the big city.
Although Jules Bourdais' tower never saw the light of day, Paris did, after all,
ultimately get "its master-image, the one structure that seemed to gather all the
meanings of modernity together"—the Eiffel Tower.[14] For the Eiffel Tower can
indeed be seen from almost every point in the city, and from its top the visitor
enjoys a seemingly limitless, comprehensive view of the city below. This image of
centralization also inspired Baron Haussmann's transformation of Paris from a
slovenly conglomerate of medieval neighborhoods into the triumphant city of
light. Haussmann's architectural scheme is paradigmatic for modernity's impulse
to bring order into chaos. The rebuilding of the Place de l'Étoile during the 1860s
exemplifies the absorption of centuries-old city growth into the lucidity of a geo-
metrically structured urban space generally depicted via a divine point of view
from above (**3**).[15] This ideal perspective emphasizes the rational grid underlying
the modern city, a kind of hard-wired skeleton meant to provide stability and
allow for some predictability in an otherwise all too chaotic world.

For many German intellectuals at the beginning of the twentieth century, this
abstract rationality that literally shapes the metropolis was fundamentally at odds
with both authentic national culture and genuine humanity. Stefan Zweig, for
example, argued that the chess-board structure of American cities contributed to
the "monotonization of the world" which was indicative of the hegemony of
American capitalism over Europe.[16] Oswald Spengler, in his highly influential
work *Decline of the West*, went even further and regarded the metropolis in general
as "the symbol of soullessness" of all modern civilization which has become sterile
and severed from the life-giving forces of nature: "Man as civilized, as intellectual
nomad, is again wholly microcosmic, wholly homeless."[17] According to Spengler,
this homelessness of modern man is concomitant with the rise of the "abstract

3 Aerial view by Nadar of the Place de l'Étoile and Arc de Triomphe in Paris, 1858

city" distinguished by its "multiplied barrack-tenements and utility buildings" and perceived by the disembodied gaze from above:

> Looking down from one of the old towers upon the sea of houses, we perceive in this petrification of a historic being [i.e. the old town—*author's note*] the exact epoch that marks the end of organic growth and the beginning of an inorganic and, therefore, unrestrained process of massing without limits. And now, too, appears that artificial,

mathematical, utterly land-alien product of a pure intellectual satisfaction in the appropriate, the city of the city-architect.[18]

Spengler's juxtaposition of the old town and the modern city enlists a plethora of binary oppositions to support his claim that traditional values such as life, organicity, and the human soul have been put to death by the lifeless artificiality that haunts the metropolis. He particularly emphasizes that this development is by no means peculiar to capitalist America, but can indeed be found in "all Civilizations alike," since "all these cities aim at the chessboard form, which is the symbol of soullessness."[19]

It is crucial to point out that Spengler's cultural pessimism about the "petrification" of Being exemplified in modern city structures did not remain unchallenged. Robert Park, a founding member of the Chicago School, explicitly rejected Spengler's view and juxtaposed the artificial appearance of the city with its "moral [and] physical organization," both of which imposed a "limit to arbitrary modification which it is possible to make."[20] For Park, the migration of its population as well as the distinct characters of various neighborhoods once again endow the modern city with an organicity of its own. According to Richard Sennett, the entire Chicago School initiated a shift from "defining city culture as a unitary phenomenon" toward a mode of analysis that "took the city as a world in itself, and sought to define what the city was in terms of the relations between the parts in this world."[21] Although this approach fully recognized the constructed artificiality of the metropolitan space, it primarily focused on the startling complexity of city life and individual experience. This crucial shift literally entailed a different point of view as it juxtaposed the translucent, organizing gaze from above the city with the multiplicity of conflicting perspectives experienced down below. Such visions, of course, had already been alive during the second half of the nineteenth century. They describe the home of Baudelaire's *flâneur* who aimlessly wanders the streets of Paris enjoying the bombardments of visual impressions he encounters in the labyrinths of the modern city.

The chaotic experience of spatial incoherence and disorientation characteristic of the metropolis is strikingly illustrated by one of Ludwig Meidner's drawings, entitled "Berlin," from 1913 (**4**). The picture creates a kind of vortex that captures the gaze of the beholder and draws it toward the heart of the city as if trying to

4 Ludwig Meidner, "Berlin," 1913

devour the spectators themselves. Looking at the image, it becomes increasingly difficult to position oneself outside of it—instead, one feels the urge to physically enter the scene and mingle with the crowds. And yet, Meidner's image is not completely without structure itself, since the diagonal vanishing lines created by the flow of people, traffic, and buildings all converge at an endlessly retreating and ultimately void center. Meidner's "Berlin" thus provides an intriguing comparison with Haussmann's vision of Paris and his design of the Place de l'Étoile for two reasons: first, because Meidner contrasts the disembodied gaze from above with the anxious view of the immersed city-dweller down below, and, second, because both pictures nonetheless share a diagonal composition which, in spite of their different perspectives on the city, demonstrates a formal complicity between them. Contrary to first appearances, Haussmann's geometric city is still present in Meidner's picture, yet it has literally been painted over with the chaotic, fragmentary life taking place within urban space. Meidner's "Berlin," one might conclude, illustrates the fact that, as James Donald argues in a chapter on Ruttmann and Vertov, "however rationalized and disenchanted modern societies may become, at an experiential level (that is, in the unconscious) the new urban-industrial world has become fully *re*-enchanted."[22]

A variety of recent studies have sought to examine this simultaneity of map and labyrinth, transparency and obscurity with reference to the uncanny.[23] The latter is generally understood as a symptom of this irreconcilable ambiguity lurking in the metropolis. According to Anthony Vidler, it is precisely the modern attempt to classify and make the city transparent that causes it to re-emerge as the locus of the modern unhomely. A similar observation has been advanced by Michel de Certeau who, in his analysis of *The Practice of Everyday Life*, regards individual behavior as undermining the efficiency of modern systems of surveillance. According to de Certeau, the practice of everyday life in the city might be read as subversive acts of resistance able to disrupt the abstract text that informs and structures the metropolis.[24] However, if cinema is the main facilitator for modernity's negotiation of urban space, then the city is not a "text" to be "read," as de Certeau incessantly claims, but a sight to be seen. A visual rather than textual experience, both cinema and the metropolis gave rise to a new "language" fundamentally at odds with the traditional, contemplative gaze carefully "reading" the world.[25] This is not to disavow the continued importance of literary and artistic endeavors of the avant garde to mediate what Robert Hughes has called "the shock of the new" at the beginning of the twentieth century. Yet one cannot deny the primary significance of film aesthetics as a means to capture the essence of modern urban experience which presented the metropolis itself as one big intersection of "moving images":

> What on earth gives this city [Berlin] its charm! Movement in the first place. There is no city in the world so restless as Berlin. Everything moves. The traffic lights change restlessly from red to gold and then to green. The lighted advertisements flash with the pathetic iteration of coastal lighthouses.[26]

Dominated by rapid industrialization and urbanization at the turn of the century, cultural modernity presented the entire world in a constant state of flux.

Moreover, the so called "perceptual revolution" in science and the arts around 1900 was fortified by the rapid development of modern means of transportation.[27] Wolfgang Schivelbusch alludes to film as the artistic correlative to the psychological effect of the railway journey: "He [the traveler] perceives objects, landscape, etc., through the apparatus with which he is moving through the world."[28] The world outside was indeed converted into a tableau, a complex of "moving pictures" whose unprecedented speed caused passengers to feel dizzy or even lose consciousness. In short, metropolitan life was characterized by the same overload of visual stimulation that also distinguishes the aesthetics of film, meaning that "modern culture was 'cinematic' before the fact," as Leo Charney and Vanessa Schwartz have argued.[29] The film-screen becomes the mirror of modern life. This structural homology between cinema and the city was already noted before World War One and repeatedly scrutinized thereafter by members of the Frankfurt School—most forcefully by Walter Benjamin in his classic chapter on "The Work of Art in the Age of Mechanical Reproduction," published in 1936.[30]

However, the complicity between cinema and the metropolis far exceeds this particular socio-historical juncture generally alluded to by critics, for film also shares the city's ambivalent relationship toward modern fantasies of visual transparency. Just as the metropolis becomes a site of conflict between surveillance and obscurity, so does the cultural sphere of cinema oscillate between the destruction and the re-invention of visual coherence. On the one hand, film is at once constituted by and constitutive of the "perceptual revolution" of modernity in that it both exemplifies and corroborates the loss of a centralized Archimedean point of reference through the use of montage and the constant change of perspective. Yet, on the other hand, as later theorists of the cinematic apparatus have argued, one of the functions of cinema was to undo the damaging effect of the multi-perspective field by inviting the spectator to identify with the camera as the locus of an ubiquitous, all-perceiving subject. According to Jean-Louis Baudry, for example, "the spectator identifies less with what is represented, the spectacle itself, than with what stages the spectacle, makes it seen, obliging him to see what it sees; this is exactly the function taken over by the camera as a sort of relay."[31] A similar argument was advanced by Christian Metz, who distinguished between primary and secondary cinematic identification, defining the former as the "[i]dentification [of] one's own look" with that of the camera.[32] Since every single film image relies on monocular perspective, this identification process stabilizes the perceptual field of the spectator and allows her to occupy a unified and central position *vis à vis* the flow of images. The world in film, to summarize Baudry's and Metz's argument, is meant to confirm the spectator's narcissistic pleasure in exercising an albeit illusory form of visual control.

Hence, the role played by film with regard to the "perceptual revolution" of modernity is profoundly ambivalent. Although part of the socio-historical development that destroyed the traditional belief in the existence of Archimedean perspective—that is, the superior gaze from above—on the level of each individual shot, film nonetheless reintroduced the very same experience of a totalizing vision it allegedly superseded. Given this structural ambiguity inherent in the aesthetics of film, it is hardly surprising that the cinema became the battle-ground for the new laws of urban perception as it gave rise to uncanny visions of a world devoid of the "human."

"Cinema is war, and war is cinema," Abel Gance proclaimed in 1914.[33] This combative description characterizes both the genre of the city film in general and Vertov's and Ruttmann's films in particular. The simultaneity of order and chaos, for example, is strikingly exemplified in Vertov's opening shot which shows the cameraman climbing a gigantic movie-camera placed directly opposite the film audience. This endorsement of absolute cinematic vision is fortified by a similar image toward the end of the film, depicting the "man with his camera" looming large above the city crowds. Both images identify the eye of the camera with the disembodied, omniscient gaze high above the metropolis as envisioned by Bourdais, the modern architect.

And yet Vertov also strongly relies on montage effects to picture life in the city as a rapid succession of disparate and incoherent images. The film thus exploits a contrast between an ordering perspective from above and the disorienting fragmentation of life experienced below. This antagonistic rivalry of two opposed concepts wrestling for dominance as each alternately forces the other to literally go underground, not only informs the structure of Vertov's film but exemplifies its primary goal: armed with his movie camera, the cameraman plunges into the city to seek out and shoot the "facts of life" (Vertov) surrounding him. During the course of the film, the camera indeed becomes a weapon which increasingly dominates and ultimately emerges as its sole hero. The uncanny moment in Vertov's film consists precisely in the realization that the modern ideal of total vision necessarily supersedes the human and thus undermines rather than strengthens the notion of the individual or of class. Instead of augmenting human perception, the cinematic eye is unwittingly unveiled as a self-sustaining, autonomous form of vision that eradicates what it ought to liberate—the (bourgeois/Marxist) subject understood as the agent of history.

If Bourdais' imagined tower sheds light on Vertov's failed project to conquer the dark territory of the modern city in the name of class consciousness, it also makes an appearance in the closing sequence of Walter Ruttmann's *Berlin, The Symphony of a Great City* (1927) in the image of a radio tower shining powerful searchlights across the urban landscape. A source of artificial illumination, the tower provides a striking contrast with the film's opening shots of the sun describing several half-circles over a body of water, indicating the natural passing and the eternal recurrence of time. While Ruttmann, much like Vertov, confronts his audience with a stunning array of city impressions, he is not primarily concerned with the self-conscious exploration of cinematic representation. Instead, he focuses on the conflict between culture and nature, trying to reconcile them through the deliberate merging of linear and cyclical movements meant to identify the metropolis as the new, yet nonetheless "natural," home of modern man. Ruttmann, therefore, depicts the city as a cyborg-like organism imbued with a life of its own, which leads him to eschew individual life-stories within his film in favor of a mere surface network of rhythmic changes that need to be enjoyed visually rather than analyzed cognitively, as Ruttmann himself emphasized repeatedly in his interviews.

Since both Vertov's and Ruttmann's films lack distinct plot-lines, their popularity among contemporary audiences was indeed mostly based on the spectator's experience of thrill and excitement evoked through the use of accelerated montage, as contemporary critics pointed out. Siegfried Kracauer, for example, reprimanded the inherent social indifference of Ruttmann's "surface approach" to city life, arguing that the film "relies on the formal qualities of the objects rather than on their meanings," and thus provides visual pleasure devoid of a deeper meaning.[34] Vertov's *Man with a Movie Camera*, too, was judged inaccessible and denounced as "confused, formalistic, aimless, and self-satisfied trickery," a verdict echoed by Sergei Eisenstein, for whom the film consisted of "mere formalistic jackstraws and unmotivated camera mischief."[35] Instead of presenting a critical analysis of modern city life, Ruttmann and Vertov used both the camera and the city as mere tools for the production of mindless entertainment and voyeuristic pleasure. In psychoanalytical terms, one might say that these films were judged regressive in spite of their apparently novel and progressive mode of filming. Not only did they invite their audience to enjoy the childish pleasure of looking for looking's sake, but they also reoriented the medium of film back toward its origins by reviving the early "cinema of attraction" that had preceded narrative film and its focus on individual stories.[36]

In fact, given both films' reference to ordinary city life seemingly devoid of visual manifestations of the uncanny, one might even argue that *Berlin, The Symphony of a Great City* and *Man with a Movie Camera* are anything but uncanny. Rather than centering on the perception of lack, they glorify visual plenitude and the ubiquity of the camera enjoyed by the audience. Instead of a "nothing" (that is, the lack of castration), the audience sees everything and every aspect of the city. Celebrating the visual omniscience provided by the camera, Vertov indeed anticipated what Christian Metz called "primary cinematic identification," in expressing the basic principles of the theory of the cinematic apparatus *avant la lettre*:

> I am the camera's eye. I, a machine, am showing you a world, the likes of which only I can see. Starting from today, I am forever free of human immobility. I am in perpetual movement. I approach and draw away from things—I crawl under them—I climb on them. My road leads toward the creation of a fresh perception of the world. I decipher, in a new way, a world unknown to you.[37]

However, as suggested earlier in this chapter, the Lacanian uncanny is not bound to an event or a tangible object, but to a crisis in perception which jeopardizes the integrity of the body and the identity of the subject. According to Samuel Weber, the perception of lack—that is, the wound of castration understood as a general sign of human imperfection—causes a fundamental denial, a defense mechanism spurring the "desire to penetrate, discover and ultimately to conserve the integrity of perception: perceiver and perceived, the wholeness of the body, the power of vision."[38] The question, in other words, is whether there exists something in these films that has been "castrated," so to speak, or excluded from sight precisely in order to "conserve the integrity of perception." What is the price to pay for obtaining the omniscient and ubiquitous gaze celebrated by Ruttmann and Vertov? The answer clearly relates to the classical notion of human subjectivity and historical agency. What is lost in the city films is a sense of visual control over the images on the screen. Disregarding individual or class consciousness, both films unveil visual plenitude to be a post-human ideal that cannot be reconciled with bourgeois humanism or traditional Marxism. The gap between our own limited visual field and the seemingly limitless visual scope of the cinematic apparatus is too wide to be bridged anymore through the spectator's identification with the "eye" of the camera.

If it is not "us" who is controlling these images, it must be somebody else. Indeed, both films triumphantly announce the arrival of "l'homme machine" as the inevitable product of modernity's attempt to see and reveal "everything." It follows that the alleged "lack of lack" in these films—that is, their preoccupation with the delirious pleasure of showing and looking—can be conceptualized as part of the defense mechanism to which Weber alludes. Both the exclusion of self-determining historical agents shaping history and the preoccupation with total transparency suggest the fundamental denial that causes the uncanny to erupt elsewhere, at some "other" place in the form of another being. This "other" is the metropolis.

The uncanny in Vertov's and Ruttmann's films, in other words, resides in the absence of the "human" who is being absorbed into the cyborgian complex of city life. Vertov's film, of course, was not meant to endorse sentimental bourgeois values or notions of individuality, and Walter Benjamin admired Russian film precisely for its representation of faces that "no longer" functioned "as a portrait," but rather showed "facial types."[39] Yet the real protagonists in Vertov's film are not individuals or types or, as one might expect, the working class as the meta-subject of history. Rather, the protagonists are the camera and the metropolis itself as experienced by the fictional audience within the film. The latter in particular makes it clear that there remains nothing "outside" of Vertov's film, since this audience, understood as the official representative of the proletariat, is already situated within and literally envisioned as a part of the picture it watches. Instead of critically judging the film from the outside as a means to gain class consciousness, the masses are simply shown to play their part, laughing and enjoying "their" movie.

Similarly, the often-voiced critique regarding the abstraction and surface character of *Berlin* as well as its lack of a deeper inquiry into the socio-historical roots and effects of modernity might itself be read as a symptom: it marks critics' unease with a film which celebrates rather than condemns the loss of an objective insight into the essence of things.[40] Instead of testifying to the ability of the mind's eye to penetrate into and analyze the socio-economic or political structures that shape history, Ruttmann's film dispenses entirely with such crucial Marxist/humanist distinctions as surface vs. essence or alienation vs. freedom or man vs. machine, since all of these elements and categories are being dissolved within the new life organism of the metropolis. The hero of *Berlin*, in other words, is the city itself, and Ruttmann repeatedly emphasizes how difficult it was to work with his only actor: "With insidious treachery and malice, Berlin tried to escape the relentlessness of my camera," he emphasized, insisting that his goal was "not to create a picture-book, but rather something like a network of a complicated machine that can only gain momentum if every little piece fits into the other with the utmost precision."[41] Or, as he phrased it during another interview: "A counter-point had to emerge from the rhythm of man and machine."[42]

The fusion of man and machine clearly underlies the montage rhythm both of Vertov's film and of Ruttmann's. Their ultimate purpose is to enable the urban masses to recognize themselves on the screen not as particular individuals, but as organic parts of a larger entity called the metropolis. Vertov repeatedly cross-fades human faces with machine parts of similar shape or presents human mechanics surrounded by, and thus part of, the powerful machines they supervise and maintain. In his theoretical writings, Vertov consciously embraces this fusion of man and machine and acknowledges the creation of a machine-man as the ultimate goal of his films:

> I am kino-eye. I am a builder . . . I create a man more perfect that Adam, I create thousands of different people in accordance with preliminary blueprints and

diagrams of different kinds . . . From one person I take the hands, the strongest and most dexterous; from another I take the legs, the swiftest and most shapely; from a third, the most beautiful and expressive head—and through montage I create a new, perfect man.[43]

Man with a Movie Camera is meant to explore and put to the test Vertov's theory of the spectator's identification with the camera. The film literally merges the "Man" with the "Movie Camera" as it presents numerous match-cuts between the human eye and the camera lens, suggesting a powerful union that culminates in several shots superimposing the two. In theory, according to Vertov, this fusion is meant to overcome "the slavery of the imperfect and limited human eye" by making the "eye submit to the will of the camera."[44] Vertov's language is telling indeed, for he endows the camera with a subjective will of its own which he explicitly denies the human individual. Vertov, of course, believed in film mainly as an aesthetic means to a political end. Since he trusted the power of the camera to penetrate beneath the surface of apparent reality and to record the facts of "life-as-it-is," he fully shared Walter Benjamin's well-known optimism about the emancipatory power of cinematic perception to reverse the ongoing process of modern alienation. Similarly to Benjamin, Vertov's goal is to burst open reified social relations, hoping to create a new cinematic "truth" of modern life by means of an "absolute vision" which can be understood universally and judged accordingly.[45]

His cinematic practice, however, celebrates the inherent psychological complicity between film and urban life to the point of complete (con)fusion: the incredible speed of Vertov's montage—that is, the cinematic manipulation of images via the editing process—merges with the documentary recording of real city flux and traffic: "life-as it-is" becomes "life-as-seen-through-and-enjoyed-by-the-movie-camera," a crucial transformation that blurs the borderline between inside and outside, man, and machine, without leaving any space for the consciousness Vertov allegedly seeks to activate. Rather, class consciousness is relocated from the common mind of the class-proletariat within the cinematic apparatus itself. The film seems made not only *with* the camera, but *for* the camera as well.

Vertov's celebration of *l'homme machine* finds its most striking expression in the sequence of the anthropomorphized camera dancing and celebrating the demise of human individuality toward the end of his film. At this point, it becomes obvious that Vertov's project must fail. *Man with a Movie Camera* seeks to improve technologically the limits of human perception in an effort to render the metropolis utterly transparent; yet by trying to look this fantasy straight in the eye instead of staging it indirectly by means of narrative closure and cinematic suture, the film cannot but function as a fetish for modernity at large.[46] Against "its will", the virtuosity of Vertov's dancing camera reveals the new visual paradigm to be inhuman and human perception itself to be inadequate and unable to compete with the cinematic apparatus.

The correlative to Vertov's ideal fusion of man and machine can be found in the latent anthropomorphization of the city in Ruttmann's *Berlin*. Ruttmann presents the city itself as a gigantic organism coming to life in the morning, opening its "eyes" in a series of match-cuts as blinds and curtains are drawn and windows and doors are opened. His "symphony" depicts the instrumentalization of people as part of the city's interior machinery—for instance, in the telephone switch-room or within the trains and trams which represent the blood-stream of modern life that transports the masses from one place to another. Before we ever see any people, we are already presented with their substitutes in the form of mannequins prominently displayed in a shop window. Ruttmann also repeatedly cross-cuts human behavior on the streets with the repetitive movements of mechanical toys and automata, suggesting an affinity that finds its most adequate expression during the cabaret sequence. The scene depicts a female dance group resembling the Tiller Girls who imitate the exact movements of the speeding train depicted several times in the film. Not surprisingly, most of these shots de-accentuate the face and focus on various body parts instead. While Ruttmann's celebration of the mass ornament effaces living people by transforming them into machines, his film, in turn, endows the train with a human face of its own as it emerges out of its hangar and menacingly confronts the camera.

Ruttmann's efforts to endow the metropolis with a soul of its own are mirrored in the film's attempt to "naturalize" technology—that is, to reconcile the conflict between nature and culture by merging cyclical and linear movements, static and moving imagery. In many sequences, the dramatic accentuation of open, off-screen space through traffic and people speeding across the screen in straight (vertical, horizontal, or diagonal) lines is contrasted with closed circular forms such as those of rotating machines, roulette tables, and fireworks as well as the repeated presentation of the clock and the spiral. Unlike Vertov, Ruttmann rarely makes use of the "unleashed" camera except to present a roundabout view of city space juxtaposed with the linear movements taking place within it. *Berlin* thus introduces the metropolis itself as a form of "second nature" by fusing the linear time of technological progress with the cyclical time of nature. The definitive reconciliation of the two principles is represented in the final shot of the phallic radio-tower endowed with a revolving search light. People are absent at the end of Ruttmann's film just as they were at the very beginning because they are implicitly present and presented as part of the city organism that came alive during the movie itself. The "human" has finally ceased to exist. This demise is at the heart of critics' discomfort with Ruttmann's film and its enthusiasm for the cyborgian complex of city-life.

I deliberately refer to Ruttmann's and Vertov's vision of urban space as "cyborgian" in spite of the obvious fact that the term itself is a recent one and indeed relates more closely to our contemporary debate about *postmodernity* rather than modernity.[47] As Donna Haraway points out with reference to late-twentieth-century society, the cyborg—far from being a mere fantasy image sprung forth from recent science fiction novels and films—actually describes today's total interdependence of human and technological resources in a globally connected environment.[48] The cyborg represents both a threat and a promise: it can be pictured either as the annihilation and mechanization of the human spirit or as an embodied reminder of the irreducible heterogeneity that haunts "humanity." For Haraway, the latter is the more apt and productive reading in so far as it serves to undermine the ideological validation of notions such as human subjectivity, national unity, or natural origin. My own discussion of Ruttmann's *Berlin, The Symphony of a Great City* and Vertov's *Man with a Movie Camera*, on the other hand, has aimed to highlight the political ambivalence of these cyborgian visions which, historically speaking, have lent themselves much more readily to the totalitarian eradication of difference than to Haraway's demand for cultural hybridity and political freedom. The latter represents a utopian vision, the former a historical reality. Ruttmann's and Vertov's films, however, remain caught in the interstices between the two.

In fact, the striking similarities between fascist aesthetics and modernist film have often been noted—for example, with regard to Fritz Lang's masterpieces *Siegfried* (1924) and *Metropolis* (1927)—both of which depict crowds of people shaped into various geometrical patterns that often appear to be part of the architectural space surrounding them. Lang's films provide visual evidence of the Nazis' appropriation of cinematic set designs and mass choreography for the staging of its own rituals of cultural renewal.[49] Siegfried Kracauer aptly discussed Weimar culture and Nazi Party rallies in terms of a "mass ornament" whose propagandistic function was to celebrate the merging of multiple individuals into a machine or a single organism.[50] Indeed, German fascism portrayed the choreographed "movement" of the German Volk as if it represented the very reincarnation of the organic being Ruttmann and Vertov envisioned in the idealized image of the cyborg-city. Like Ruttmann and Vertov, Nazi propaganda pictured the creation of the "new man" as a gigantic body with many indistinguishable faces that literally merge with the architectural and social space they inhabit. To be sure, this is not to denounce Vertov's and Ruttmann's work as inherently fascist, as some critics have done.[51] Rather, it is to question the allegedly self-evident aesthetic differences said to separate the leftist avant garde from fascist aesthetics.[52]

For the major difference between the two lies less in their idealized vision of cultural renewal than in the stylistic features used to portray this vision. Contrary to the avant garde, German fascism hides the coercive and rigid production mechanism that underlies its aestheticization of politics. Nazi film and propaganda do not openly acknowledge the work of the camera and its potentially totalitarian vision, but instead rely on sophisticated cinematic and narrative techniques to suture the picture and counterfeit a sense of ideological closure which ensures its efficiency.[53] Although Leni Riefenstahl's *Triumph of the Will* (1934) also employs cinematic montage in order to accentuate movement, it appropriates these stylistic features for the glorification of the unified German *Volk* instead of the mobile camera or the abstract city, both of which become subservient to, rather than taking control of, this new organism. In light of fascism's propagandistic power, one might conclude that Ruttmann's and Vertov's belief in direct reference and visual immediacy—that is, their effort to picture the lack of lack by openly celebrating the fusion of man and machine—is, paradoxically, more ambivalent (uncanny) and hence less effective than the conservative attempt to obscure the fact yet implement its effects. In Riefenstahl's film, it is the new "human" who makes history—not the machine whose secret mechanism, precisely because it remains hidden, literally enables this totalitarian body to begin moving. In its day, therefore, the avant garde's effort to fully expose these mechanisms and raise them to the level of consciousness remained caught in a modern dialectic of exposure and displacement which could not but result in its own undoing. Thus, the cinematic avant garde ultimately undermined what it had hoped to achieve, namely to render the modern world transparent in order to enable the masses to both critically examine and radically change it.

Seen in this light, recent calls by critics for an exhaustive analysis of the complex compositional structure of Vertov's film in order to "fully understand" or "fully decipher" it seem ironic: firstly, because such calls misidentify the film's main concern, which is not to provide a rational socio-political critique but to focus on the visual appropriation of reality; and secondly, because such efforts at rational explanation mirror precisely Vertov's and modernity's own failed attempt to render "fully" transparent that which ultimately remains obscure, giving rise to the uncanny as marked not by a tangible object there to be seen but by an absence that eludes perception.[54] For the city, much like the cinema, presents an inherently ambivalent picture of modern life which cannot be rendered fully present in its entirety. There is always more to the picture than meets the eye, and Ruttmann's and Vertov's attempt to "see it all" remains as illusory as Bourdais' tower of light illuminating the urban spaces of modernity.

NOTES

1. Wolfgang Schivelbusch, *Disenchanted Night: The Industrialization of Light in the Nineteenth Century*, trans. Angela Davies, Berkeley, CA: University of California Press, 1988, p. 3.
2. Michel Foucault, "The Eye of Power," in Bolin Gordon, ed., *Power/Knowledge: Selected Interviews and Other Writings 1972–1977*, New York: Pantheon, 1980, p. 153.
3. Max Horkheimer and Theodor Adorno, *The Dialectic of Enlightenment*, trans. John Cumming, New York: Continuum, 1972, p. 16.

4. Sigmund Freud, "The Uncanny," *The Standard Edition of the Complete Psychological Works of Sigmund Freud*, trans. James Strachey, vol. XVII, London: Hogarth, 1966, p. 253.

5. Mladen Dolar, "I Shall Be With You On Your Wedding-Night: Lacan and the Uncanny," *October* 58, Fall 1991, pp. 5–24. Similarly Terry Castle, who situates the rise of the uncanny during the latter half of the eighteenth century and its attempt to valorize reason over superstition. See Terry Castle, *The Female Thermometer: Eighteenth-Century Culture and the Invention of the Uncanny*, New York: Oxford University Press, 1995. The gaps in Freud's argument are analyzed in depth by Samuel Weber, "The Sideshow, or: Remarks on a Canny Moment," *Modern Language Notes*, vol. 88, no. 6, December 1973, pp. 1,102–1,133; and by Hélène Cixous, "Fictions and its Phantoms: A Reading of Freud's 'Das Unheimliche'," *New Literary History*, vol. VII, no. 3, Spring 1976, pp. 525–48. For a more recent discussion of Freud's text, see Robin Lydenberg, "Freud's Uncanny Narratives," *PMLA*, vol. 112, no. 5, October 1997, pp. 1,072–1,086.

6. Lydenberg, "Freud's Uncanny Narratives," p. 1,081.

7. Jacques Lacan, *The Four Fundamental Concepts of Psychoanalysis*, trans. Alan Sheridan, New York: Norton, 1978, pp. 85–90.

8. As Mladen Dolar states: "The uncanny is always at stake in ideology—ideology perhaps basically consists of a social attempt to integrate the uncanny, to make it bearable, to assign it a place . . . Thus the criticism of ideology helplessly repeats the modern gesture—the reduction of the uncanny to its 'secular basis' through the very logic that actually produced the uncanny in the first place as the objectal remainder." Mladen Dolar, p. 19.

9. One is reminded of the paradox implicit in Lacan's concept of the mirror-stage, in which the "corps morcelé" appears as a retrospective projection engendered only after the child has identified with the mirror-image, although, chronologically speaking, it must have preceded the identification process. See Jane Gallop, *Reading Lacan*, New York: Cornell University Press, 1985, pp. 72–94.

10. Gilles Deleuze and Félix Guattari, *Anti-Oedipus: Capitalism and Schizophrenia*, trans. Robert Hurley et al., Minneapolis: University of Minnesota Press, 1983, p. 34.

11. See Anthony Vidler, *The Architectural Uncanny. Essays in the Modern Unhomely*, Cambridge, MA: MIT Press, 1992.

12. I am referring, of course, to the Lumière brothers' first public presentation of *L'Arrivée d'un train à La Ciotat* which is generally regarded as the literal arrival of motion pictures. Rumor has it that during its first showing, the spectators dodged aside for fear of being run over by the train. The accuracy of this anecdote has been subjected to doubt ever since, as the spectators' terror seems inconsistent both with their overall level of education and with their familiarity with photography in particular.

13. Georges Demenÿ, quoted in Noël Burch, *Life to those Shadows*, trans. Ben Brewster, Berkeley, CA: University of California Press, 1990, p. 26. Indeed, Dziga Vertov's *Man With a Movie Camera* somewhat redeems Marey's futuristic vision as it presents an array of single frames focusing on individual faces and subsequently grants them "life" as they begin to move.

14. Robert Hughes, *The Shock of the New*, New York: Knopf, 1998, p. 10.

15. See David P. Jordan, *Transforming Paris: The Life and Labors of Baron Haussmann*, New York: Free Press, 1995.

16. Stefan Zweig, "The Monotonization of the World," in Anton Kaes et al., eds, *The Weimar Republic Source Book*, Berkeley, CA: University of California Press, 1994, p. 397.

17. Oswald Spengler, "The Soul of the City," in Richard Sennett, ed., *Classic Essays on the Culture of Cities*, New Jersey: Prentice-Hall, 1969, p. 65.

18. Spengler, "The Soul of the City," p. 77.

19. Ibid.

20. Robert Park, "The City: Suggestions for the Investigation of Human Behavior in the Urban Environment" in Richard Sennett, ed., *Classic Essays on the Culture of Cities*, New Jersey: Prentice-Hall, 1969, p. 93f.

21. See Richard Sennett, ed., "An Introduction," *Classic Essays on the Culture of Cities*, New Jersey: Prentice-Hall, 1969, p. 12.

22. James Donald, "The City, the Cinema: Modern Spaces," in Chris Jenks, ed., *Visual Culture*, London: Routledge, 1995, p. 83.

23. See Vidler, *The Architectural Uncanny*.

24. Michel de Certeau, *The Practice of Everyday Life*, trans. Steven F. Rendall, Berkeley, CA: University of California Press, 1984.

25. As Christian Metz has argued, we need to distinguish between language and language system: cinema certainly qualifies for the former, but not for the latter, since it does not have a prescribed grammar. Instead, its grammar is continuously being invented as actual films are being produced. See Christian Metz, *Film Language. A Semiotics of the Cinema*, trans. Michael Taylor, Chicago, IL: University of Chicago Press, 1974, pp. 60, 75.

26. Harald Nicolson, quoted in Patricia Petro, *Joyless Streets: Women and Melodramatic Representation in Weimar Germany*, Princeton, NJ: Princeton University Press, 1989, p. 40.

27. The term was coined by Donald M. Lowe in his *History of Bourgeois Perception*, Chicago, IL: University of Chicago Press, 1982.

28. Wolfgang Schivelbusch, *The Railway Journey: The Industrialization of Time and Space in the Nineteenth Century*, Berkeley, CA: University of California Press, 1986, p. 61.

29. Leo Charney and Vanessa R. Schwartz, eds, *Cinema and the Invention of Modern Life*, Berkeley, CA: University of California Press, 1995, p. 1.

30. Walter Benjamin, "The Work of Art in the Age of Mechanical Reproduction," in *Illuminations*, trans. Harry Zohn, London: Fontana/Collins, 1982, pp. 211–44. Erhard Kienzl, for example, stated as early as 1911 that "the psychology of the cinematographic triumph is metropolitan psychology. Not only because the big city constitutes the natural focal point for all manifestations of social life, but especially because the metropolitan soul, that ever-harried soul, curious, and unanchored, tumbling from fleeting impression to fleeting impression, is quite rightly the cinematographic soul." Quoted in Anton Kaes, "The Debate about Cinema: Charting a Controversy (1909–1929)," *New German Critique*, vol. 40, Winter 1987, pp. 7–33. Similarly Emilie Altenloh in her empirical study of early German film, published in 1914: "The cinema belongs above all to modern man, those who drift along and live accordingly to the laws of the moment." (Emilie Altenloh, *Zur Soziologie des Kino: die Kino-Unternehmung und die sozialen Schichten ihrer Besucher*, Jena, Diederichs, 1914.)

31. Jean-Louis Baudry, "Ideological Effects of the Basic Cinematographic Apparatus," in Gerald Mast et al., eds, *Film Theory and Criticism*, New York: Oxford University Press, 1992, 4th edition, p. 311.

32. Christian Metz, *The Imaginary Signifier: Psychoanalysis and the Cinema*, Bloomington, IN: Indiana University Press, 1982, p. 56.

33. Abel Gance, quoted in Paul Virilio, *War and Cinema: The Logistics of Perception*, trans. Patrick Camiller, London: Verso, 1989.

34. See Siegfried Kracauer, *From Caligari to Hitler*, Princeton, NJ: Princeton University Press, 1947, p. 184.

35. Quoted in Vlada Petric, *Constructivism in Film: Man With a Movie Camera—A Cinematic Analysis*, Cambridge: Cambridge University Press, 1987, pp. 65 and 56 respectively.

36. The term was introduced by Tom Gunning, "An Aesthetics of Astonishment: Early Film and the (In)Credulous Spectator," *Art and Text*, 34, 1989, pp. 34–45.

37. Dziga Vertov, "Kinoks. A Revolution," in Annette Michelson, ed., *Kino-Eye: The Writings of Dziga Vertov*, trans. Kevin O'Brien, Berkeley, CA: University of California Press, 1984, p. 17.

38. Samuel Weber, "The Sideshow, or Remarks on a Canny Moment," *Modern Language Notes*, 88, December 6 1973, p. 1,133.

39. Benjamin, "A Short History of Photography," p. 252.

40. Most critics have pointed out that Ruttmann's *Berlin* does not show any individuals at all, but "is more concerned with people as a mass," thus pointing to the central issue at stake in Ruttmann's film, namely that "the human being is missing." See Jay Chapman, "Two Aspects of the City: Cavalcanti and Ruttmann," in Lewis Jacobs, ed., *The Documentary Tradition. From Nanook to Woodstock*, New York: Hopkinson, 1971, p. 37; and Bernhard von Brentano, quoted in Jean Paul Goergen,

Walter Ruttmann: Eine Dokumentation, Freunde der Deutschen Kinemathek, 1989, p. 28. For a more comprehensive overview regarding critical literature on Ruttmann's film, see also Sabine Hake, "Urban Spectacle in Walter Ruttmann's *Berlin, The Symphony of a Great City*," in Thomas W. Kniesche and Stephen Brockmann, eds, *Dancing on the Volcano: Essays on the Culture of the Weimar Republic*, Columbia, SC: Camden, 1994, pp. 127–42.

41. "Interview with Licht-bild-Bühne," October 8 1927; quoted in Goergen, p. 80.

42. "Spielplan des Tauentzien-Palast," Berlin, September 23–9 1927; quoted in Goergen, p. 80.

43. Vertov, "Kinoks: A Revolution," p. 17.

44. Ibid., p. 16.

45. In Benjaminian terms, Vertov's and Ruttmann's films provide an excellent opportunity for the metropolitan masses to "rehearse" and "master" the new paradigm of modern perception. Again, the question arises as to the emancipatory or reactionary teleology implicit in this rehearsal, which indeed may serve only to transform human beings into well-programmed, functional machines rather than critical subjects.

46. Jean-Pierre Oudart and Daniel Dayan were among the first critics to apply Lacan's concept of "suture" to the analysis of mainstream film. See Jean-Pierre Oudart, "Cinema and Suture," *Screen*, vol. 18, no. 4, Winter 1977/78, pp. 35–47; Daniel Dayan, "The Tutor Code of Classical Cinema," in Gerald Mast et al., eds, *Film Theory and Criticism*, New York: Oxford University Press, 1992, pp. 179–91. Dayan's text was originally published as the English exposition of Oudart's work.

47. The term "cyborg" was coined by NASA scientists in 1950. It is used as an acronym for "cybernetic organism" and refers to any kind of fusion of human and mechanical parts into a single living organism. For a more thorough discussion of the term, see Chris Hables Gray, ed., *The Cyborg Handbook*, New York: Routledge, 1995.

48. Donna J. Haraway, "A Cyborg Manifesto," in *Simians, Cyborgs, and Women: The Reinvention of Nature*, New York: Routledge, 1991.

49. See Dieter Bartetzko, *Zwischen Zucht und Ekstase: Zur Theatralität von NS-Architektur*, Berlin: Mann, 1985.

50. Siegfried Kracauer, "The Mass-Ornament," in Anton Kaes et al., eds, *The Weimar Republic Sourcebook*, Berkeley, CA: University of California Press, 1994, pp. 404–7.

51. See Jeremy Murray-Brown, "False Cinema: Dziga Vertov and Early Soviet Film," *The New Criterion*, November 1989, pp. 21–33. A more balanced approach is presented by William Uricchio, "Ruttmann nach 1933," in Jean Paul Goergen, pp. 59–66.

52. In an article on Ruttmann, Barry A. Fulks rightly contends that "the basic motif of the cinematic avant garde, namely the search for a visual culture and a purely cinematic form of expression, was being appropriated by the Nazi regime . . . without

any problems." See Barry A. Fulks, "Walter Ruttmann, der Avantgardefilm und die Nazi-Moderne," in Jean Paul Goergen, p. 67. James Donald, by contrast, acknowledges that Vertov's film prefigures "the city of total surveillance," yet immediately distinguishes Vertov's formalist politics from the aestheticized "kitsch of fascism" by means of Vertov's "romantic ethic of personal and social perfectibility"—a surprising criterion given fascism's own indebtedness to Romantic imagery. James Donald, "The City, the Cinema: Modern Spaces," in Chris Jenks, ed., *Visual Culture*, London: Routledge, 1995, p. 90.

53. See Eric Rentschler, *The Ministry of Illusion: Nazi Cinema and its Afterlife*, Cambridge, MA: Harvard University Press, 1996; and Linda Schulte-Sasse, *Entertaining the Third Reich: Illusions of Wholeness in Nazi Cinema*, Durham, NC: Duke University Press, 1996.

54. Recent studies of Vertov's *Man With a Movie Camera* suggest the important role of the spectators as "decipherers of its images," which in turn requires an exhaustive analysis of the entire "film as a whole." See Noël Burch, "Film's Institutional Mode of Representation and the Soviet Response," *October* 11, Winter 1979, p. 94. Similarly Petric, p. 78f.

2

RUTTMANN'S BERLIN: FILMING IN A "HOLLOW SPACE"?

MARTIN GAUGHAN

When Walter Ruttmann's film *Berlin, Symphonie einer Großtadt* (*Berlin, The Symphony of a Great City*) was released in 1927 both subject matter (the city of Berlin) and aesthetic mode (montage) were already the focus of intense ideological and cultural discussion. More visibly marked since the beginning of the twentieth century than London or Paris by the processes of an accelerated modernization and rapid urbanization, Berlin's transitory character was the occasion for concerned commentary from both the right and left of the political spectrum. A couple of years prior to Ruttmann's film that modernizing process was intensified through the Americanization of the German economy, with its automated technology and the increasing mechanization of the labor process in factory and office. This revolution in everyday life brought about related changes in the social (for example, newly emerging subjectivities, among which were those of the white-collar consumers of a vastly expanded mass culture arena) and in the cultural (stylistic innovation characterized as the New Objectivity). The term New Objectivity (*Neue Sachlichkeit*) became the designation for changes both in the economic order, with its precisely stamped mass production, and in the cultural sphere, with photographic replication in close-up of machines, machine parts, and products, and a pronounced fascination among some artists with surface sheen and appearance. Ruttmann's *Berlin, The Symphony of a Great City*, as we shall see below, was criticized on grounds of such replication and fascination, for being lured by the appearance of Berlin's modernity, unconcerned with its more complex workings, for presenting an unmotivated series of images, simply mirroring the city.[1] While the designation "New Objectivity" is not unproblematic, there was a general consensus in German critical debate on its key characteristics, and especially its difference from its two immediate cultural predecessors, Expressionism and Dada. Both of these were considered as disruptive to the system; but the New Objectivity was perceived, certainly by critics on the left, as being compliant with an increasingly rationalized social order and, consequently, as reactionary.

Undoubtedly an innovative contribution to filmic representation of the city, *Berlin, The Symphony of a Great City* is worth revisiting in its own right; but refamiliarization with the issues raised in the critical debates it gave rise to is equally rewarding. Together, the film and its reception constitute a paradigmatic moment in the visualization and theorization of the experience of modernity in Weimar Germany. This chapter initially establishes the "narrative" of Ruttmann's film and his intentions for it. It then proceeds to consider what kind of object or process the urban was, how its dynamics were theorized, before Ruttmann pointed his camera at it—to ascertain, in other words, how the city was "understood," not just "experienced," and how discourse and representation interrelated. Finally, the chapter engages with crucial moments in the critical reception of Ruttmann's film, then and now.

In preparation for the film, Ruttmann recorded impressions, ideas, images, and details, in an ad hoc manner on card indexes, several hundred of which constituted a kind of script, a system which allowed him to cross-reference, plan shots, and compose the rhythmic analogies he was working toward. The film was shot over a year, throughout Berlin. With the exception of two passages all the episodes were unstaged.

Berlin, The Symphony of a Great City belongs to that genre characterized by Siegfried Kracauer, then cultural correspondent for the *Frankfurter Zeitung*, as "cross-section"—here, the cross-section of a Berlin working day in late spring. A description of its unfolding may be briefly attempted: an early morning express train rushes toward the city, slowing down through its suburbs and arriving at the Anhalter terminus. Then shots of empty streets, where a clock shows 5 a.m. Some slight activity, night revelers returning, a billboard sticker, then, at about 7 a.m., some industrial workers setting off. The pace quickens, more workers, the urban transport system and subways becoming more crowded, visually carried by quick cutting on movements to and from platforms, up and down steps. Factory wheels begin to turn, close-ups of machines and products but not workers. As the clock shows 8 a.m., business begins its day, filing cabinets open, hands lift telephones—we are introduced to the world of the white-collar worker, a world visibly different from that of the industrial workers seen earlier, in which the presence of the New Woman (*Die neue Frau*), fashionably dressed, is notable. Slightly later the entrepreneurs and professionals set out from their luxury flats or suburban villas. By mid-morning, Potsdamer Platz, the energizing hub of Berlin's distinctive tempo, is in full flow. Street incidents multiply. Past midday the city slows down, inhabitants eat and rest. Then the tempo picks up again. Production, including the printing of an evening newspaper, starts up again. A woman commits (a staged) suicide. The end of the working day is signaled by the reverse of its beginning: factory wheels stop, files are closed, telephones unplugged. Various sporting and leisure activities are pursued. Darkness falls, the city is dramatically lit, its prominent street, the Kurfürstendamm, illuminated. We enter a cinema, see a stage show, sporting events, a high class restaurant and a local *Kneipe*. The day closes with a firework display set against the silhouette of the radio tower, a recently built landmark of Berlin's striking modernity.

Ruttmann, who had trained as a painter and had made purely abstract films since 1921, emphasized the formal innovation of the film in his stated program. In a brief pre-release contribution to the journal *Filmspiegel* in May 1927 he set down four points, the first of which insisted on "the consistent realization of the musical-rhythmic demands" of his montage practice.[2] Immediacy of effect would be achieved through concealed filming—Berlin's citizens and their behavior would be taken unawares. "The life of the city must be surprised and non-consciously filmed," he wrote in the Berlin paper *BZ am Mittag*.[3] Each incident would be "visually self-sufficient . . . [with] no intertitles."[4] In a longer article entitled "How I Shot My Berlin Film," he referred to his interest since 1921 in representing movement through the mobilization of abstract geometric forms while always retaining the desire "to construct from living material, to create a film symphony from the million-fold actual energies of the great city organism."[5] Indeed, his concluding passage to the article would seem to confirm the charge of formalism made against him by hostile critics: "I believe that most of those who experience the intoxication of speed during my *Berlin* film will not know where that comes from. And if I have succeeded in bringing them to the pitch which allows them to experience the city of Berlin, then I have achieved my objective."[6] Ruttmann explicitly rejected the category of *reportage*, a distinctive element in the emerging formation of the New Objectivity,[7] and insisted that "art was not anymore a flight from the world but an immersion in it and the clarification of its essence. Art is no longer abstraction but a point of view."[8] Ruttmann hoped that he had "allowed his audience to experience the city," and had enabled a heightened awareness of the "tense, gripping qualities of everyday life."[9]

Critical reception of *Berlin, The Symphony of a Great City* can be roughly grouped into three categories. Firstly, there were those who generally accepted the aesthetic premise articulated by Ruttmann and praised the film for its articulation of the real. The Catholic Center Party paper *Germania*, for example, described it as "a magnificently successful attempt to let reality speak for itself," while *BZ am Mittag* declared it to be a lesson for artists "to show the real, always the real! There is nothing more beautiful or fantastic."[10] But then there were those, mainly on the left, who rejected the film for its inability to deal with immediate social issues—for example, the German Communist Party paper, *Die Rote Fahne*, in which Paul Friedländer argued that the film's overall "economic, social and political content was limited."[11] And, finally, there was Siegfried Kracauer, who, specializing in theories of photography and film and developing as a historical materialist rather than a political Marxist, was more questioning of Ruttmann's aesthetic claims than most and somewhat distanced from the immediate concerns of the Socialist or Communist Party responses.

Of course, Berlin, the city, as material fabric and social organism, industrial center and communications network, was probably buffeted more than most cities in the early twentieth century by those maelstrom-like forces of the modernizing process characterized by Marshall Berman.[12] The particular qualities of the maelstrom of modernity as it affected Berlin may be indicatively traced by reference to three of the city's most important commentators. In his 1910 book, *Berlin: The Destiny of a City*, Karl Scheffler concerned himself with the rapidity of the physiognomic and cultural changes then taking place in the city, and remarked strikingly that "Berlin is condemned ever to becoming, never to being."[13] A quarter of a century later, in 1935, the unorthodox Marxist cultural philosopher, Ernst Bloch, writing from exile in Switzerland, updated Scheffler's perceptions in his aphoristic-cum-essayistic reflections on the Weimar period, *Heritage of our Times*. In a section titled "Transition: Berlin, Functions in Hollow Space," Bloch went deeper beneath the surface than Scheffler had, claiming that "Berlin . . . is a constantly new city, built hollow, on which not even the lime becomes or is really set."[14] Finally, Siegfried Kracauer responded to the series of Berlin "Street" films, in particular to Walter Ruttmann's *Berlin*, by writing "These films are like the dreams called forth by the paralyzed authoritarian disposition for which no direct outlet is left. *Berlin* is the product of the paralysis itself."[15]

What the above quotations from Scheffler, Bloch, and Kracauer share is a suggestion of the presence of problems in the representation of what it is that Berlin is, of what the experience of its modernity might be. Both Bloch and Kracauer, in particular, as historical materialists, are intent on excavating beneath the surface to one degree or another in order to discover the plan of the city, its origins, its governing forces, rather than just contenting themselves with the changing appearance of the fabric of the city and its forms of social circulation as a spectacle for consumption. In other words, both Kracauer (directly) and Bloch (indirectly) challenge the status of knowledge of urban experience under the conditions of modernity provided by films such as Ruttmann's *Berlin*. It is necessary, therefore, to address some of the grounds upon which their claims to a counter-knowledge of the city might be staked. While there are parallels between the operations of Kracauer and Bloch, on the one hand, and of Ruttmann, on the other—for example, their *flânerie*, their urban explorations and excursions, their observations and recording of the city—there are also crucial differences. To establish these it is necessary to discuss briefly the rich tradition of Berlin urban sociology which informed contemporary cultural criticism.

The urban sociology that Kracauer, Bloch, and Benjamin were initially introduced to was that of Georg Simmel, whose lectures they attended or whose circle they frequented. Simmel's 1903 essay, "The Metropolis and Mental Life," is still a classic contribution to the subject.[16] Characterized at one level as "sociological impressionism" (embodied in the title of David Frisby's 1981 study) Simmel's work was speculative, non-empirical, and culturalist.[17] If this were the extent of his contribution then the status of a claim to knowledge would be highly dubious, defective as it would appear to be by its reliance on the immediate, the absence of a mediated process. While antipathetic to Marxism and not philosophically an historical materialist, Simmel nevertheless recognized the operations of what he termed "the money economy" and its systemic role in urban formation. Roy Pascal writes of Simmel's 1908 book, *The Philosophy of Money*, that Simmel referred to the urbanizing process as "the typical crystallization of high capitalism."[18] Indeed, we might speculate that when Kracauer and Benjamin were botanizing on the asphalt they too were informed, particularly after the November Revolution of 1918, of this dimension of urban sociology. They might be seen as ideal representatives of the procedure described by Joachim Schlör in his recently translated *Nights in the Big City: Paris, Berlin, London, 1840–1930*. In a section entitled "Insight while walking," he writes that

> the structure of the city cannot be taken in while walking, just walking past: the functioning of its different individual parts demands thorough systematic examination. It could be, however, that there are aspects of urban life that evade the penetrating gaze of systematic research, while disclosing themselves for an instant to the person who walks past by chance.[19]

It would appear that the trained architect, social, film, and photographic theorist, Kracauer, had, as it were, a more multi-layered perspectival range than the abstract filmmaker, Ruttmann; that Kracauer was in a better position to seize the instant disclosure because of his systematic understanding of the urbanizing process. These are the grounds upon which his evaluation of *Berlin* might be judged, that the montage is structured on "fictitious transitions which are void of content" and consequently that "(t)his symphony fails to point out anything, because it does not uncover a single significant context."[20]

Simmel's contemporary and fellow social theorist, Werner Sombart, proposed another important connection between capitalism and the urban, recognizing the systemic relationship and its impact on cultural production. "Metropolitan *Kultur*" he writes, "is thus the *Kultur* of the capitalist programme of planning."[21] Whether or not Kracauer or Bloch were familiar with this somewhat deterministic account of the relationship, it bears striking resonance with their own slightly later descriptions of the relationship in the context of mid-1920s Weimar Berlin, at the time Ruttmann began working on his film. In their account, the rationalization of the economy was characterized as a reified social process underpinned by scientific work practices and the mechanization and fragmentation of human participation. The charge leveled by Kracauer at Ruttmann's *Berlin* was that he failed to see the relationship between the technological and the representational. It is important to remember at this point that there was a rich and generally critical set of representations of Berlin's modernity already to hand in the work of the artists Kirchner, Grosz, and Dix. The critical qualities of Expressionism and Dada were seen as having been displaced by the conformism of the New Objectivity. Bloch in particular was exercised by the oppositional potential of Expressionism.

With the above perceptions in place—urbanization as the systemic growth of capital, its determining influence on culture and subjectivity, and its displacement of more radical visual forms—we can now return to the Berlin of the mid-1920s as perceived by Bloch and Kracauer.[22] In "Transition: Berlin Functions in Hollow Space," Bloch writes that "the city is right *in front* in late bourgeois terms."[23] It seems "in fact extraordinarily 'contemporaneous'," but he qualified this contemporaneity: "it is for the present only 'contemporaneous' in the limited, indeed inauthentic sense, namely that of being merely up to date."[24] Its inauthenticity, its limited contemporaneity, results from the absence of reason (*ratio*) in the capitalist rationalization process. Bloch comments: "*Ratio* in (an) anarchistic profit economy is an active contradiction," a judgment with which Kracauer was in agreement, when he characterized the *ratio* of capitalism as "not reason itself but a reason rendered dreary . . . It does not rationalize too much but rather too little. The thought which it bears resists the completion of reason which speaks from the foundations of humanity."[25] Concerned with the façadism, both literal and symbolic, of the cultural products of that rationalization process, Bloch claims with regard to this objectivity that "nothing is expressed in this except emptiness," an emptiness that is "so nickel-plated that it gleams and captivates."[26] He writes of "the naked, apparent overbright Objectivity" that it is "the highest, also the most unrecognizable form of diversion," and, echoing Sombart, that it corresponds to the "capitalist planned economy."[27] The theme of façadism is also highlighted by Michael Bienert in his study *The Imagined Metropolis: Berlin in the Feuilletons of the Weimar Republic*, in which Bienert refers to a 1928 publication on contemporary Berlin architecture in which the shopfronts on the Kurfürstendamm, a major West End boulevard featured in Ruttmann's film, are described as "Potemkin fronts" (*Potemkinkulissen*), painted scenography behind which there is nothing.[28] Reacting to the ever-changing profile of the street under directionless modernization, Kracauer titled his short street-essay on the Kurfürstendamm "Street without Memory" (*Strasse ohne Errinerung*). Anticipating Benjamin's conceptualization of time in *Theses on the Philosophy of History*, Kracauer wrote: "Some streetscapes . . . appear to have been fashioned for eternity; today's Kurfürstendamm is the embodiment of an empty flowing time in which nothing is allowed to last."[29]

The idea of Berlin as a permanent film set is nicely evoked in a 1926 observation by the cultural commentator Alfred Polgar: "Film occupies Berlin . . . Confused by klieg lights, the stranger often has the impression that the true Berlin, at this moment, could very well be a film vision built out of cardboard, and that the real houses are only placed there in order to feign a little bit of 'real city'."[30] The interplay between façade and the real is perceptibly on the surface here, and as such relatively unproblematic. But given the theorization of the experience of urban modernity provided by Simmel, Sombart, Bloch, and Kracauer, we must question the adequacy of Ruttmann's montage in the representation of the "real life" (*wirkliches Leben*) of Berlin through, as Ruttmann claimed, "a heightened awareness of everyday life, tense, gripping, dramatic."[31]

An immediate context for Kracauer's engagement with issues raised by *Berlin* was his work on white-collar workers, their leisure pursuits, their cinema interests and mode of spectatorship, particularly as it was excited by tempo, a quality Kracauer recognized as central to Ruttmann's film, "a formal idea which does not imply content either and perhaps for that reason intoxicates the petty bourgeoisie in real life and literature."[32] In a sense it might be claimed that he saw them as a "hollow class," the products of an economically rationalizing social order, the inhabitants of Bloch's "Hollow Space." For Kracauer, Ruttmann's film was essentially the cultural offspring of economic rationalization, made in the aesthetic mode of New Objectivity, its montage answering to the need for distraction of the petty bourgeois spectator. Here is Kracauer's characterization of the white-collar worker:

In the evenings one strolls through the streets, filled with a frustration from which no fullness can grow. Over there, flickering words pass into this exotic advertisement. The body puts down roots in the asphalt, and the mind, which is no longer ours, wanders endlessly with these enlightening slogans of light, of the night into the night.[33]

In such a state, Kracauer indicates later in this essay on boredom, the white-collar worker may enter the cinema to be distracted. He returns to the subject in a passage on *Haus Vaterland*, one of those new centers of pleasure he would describe as *Vergnügenskaserne*, barracks of pleasure, an ironic reference to Berlin's notorious tenements or rental barracks, *Mietskaserne*:

At the same time as the offices are being rationalized, the big cafes rationalise the pleasure of the office workers' armies. The ambiance is especially opulent at Haus Vaterland, which is the perfect prototype for the style also aimed at in movie palaces and the establishments frequented by the lower middle classes.

For Kracauer, one of the characteristics of this style "is to present a façade which hides nothing, which does not emerge from a depth but merely simulates one."[34]

This relationship between economic rationalization, cultural rationalization, and the production of subjectivities (the white-collar worker) is crucial for an understanding of Kracauer's critique of Ruttmann's film. In a recent chapter on the film, "Urban Spectacle in Walter Ruttmann's *Berlin, The Symphony of a Great City*," Sabine Hake expands on Kracauer's perceptions but keeps this nexus firmly in mind.[35] For her, as for Kracauer, both the origin and focus of the film's spectatorship is the white-collar worker, the structuring of whose gaze "legitimizes the authority of modern mass culture and its obsession with visual spectacle."[36] Drawing upon concepts of voyeurism, scopophilia, and visual pleasure, she claims that the basis of "a new kind of urbanism rooted in imagination and desire" is being established, in which "the celebration of the image as such confirms spectatorship as the dominant mode of relating to the outside world," essentially a conflation of "visual perception and social experience."[37] She sees the film as "bringing to perfection the fetishization of spectacle and specularity," but "without critical awareness."[38]

What I have concentrated on mainly to this point has been the pre-filmic configuration of the urban. I have been mostly concerned with the production of a set of representations resulting from a largely historical materialist theorization of the urban. Flexible and accommodating, its rhetorical modes, not unlike the mobility of a camera, ranged from the observational *flânerie* of Benjamin and Kracauer, to the cultural philosophy of Bloch, to the empirically informed investigation of white-collar workers by Kracauer. As such, this theorization might have provided the basis for an excellent cross-section film, but not the one Ruttmann produced. Ruttmann's film was panned.

In recent years, attempts have been made to challenge the film's original critical rejection, most recently by Wolfgang Natter, in his 1994 essay, "The City as Cinematic Space: Modernism and Place in *Berlin: Symphony of a Great City*."[39] Natter questions the basis of Kracauer's negative response to the film, beginning with a crucial distinction between "cinematic space," which he defines as "the submerged spatiality inherent to film and the filmic apparatus," and, on the other hand, the pre-filmic "place."[40] Natter claims that Kracauer paid too little attention to "cinematic space" (the imaginary Berlin) and too much attention to "place" (the real Berlin of his experience), therefore mis-reading the film as a documentary. This claim derives from Natter's preference for Benjamin's sensitivity to "filmic spatiality" as mobile and dialectical in contrast to Kracauer's perception of it as "inert, undialectical and immobile."[41] The crucial Benjamin passage which Natter draws upon is:

> Our taverns and our metropolitan streets, our offices and furnished rooms, our railroad stations and our factories, appeared to have us locked up hopelessly. Then came the film and burst this prison world asunder by the dynamite of the tenth of a second. So that now, in the midst of its far-flung ruins and debris, we calmly and adventurously go traveling.[42]

As Natter explains, the principal agent of this new freedom is "the cut" which "thoroughly defines film as spatial."[43] Natter invokes Benjamin's idea of an "unconscious optics," allowing him to claim that "unconsciously experienced space is substituted in film for a space consciously explored by human beings."[44]

The argument is conducted at a complex theoretical level but a couple of important reservations must be put in place. Kracauer is not unaware of the unconscious dimension in our experience of space. Exploring sites not frequented by Benjamin—for example, employment exchanges in working class

Berlin—he set down one of the principles governing his understanding of the social production of space:

> Each typical space is brought into being by typical social relationships that, without the distorting intervention of consciousness, express themselves in it. Everything that consciousness has disavowed, everything that has been intentionally overlooked, participates in that space's structuring. Spatial images are the dreams of society. Wherever the hieroglyph of any spatial image is deciphered, there the basis of social reality presents itself.[45]

Bienert's caution that one should not succumb to a Freudian reading of this passage is to be commended, emphasizing as it does the hieroglyphic presence, the word/picture relationship, whose meaning is decipherable from others in the same series, the outcome of a deliberate procedure. Bienert quotes Inka Mülder, who characterizes Kracauer's deployment of the "dream" conceit as "dreams without the dream work."[46]

Natter further writes of Ruttmann that he is "intoxicated with geometry." He discovers Benjamin's "unconscious optics" in the filmmaker's "disclosure of geometric space" and criticizes Kracauer for "his suspicions regarding the presumed asocial context of geometric-spatial representation."[47] Kracauer was acutely aware of the structuring role of abstraction and the geometric in the social, as elaborated in his collection of essays *The Mass Ornament* (1927), in which he wrote of the "geometric precision" of the Tiller Girls, "who radiantly illustrated the virtues of the conveyor belt . . . when they kicked their legs high with mathematical precision, they joyously affirmed the progress of rationalization."[48] For Kracauer, abstraction was a vital element in moving toward reason, but under what he theorized as the defective reason of the rationalizing process abstraction became a merely decorative element in the culture of the New Objectivity, shaping the architectural fabric of Berlin, the movements of its dancing girls, the stadium patterns of physical culture. Although Natter fails to take into account major aspects of Kracauer's theory which informed his negative response to Ruttmann's *Berlin*, his essay nonetheless usefully questions Kracauer's account, particularly as it mobilizes Benjamin's ideas.

In this light, one might now suggest that Ruttmann's film was far more sophisticated than Kracauer understood it to be. Sabine Hake writes:

In simulating the urban experience, *Berlin* offers a view of the modern city that is more radical in its formal solution to the crisis of representation than melodramatic street films or class-conscious leftist films. Reification, mechanization and the cult of functionality return as the essence of modern urban life.[49]

Hake's understanding of the crisis of representation is indebted to the critical tradition established by Kracauer, Benjamin, and others. She recognizes in Ruttmann's formalism a provocative limit case of representational strategies. It is not that Ruttmann's film fails to tell us anything about Berlin's experience of modernity—even the reviewer for the Communist Party newspaper, Paul Friedländer, admitted that there were some significant juxtapositionings—but that filmic space is not as autonomous as Natter would have it, that there is a greater porosity between its space and the more overtly present social space as characterized by Bloch and Kracauer. We now come to recognize just how problematic that representation is.

There is much at stake in the debate between Kracauer's conjunctural reading of the late 1920s and more recent attempts to liberate the film from the constraints Kracauer's reading imposed. Jean Paul Goergen, in his introductory essay in the catalogue, *Walter Ruttmann: Eine Dokumentation*, argues that *Berlin* marked a turning point in the filmic representation of the city in its "transposition of observation, in the transition from the documentation of an object to the documentation of an experience."[50]

The representation of experience was, of course, central to Kracauer's concern but so too was the constitution of experience. Suspicious at best of the possibility of "concrete" experience within the impaired *ratio* of capitalist modernization, he would have shared Benjamin's distinction: "concrete experience (*Erfahrung*) is the product of labor; individual lived experience (*Erlebnis*) is the phantasmagoria of the idler."[51] With the rationalization of work, and particularly the office work of the white-collar worker, individual experience was becoming more phantasmal and, consequently, satisfaction was increasingly sought through distraction, no more so than in the city itself and its filmic representations. For Kracauer, therefore, Ruttmann's *Berlin* did not mark a transition to the "documentation of experience" but another moment in its impoverishment; Ruttmann's transitions were merely formal, "fictitious transitions which are void of content," not uncovering a "single significant context."[52] While Benjamin was not to write about the aestheticization of politics by Fascism until the 1930s, Kracauer was already alert to such tendencies.[53] "During the Third Reich, for example," the American historian Barry A. Fulks informs us, "Ruttmann's *Berlin*, by dint of the virtuosity of its montage and its revelation of the beauty of technology, was considered to be among the foremost paradigms of the *Kulturfilm*."[54] Ruttmann was also assistant to Riefenstahl on *Triumph of the Will* and made a number of documentaries for the regime.[55] This reference to his post-1933 career is not mobilized to condemn the *Berlin* film but to point up the complex dimensions of Kracauer's theorization of urban experience and its representation in the "empty flowing time" of capitalist modernization and its New Objectivity culture.

NOTES

1. To anticipate dimensions of the criticism to be encountered below a distinction may be proposed between the montage practice of Eisenstein and of Ruttmann, indebted to Lukács' attempted definition of realism. For Lukács a "realist" practice recognizes the difference between (social) appearance and (social) essence, the requirement to get below the surface, to disclose what was being veiled. Eisenstein's montage, characterized as conceptual or intellectual, operated with that distinction, Ruttmann's did not.

2. Jean Paul Goergen, ed., *Walter Ruttmann: Eine Dokumentation*, Freunde der Deutschen Kinemathek, 1989, p. 79: "Konsequente Durchführung der musikalisch-rhythmischen Forderungen des Films."

3. Ibid., p. 79: "ich mußte hineingehen in das Leben der Großstadt, *unbemerkt* aufnehmen, denn keines der Objekte durfte etwas von der Aufnahme wissen und im Bewußtsein 'gefilmt' zu werden."

4. Ibid., p. 79: "Jeder Vorgang spricht durch sich selbst—also: keine Titel."

5. Ibid., p. 80: "aus Lebendigen Material zu bauen, aus den millionenfachen, tatsächlich vorhandenen Bewegungsenergien des Großstadtorganismus eine Film—Sinfonie zu schaffen."

6. Ibid., p. 80: "Ich glaube, daß die meisten, die an meinem Berlin—Film den Rausch der Bewegung erleben, nicht wissen, woher ihr Rausch kommt. Und wenn es mir gelungen ist, die Menschen zum Schwingen zu bringen, sie die Stadt Berlin erleben zu lassen, dann habe ich mein Ziel erreicht und damit den Beweis gegeben, dass ich recht habe."

7. Ibid., p. 190: "I do not accept that *Symphony of a Great City* can be designated a reportage film." ("Ich bin nicht damit einverstanden, daß man die *Sinfonie der Groß-tadt* Reportagefilm nennt.")

8. Ibid., p. 82. "Denn Kunst . . . Nicht mehr eine Flucht aus der Welt in höhere Sphären, sondern ein Hineinsteigen in die Welt und die Verdeutlichung ihres Wesens. *Kunst ist nicht mehr Abstraktion, sondern Stellungnahme!*"

9. Ibid., p. 80: "das Leben, alltägliches Leben, spannend, erschütternd, dramatisch ist."

10. See "Ein grandiös gelungener Versuch, die Wirklichkeit aus sich sprechen zu lassen," in ibid., p. 30; and "Welche Lehre für Künstler, Wirkliches nur Wirkliches anzuschauen. Es gibt nichts Schöneres und Phantasticheres," ibid.

11. Ibid., pp. 117–18: "Darum ist dieser Film . . . ein Film, dessen wirtschaftliche, soziale, politische Ausbeute gering ist."

12. Marshall Berman, *All That Is Solid Melts Into Air: The Experience of Modernity*, London: Verso, 1983, p. 15.

13. *Berlin: Ein Stadtschicksal*, Berlin: Erich Reiss Verlag, 1910, p. 267. "Berlin ist dazu verdammt immerfort zu werden, niemals zu sein." Translation from the German, unless otherwise indicated, is by me. Scheffler was the editor of *Kunst und Künstler* (*Art and Artist*), and wrote widely about Berlin culture. In the above book he notes that the accelerated "tempo" of modernization has accelerated the production and consumption of high art, a concern which animates much of the debate that follows.

14. Ernst Bloch, *Heritage of Our Times*, trans. Neville and Stephen Plaice, London: Polity Press, 1991, p. 195.

15. Siegfried Kracauer, *From Caligari to Hitler: A Psychological History of the German Film*, Princeton, NJ: Princeton University Press, 1947, p. 187. Kracauer's characteriza-tion here is not unlike James Joyce's comment on his *Dubliners*: "I call the series *Dubliners* to betray the soul of that hemiplegia or paralysis which many consider a city" (quoted in Patrick Parrinder, *James Joyce*, Cambridge University Press, 1990, p. 34). This is not the only connection between the great novelist of urban experi-ence and representations of the city in Weimar Germany. Joyce expressed interest in having the filming of *Ulysses* undertaken by Ruttmann. I have addressed the paral-lels in greater detail in "The Experience of Modernity at the Centre and the Periph-ery," in *Circa Art Magazine: Contemporary Visual Culture in Ireland*, no. 51, May/June 1990, pp. 16–19.

16. Georg Simmel, "The Metropolis and Mental Life," reprinted in *On Individuality and Social Forms: Selected Writings*, Donald M. Levine, ed., Chicago, IL: University of Chicago Press, 1971.

17. David Frisby, *Sociological Impressionism: A Reassessment of Georg Simmel's Social Theory*, London: Routledge, 1992.

18. Roy Pascal, *From Naturalism to Expressionism*, Manchester: Manchester University Press, 1973, p. 152.

19. Joachim Schlör, *Nights in the Big City: Paris, Berlin, London, 1840–1930*, trans. Pierre Gottfried Imhof and Dafydd Rees Roberts, London: Reaktion, 1998, pp. 235–6.

20. Kracauer, *From Caligari to Hitler*, p. 188.

21. Werner Sombart, cited in Massimo Cacciari, *Architecture and Nihilism: On the Philosophy of Modern Architecture*, New Haven, CT: Yale University Press, 1993, p. 32.

22. In relation to the social role of white-collar workers, see Kracauer's groundbreaking 1929 study, *Die Angestellten*, Frankfurt am Main: Suhrkamp Taschenbuch Verlag, 1971 (1929).

23. Bloch, *Heritage of Our Times*, p. 195.

24. Ibid.

25. Ibid., *Heritage of Our Times*, p. 200; Kracauer, cited in David Frisby, *Fragments of Modernity*, London: Polity Press, 1988, p. 150.

26. Bloch, *Heritage of Our Times*, p. 198.

27. Ibid., pp. 197–9.

28. Michael Bienert, *Die eingebildete Metropole: Berlin im Feuilleton der Weimarer Republik*, Stuttgart: Verlag J. B. Metzler, 1992, p. 234, fn. 68: "Rasmussen, from Copenhagen, referred to the display windows on the Kurfürstendamm in 1928 as 'Potemkin fronts'" ("Der Kopenhagener Rasmussen . . . nannte die Schaufronten am Kurfürstendamm 1928 'Potemkinkulissen'"). The German title of Bienert's book may be translated as "The Imagined Metropolis: Berlin in the *Feuilletons* of the Weimar Republic."

29. Siegfried Kracauer, *Straßen in Berlin und anderswo*, Berlin: Das Arsenal, 1987, p. 15: "Scheinen manche Strassenzüge für die Ewigkeit geschaffen zu sein, so ist der heutige Kurfürstendamm die Verkörperung der leer hinfliessenden Zeit, in der nichts zu dauern vermag."

30. Alfred Polgar, cited in Sabine Hake, *The Cinema's Third Machine*, Lincoln, NE and London: University of Nebraska Press, 1993, p. 126.

31. Walter Ruttmann, in *Illustrierter Film-Kurier*, Berlin, no. 658, 1927. Reprinted in *Walter Ruttmann: Eine Dokumentation*, p. 80: "daß Leben, alltägliches Leben, spannend, erschütternd, dramatisch ist."

32. Kracauer, *From Caligari to Hitler*, p. 188.

33. Siegfried Kracauer, *Das Ornament der Masse: Essays*, Suhrkamp, 1977, p. 322: "Man schlendert des Abends durch die Strassen, gesättigt von einer Unerfülltheit, aus der die Fülle zu keimen vermag. Da ziehen leuchtende Worte an den Dächern vorüber, und schon is man aus der eigenen Leere in die fremde *Reklame* verbannt. Der Körper schlägt Wurzeln im Asphalt, und der Geist, der nicht mehr unser Geist ist, streift mit den aufklärenden Lichtbekundungen endlos aus der Nacht in die Nacht."

34. Kracauer, quoted in Thomas Elsaesser, "The Irresponsible Signifier," *New German Critique*, no. 40, Winter 1987, p. 73.

35. Sabine Hake, "Urban Spectacle in Walter Ruttmann's *Berlin, The Symphony of a Great City*," in Thomas W. Kniesche and Stephen Brockmann, eds, *Dancing on the Volcano. Essays on the Culture of the Weimar Republic*, Columbia, SC: Camden House, 1994, pp. 127–42.

36. Kniesche and Brockmann, *Dancing on the Volcano*, p. 133.

37. Ibid., pp. 130, 137.

38. Ibid., p. 128.

39. Stuart C. Aitken and Leo E. Zonn, eds, *Place, Power, Situation, and Spectacle: A Geography of Film*, Lanham, MD, Rowman and Littlefield Publishers, Inc., 1994, pp. 203–28.

40. Ibid., p. 203.

41. Ibid., pp. 204, 221.

42. Ibid. p. 211. Ruttmann anticipates that his film will have a similar effect on Berlin, "stifled behind its façades, crushed by its monumentality" ("die noch wird und nicht schon erstickt ist hinter Fassaden, erdrückt von der eigenen Monumentalität"). See Jean Paul Goergen, ed., *Walter Ruttmann: Eine Dokumentation*, p. 76.

43. Aitken and Zonn, *Place, Power, Situation and Spectacle: A Geography of Film*, p. 221.

44. Ibid., p. 212.

45. Kracauer, "Über Arbeitsnachweise," in *Straßen in Berlin und anderswo*: "Jeder typische Raum wird durch typische gesellschaftliche Verhältniße zustande gebracht, die sich ohne die störende Dazwischenkunft des Bewußtseins in ihm ausdrücken. Alles vom Bewußtsein Verleugnete, alles, was sonst geflißentlich übersehen wird, ist an seinem Aufbau beteiligt. Die Raumbilder sind die Träume der Gesellschaft. Wo immer die Hieroglyphe irgendeines Raumbildes entziffert ist, dort bietet sich der Grund der sozialen Wirklichkeit dar."

46. Bienert, p. 157: "Sie haben, wie Inka-Mülder nachgewiesen hat, den Status von 'Träumen ohne Traumarbeit'." As this is a trope Kracauer often deploys, his strategy as a critical or historical materialist must be borne in mind: for example, "Knowledge of cities is bound up with the deciphering of their dream-like expressed images." ("Die Erkenntnis der Städte ist an die Entzifferung ihrer traumhaft hingesagten Bilder geknüpft.") See Kracauer, "Aus dem Fenster Gesehen," in *Straßen in Berlin und anderswo*, p. 41.

47. Aitken and Zonn, *Place, Power, Situation, and Spectacle: A Geography of Film*, p. 222.

48. Cited in Frisby, *Fragments of Modernity*, p. 149.

49. Kniesche and Brockmann, *Dancing on the Volcano*, p. 136.

50. See Jean Paul Goergen, ed., *Walter Ruttmann: Eine Dokumentation*, p. 30: "In dieser Verschiebung der Betrachtungsweise von der Dokumentation eines Gegenstandes zur Dokumentation einer Erfahrung sieht auch William Uricchio die wesentliche Positionsbestimmung des Berlin-Films als Wendepunkt in der filmischen Repräsentation der Stadt."

51. Quoted in Frisby, *Fragments of Modernity*, p. 262.
52. Kracauer, *From Caligari to Hitler*, p. 188.
53. Walter Benjamin, "The Work of Art in the Age of Mechanical Reproduction," in *Illuminations*, trans. Harry Zohn, London: Fontana/Collins, 1982, p. 244.
54. Barry A. Fulks, "Walter Ruttmann, The Avant Garde Film and Nazi Modernism," *Film and History*, vol. 14, part 2, 1984, p. 29.
55. See Jean Paul Goergen, ed., *Walter Ruttmann: Eine Dokumentation*.

3

THE CITY VANISHES: PIEL JUTZI'S
BERLIN ALEXANDERPLATZ

PETER JELAVICH

The audience that assembled for the premiere of *Berlin Alexanderplatz* on October 8 1931 had high expectations. Not only did the film star Heinrich George, one of Germany's greatest actors, under the direction of Piel Jutzi, an acclaimed leftist director and cameraman; above all, it purported to be based on Alfred Döblin's novel of the same name, which had been a literary sensation two years earlier. In 1929 the maverick author, well-known in artistic circles but not among the public at large, had suddenly attracted a wide readership by publishing what would come to be considered *the* Berlin novel. Perhaps it was inevitable that the screen version failed to match the book's surprising success. In any case, the critical response to the film was marked by disappointment and it is a judgment that has persisted to this day.

Berlin Alexanderplatz: The Story of Franz Biberkopf is more interesting than most examples of filmed literature because of the special qualities of Döblin's novel. The book has a highly innovative montage structure, in which a variety of media play prominent roles. To be sure, there is a plot line in the novel centered on a character named Franz Biberkopf. We first meet him as he leaves the prison where he has spent four years for having killed his girlfriend in a fit of jealous rage. He is determined to remain honest as well as autonomous, but both goals prove elusive. He tries his hand at different small jobs hawking a variety of wares, from necktie-holders to shoelaces, from gay magazines to Nazi newspapers. Unable to settle into any occupation, swayed this way and that by the conflicting advice of the people he meets, he suffers a series of blows. Some gangsters try to trick him into standing watch during a robbery. Infuriated by his unwillingness to play along, they push him from a speeding car, and he is run over by another vehicle, an accident that costs him his right arm. Franz concludes that he was wrong to try to be independent and morally upright, and he joins the gang—prompted in part by what is perhaps a homoerotic attraction to one of its members, Reinhold, the very person who had thrown him from the getaway car. Yet Reinhold punishes Franz again, by murdering his lover, Mieze. After suffering a nervous breakdown, a cautious and chastened Franz takes his place in society by becoming a doorman in a midsize factory.

Told as a straightforward narrative, this tale is somewhat unusual, but generally innocuous. Its value lies in Döblin's mode of telling: the story continually is interrupted and entangled by media-generated discourses. A major theme in the novel is the manner in which human thought and action are shaped, but also confused, by a variety of competing and often contradictory messages—a complex of discourses which, in their incommensurate totality, constitute the city of Berlin. A barrage of messages—drawn from the realms of advertising, commerce, fashion, journalism, politics, sexuality, religion, popular culture, and literature—are relayed to the individual through mass media: via newspapers, journals, posters, radio, phonographs, and not least of all, film. The novel illustrates how Biberkopf is buffeted and confused by the profusion of what we now would call "info-bites": he sways between respectability and criminality, self-employment and willful unemployment, leftist slogans and Nazi jargon, heterosexuality and bisexuality. In the process, Döblin seems radically to question the autonomy and the coherence of the self in the modern metropolis.

What is paradoxical is the fact that when this tale is retold in the medium of film, the critical and innovative aspects are lost. The most basic paradox resides in the fact that the novel shows how a human personality dissolves in the modern, media-saturated environment; yet when the story is retold through one of those mass media—film—Biberkopf is presented as a coherent, autonomous individual. In short, the very image of humanity that is supposedly dissolved *by* the modern media celebrates its resurrection *in* the modern media. Furthermore, the political, socially critical, and sexual discourses that occupy such commanding roles in the novel disappear in the film. Indeed, the city of Berlin, which dominates Döblin's book, is reduced to a marginal bit-player on the screen. Hence this chapter poses the question: what was happening in Germany in 1931 to prevent a cinematic novel about the metropolis finding adequate expression in film? Why did Berlin vanish from *Berlin Alexanderplatz*?

In order to answer this question, we will have to examine not only the media aesthetics of the era—the parameters of what was presentable on screen in Germany during the early years of sound film—but also the historical conditions of the time. *Berlin Alexanderplatz* is set in 1928, the last of the "golden years" of the Weimar Republic after it recovered from the disastrous hyperinflation of 1923. The fact that even those years were not very "golden" for the average citizen is underscored in the novel, since Biberkopf's difficulty in finding a job reflects the relatively high unemployment which persisted throughout the 1920s. But that was nothing compared to the Great Depression, which commenced in the fall of 1929, when Döblin's novel was published. By the time the work came to be filmed, unemployment had swelled to crisis proportions, and an aggressive force had emerged on the political scene that openly threatened to destroy Weimar Germany's cultural vitality: the National Socialist Party of Adolf Hitler.

Like his friend Bertolt Brecht, Alfred Döblin was not only an innovative author, but also a major theorist who welcomed the challenges and opportunities of new media. As early as 1913, in his so-called "Berlin Program," Döblin proposed that novels adopt a constructivist *Kinostil* that would break out of the "narrative rut" of storytelling. He contended that authors should eschew simplistic psychologizing and metaphorical language. Instead, they should learn from film to become radically objectivist by focusing on things (rather than moods), and by juxtaposing simultaneous events (rather than forcing the story into a straightforward narrative flow). This project was, for Döblin, explicitly anti-humanist: authors would have to deny both themselves and their conventional conceptions of individual coherence and autonomy. The essay concluded with a call for "*Depersonisation*": "Cut loose from human beings! Have courage for kinetic fantasy [. . .]!"[1] Sixteen years later, in 1929, Döblin repeated his call for a radically objective, anti-psychological literature in his essay on "The Construction of the Epic Work." Among other things, he noted with approval that playwrights were beginning to replace dialogue and conventional plots with more cinematic and visual devices, and he concluded the essay with the question: "Who knows to what interesting intermediate zone the talking film will lead us one day?"[2]

Not surprisingly, when the novel *Berlin Alexanderplatz* appeared that same year, a number of reviewers noted its cinematic quality. For example, Herbert Ihering, arguably the greatest critic of the time, wrote: "Pimps and newspaper salesmen, robbers and Salvation Army soldiers, small-time gentlemen and big-time crooks, pubs and dives, subway construction sites and advertisement posters, popular hits and Bible passages, all of this comes together in a glittering, flickering strip of pictures, in the word-film [*Wortfilm*] *Berlin Alexanderplatz*."[3] The montage structure of the novel, with its juxtaposition of numerous stories and texts, was an obvious point of comparison with film, and was highlighted in particular by Walter Benjamin in his review of the book.[4] Other commentators perceived cinematic elements in the novel's mode of description. One critic wrote that "the novel—with its rapid succession of images, in which individual scenes, motives, and details are illuminated suddenly, with its cuts and its fade-overs—clearly has been created out of the experience of film."[5] Another noted that the novel was "written with camera-eyes; a hundred ideas were spliced onto every documentary page of the novel and registered with a mental microphone."[6] Other critics compared the numerous passages of Biberkopf's (often semi-conscious) impressions while walking the streets of Berlin to the traveling shots of a mobile camera. Siegfried Kracauer wrote:

> Whole sections of the book ramble all over the place, without sticking timidly to the story. They are themselves the story, which does not consist so much in a cohesive plot as in an easygoing sauntering, which rightfully forgoes fixed perspectives. But that is precisely how every film that really is a film saunters along. Its suspense derives from the camera's freedom of movement, which fulfills its task only when it pans across the surroundings and bit by bit collects the environs.[7]

Beyond the cinematic mode of composition, the novel depicts the combined impact of commodities, street life, and modern media on the urban individual. Döblin himself wrote explicitly (in a review of James Joyce's *Ulysses*): "Cinema has entered the realm of literature; newspapers have grown, they have become the most important, the most widespread written product, the daily bread of all people. Additional experiential elements of today's humans include the street, the street scenes that change every second, the advertising signs, the traffic."[8] In *Berlin Alexanderplatz*, the metropolis is portrayed as being swamped by commodities, as well as overrun by texts, slogans, and songs touted in the mass media. This flood of objects and messages constantly destabilizes, but also continually reshapes Biberkopf. At the beginning of the novel, he is released after having served four years in jail, but for him this newly found freedom represents the *commencement* of his travails: "The punishment begins."[9] During the tram ride that takes him from Tegel prison to the center of Berlin, he is overwhelmed by the sounds and commercial images hurtling by: boys crying out the titles of the latest newspapers, a multitude of stores ("shoe stores, hat shops, light bulbs, pubs"), and the mannequins in the display windows decked with "suits, coats, skirts, socks and shoes."[10]

Initially destabilized in the commodity- and media-saturated city, Biberkopf is gradually restabilized by the same media, at least to the extent that they start to arouse and direct his desires. Significantly, the first place where this happens is a cinema. Attracted by a garish poster, Biberkopf enters a working class nickelodeon. He is struck by the laughing crowd around him: "Franz found it wonderful, as people around him started to giggle. Lots of people, free people, amusing themselves, no one tells them what to do, wonderfully nice, and I'm right in the middle of it!"[11] But the novel immediately raises doubts about how "free" these people are, and questions whether "no one tells them what to do," as soon as Biberkopf gets caught up in the film. The sight of amorous couples, and women's legs in particular, arouses sexual desires that he has been forced to contain for four years. Indeed, Franz has a mental flashback to the times in prison when he and the other inmates would stare out the windows at women strolling by. Significantly, Franz's reverie indirectly equates a viewer sitting in a cinema, staring at a screen, with a prisoner locked in jail, gaping through a barred window. But now Franz is free to act on his desires, so he heads straight-away to a prostitute, only to discover that he is impotent. Film can awaken his desire, but not fulfill it. And so it goes throughout the novel: Biberkopf repeatedly allows himself to be led astray by the messages swirling around him. What is ironic about this is the fact that, unknown to him, it contradicts his overarching world view, his belief that he is an autonomous individual who does as he pleases. What is tragic about his situation is the fact that the competing discourses do not form a comprehensive whole, and he is torn apart in the process (quite literally, since he loses his right arm).

Both the cinematic form and the media-rich content of *Berlin Alexanderplatz* made the novel a prime candidate for the screen. Upon its publication, Axel Eggebrecht wrote in *Die Weltbühne*, the premier leftist intellectual journal of the day: "If we had an enterprising film industry, it would snatch up this book. Ruttmann's courageous Berlin film, in which human beings in Berlin disappear behind a lot of montages of technology and traffic, would serve as a small preliminary sketch."[12] A landmark in the history of avant garde cinema, Walter Ruttmann's *Berlin, The Symphony of a Great City* (1927) is a non-narrative film depicting a day in the life of Berlin, where scenes of industry, commerce, traffic, and entertainment represent the activities of various social classes at work and at play. It is replete with documentary scenes shot by hidden cameras, spliced together with dizzyingly dynamic cuts. Given its use of montage and eschewal of conventional narration, it was not surprising that Eggebrecht recalled Ruttmann's film when reading Döblin's novel. Indeed, after the release of Piel Jutzi's *Berlin Alexanderplatz* in October 1931, some critics deplored the fact that it was not more like *Berlin, The Symphony of a Great City*. But there were good reasons why it was not, above all the fact that—as Eggebrecht noted—in Ruttmann's work, "human beings in Berlin disappear behind a lot of montages of technology and traffic." To be sure, Döblin would have shared the anti-psychological and anti-individualist thrust of Ruttmann's film, its desire to break radically from a conventional narrative story line. But beyond that, their projects parted. Humans are just stereotypes in *Berlin, The Symphony of a Great City*. Ruttmann employed numerous cross-cuts to show how members of different classes—*haute bourgeoisie*, middle class, working class, unemployed—occupy their time at various phases of the day. He also presented another series of cross-cuts that compared humans to animals on the one hand, and to mechanized dolls and mannequins on the other. In Ruttmann's film, such general equations substituted for differentiated analysis, a strategy that infuriated Siegfried Kracauer. Speaking of his "terrible disappointment" in the work, Kracauer complained that it was cooked up in the "brains of literati" who "can think of nothing better than to get off on a senseless juxtaposition of glamour and poverty, right and left, because the meaning of their imagined metropolis resides in swallowing its unresolved contrasts."[13] Döblin obviously did not want to fall into that trap: he desired to highlight the conflicting, "unresolved" (and irresolvable) discourses of the city, and to show how those discourses met disruptively *in a single individual*. Whereas Ruttmann treated individuals as ciphers that could be lumped into social categories, Döblin believed that *within* every individual a conflict of categories was raging. He wanted to show not only the individual within the city, but also the city within the individual.

But how was that project to be projected onto a screen? Even under ideal conditions, the challenge in purely formal or aesthetic terms would have been great. But there were additional political and economic problems to consider within the context of late Weimar Germany. One of them was censorship.[14] Indeed, film was the only privately owned medium that was subject to preliminary censorship in the Weimar era. Article 118, paragraph 2 of the Weimar constitution read: "There will be no censorship, except regarding film, for which particular regulations may be legislated." These regulations, passed by the Reichstag in 1920, resulted in the creation of film review boards (*Filmprüfstellen*) in Berlin and Munich, and an appellate film review board (*Filmoberprüfstelle*) in Berlin. All films screened in Germany needed to receive prior approval from one of these commissions, which generally were staffed by people harboring conservative political and social values. By the end of the 1920s these boards had issued a number of rulings that would have caused problems for several themes in Döblin's novel. Portrayals of homosexuality generally were forbidden, as were scenes that accentuated social tensions and class differences. Explicit depictions of political conflict—such as the fights between Nazis and Communists, or the disputes between anarchists and trade unionists in Döblin's text—would have been extremely difficult to get past the censors. This did not mean that such topics could not be treated on the Weimar screen, but they had to be presented cautiously and indirectly. Producers who dared to broach such matters often had to cut or rework scenes and resubmit their films to obtain approval. In 1928, Piel Jutzi, future director of *Berlin Alexanderplatz*, was forced to excise from his docudrama *Hunger in Waldenburg* a segment in which he compared the monthly income of a Silesian mineworker (less than 100 marks per month) with the accumulated capital of a mine owner (100 million marks).[15]

Of course, some of the best producers and directors were willing to address controversial themes, but the stakes became much higher after 1929. Even under the best of conditions—that is, even if the Great Depression had not set in—the years 1929 to 1931 would have been very difficult for the German film industry, as it undertook the switch from silent to sound film. The cost of new equipment for filming and screening required great capital outlays, and production expenses soared: the cost of creating a "talkie" exceeded that for a silent film by 30 to 50 percent. Simultaneously, the Depression led to a precipitous decline in attendance. In Berlin, the annual value of tickets sold dropped 19 percent in just one year, from 57 million marks in 1930 to 49 million marks in 1931 (with a further plunge to 40 million in 1932).[16] Under such conditions, it was understandable that German film producers shied away from controversial topics that might scare away potential viewers, or that could provoke troubles with the censor (and hence increase production costs due to re-shootings and delayed releases).

Filming *Berlin Alexanderplatz* thus entailed substantial formal, political, and economic difficulties. Nevertheless, the work attracted the attention of some major actors and studios. In May 1930 the great actor Emil Jannings, who a month earlier had won accolades for his performance in *The Blue Angel*, let it be known that he wanted to play the role of Biberkopf.[17] Jannings was contracted to Ufa, Germany's largest production company, which briefly in late September considered buying an option to film the novel. However, another team beat Jannings to the project. The figure of Biberkopf had attracted the attention of another outstanding actor, Heinrich George. Indeed, George was contracted to speak the role of Biberkopf in a radio-play version of *Berlin Alexanderplatz* that was scheduled to air in late September, but the broadcast was canceled at the last moment. At the beginning of October, it was announced that George would play Biberkopf on screen under the auspices of Arnold Pressburger. As the ambitious producer of the new Allianz film company, Pressburger considered himself a representative of what was called, even then, "independent film production" (*die unabhängige Filmproduktion*)—smaller companies whose engagement in cinematic experiments made them path-breakers and, he hoped, "trendsetters for the rest of the film industry."[18] The distribution of *Berlin Alexanderplatz* was to be undertaken by Südfilm, whose director, Alfons Goldschmid, likewise prided himself on sponsoring artistic works.[19] George reported that both Pressburger and Goldschmid had a "courageous and enthusiastic" attitude to the *Alexanderplatz* project.[20]

It was not until six months later, however, that Pressburger hired a director for the film.[21] Piel Jutzi was well known as a leftist filmmaker.[22] In 1926 he had adapted Eisenstein's *Battleship Potemkin* for German distribution, and thus laid the basis for the worldwide fame of a revolutionary work that had enjoyed only moderate success in the Soviet Union. In 1928 Jutzi filmed *Hunger in Waldenburg*, a graphic account of the poverty of miners in Silesia. A year later he created the short *Blutmai 1929* (*Bloody May 1929*), which included documentary shots of the Communist May Day demonstrations in Berlin that had been suppressed with much bloodshed by the police. December 1929 saw the release of Jutzi's masterpiece, *Mutter Krausens Fahrt ins Glück* (*Mother Krause's Journey to Happiness*), a hard-hitting depiction of working class life with explicitly Marxist sympathies.

Döblin, who co-wrote the script of *Berlin Alexanderplatz*, was likewise an advocate of more audacious films.[23] He repeatedly expressed his dismay at the fact that commercial pressures hampered the artistic and political development of cinema. In 1922 he stated laconically: "Profit against art. The ghastly commodity-character of film."[24] Seven years later he cautioned that the new medium of radio must avoid following the production routine of film, "which absolutely has skidded down to the level of industry and office-workers."[25] In 1930 Döblin asserted that writers and directors needed to change in order to improve cinema: "Only the reformed author can reform film." He contended that diversionary entertainment flicks should be replaced by works addressing current issues: "Film must present cultural events that are topical, it must intervene in social concerns. A producer should not be scared of reality, he should not always say automatically 'I can't even consider that' or 'I won't be able to sell that abroad.' He must show more courage."[26]

Döblin spoke those words in an interview published on August 16 1930. A month later, events transpired that soon would have enormous repercussions in all aspects of German life, including the film industry. In the parliamentary elections of September 14 1930, Hitler's National Socialists scored a tremendous and unexpected victory. Up to that point, the Nazis had been politically insignificant. In the previous elections of 1928, they had garnered 800,000 votes, giving them only twelve seats in the Reichstag. Two years later, following the onset of the

Depression, the Nazis gained 6.4 million votes and 107 seats in the Reichstag, making them the second largest party (after the Social Democrats). The elections sent shock waves throughout liberal and leftist circles. Indeed, political fears in the wake of the Nazi victory led to the last-minute cancellation of the radio-play version of *Berlin Alexanderplatz*, which was to have aired two weeks after the election.[27] Amid the general atmosphere of anxiety and uncertainty, the management of the normally audacious Berlin radio station decided to refrain from broadcasting work by a controversial Jewish leftist author such as Döblin.

The public never learned the reason for the cancellation of the broadcast, though the Nazis would have been gratified by the news. Emboldened by their political victory, Hitler's followers were looking for a major battle on the cultural front as well. On November 25 the *Völkischer Beobachter*, the Nazis' flagship newspaper, declared: "Whoever possesses power also should exercise it. We National Socialists will do just that, and for starters, we will use our mass following to exert pressure on cinemas regarding their program selections. *Pacifist and other subversive tendentious films must disappear!*" To achieve this goal, the article—which might well have been penned by Joseph Goebbels—called for employing "our old reliable weapon, namely, attack."[28] Two weeks later the Nazis put this policy into effect with their massive, violent demonstrations against the Hollywood version of *All Quiet on the Western Front*, which was being shown at a cinema on the Nollendorfplatz in Berlin. The film seemed made-to-order as a target for Nazi resentment: it was based on the best-selling pacifist novel by Erich Maria Remarque, which had been decried by the entire right-wing press; it was filmed in the United States, which the Nazis considered a major source of "decadent" culture; and its producer, Carl Laemmle, was a Jewish *émigré* from Germany. Faced with the violence on the Nollendorfplatz, which was openly orchestrated by Goebbels, the Berlin police—under the Social Democratic leadership of the Prussian state—were more than happy to fight off the Nazi demonstrators and protect the cinema. However, conservatives appealed the decision of the Berlin film review board allowing the screening of the film. A week after its release, the appellate film review board, under massive pressure from conservatives, the Foreign Ministry, the German Army, and continued Nazi violence in the streets, banned *All Quiet on the Western Front*.[29]

This decision had disastrous consequences for the film industry and for

Weimar culture more generally. The Nazis had scored their first big success, as they proclaimed in the *Völkischer Beobachter*: "When the ruling of the appellate film board was issued, the [democratic] system of 1918 suffered its first great defeat in the eyes of all, and in a flash its complete impotence was revealed."[30] The right-wing *Deutsche Zeitung* wrote: "*For the first time* since 1918 the national opposition came forth decisively and broke the impudent despotism of foreign and naturalized Jews. The lesson that they learned will not fail to have ramifications in other areas as well."[31] The defeat of *All Quiet on the Western Front* inaugurated a general assault on progressive culture that was spearheaded by the Nazis, but backed by other conservative parties, including ones normally hostile to Hitler (such as the Catholic Center Party). The film review boards increasingly heeded this right-wing pressure, and by April 1931 producers were stunned when works by prestigious firms including Ufa and Allianz were banned. At the time, Allianz was planning to begin shooting *Berlin Alexanderplatz*, but it delayed production to see if its banned film (*Meine Cousine aus Warschau*) would be released upon appeal; otherwise, it might have scrapped the Döblin project. The *Film-Kurier*, a trade journal, noted: "You cannot blame the Allianz for postponing its next productions, above all *Berlin Alexanderplatz*, until it receives the ruling of the appellate film review board regarding this film."[32] The release of *Meine Cousine* after minor cuts allowed the firm to proceed with *Berlin Alexanderplatz*, but censorship was very much on the team's mind. One of the actors, Gerhard Bienert, said in an interview during shooting: "How will things proceed with this film? [. . .] Actors, directors, scripts, all of that is ready. But the censors keep banning; one doesn't know what to think anymore."[33]

The film *Berlin Alexanderplatz* thus was produced in a highly charged atmosphere. Economic conditions demanded that the film be neither politically nor aesthetically too radical, so that it would not alienate viewers, a scarce resource during the Depression; and the political situation was such that censorship could hold up or strike down even seemingly innocuous works. The troubled economic and political conditions left their mark on the *Berlin Alexanderplatz* film. The original script—co-written by Döblin and Hans Wilhelm, a professional scriptwriter—was largely depoliticized, although it did call for some images of prisoners and the poor. But they too were absent in the final screen version. Only in two cases were rather weak swipes made at those political forces that were causing the film industry such trouble. In a scene where Biberkopf hawks necktie-holders on the Alexanderplatz, he calls out to various listeners to come closer, including two to whom he refers as members of the "Storm-Troop." At this point, according to the script, one is supposed to see this image: "Two 14–15-year-old young men in windbreakers with fairly unintelligent faces and gaping jaws stare goggle-eyed at Franz."[34] In the actual film, the youths' rather blank expressions make the anti-Nazi message clear, but the scene flashes by so quickly that it scarcely registers with the viewer. The second slap (aimed not at the Nazis, but at government censorship) came in the film's theme song, whose refrain claimed: "Love comes, love goes / That's something that no government can prohibit" (*Liebe kommt, Liebe geht, / Das kann keine Regierung verbieten*). But these were just pinpricks. The essential depoliticization of the film becomes clearest when one compares scenes of a barroom brawl in the novel and in the movie. In the book, Biberkopf comes to blows with his erstwhile Communist comrades because he has been selling Nazi newspapers and sporting a swastika armband. In the film, the brawl occurs between Biberkopf and his gangster acquaintances because they mock him for refusing to take part in their criminal undertakings.[35]

Whereas the novel moved freely between the city of Berlin and the character of Biberkopf, the film is focused squarely on the protagonist. The verbal qualities of the book allow Biberkopf to dissolve into the city; since his thoughts, the discourses that swirl around him, and the narrator's voice (such as it is) all exist in a purely textual medium, it is possible to elide the boundaries among those three spheres. Indeed, in the novel, it often is impossible to tell who—or what—is speaking. In the film, by contrast, Biberkopf's character is fully embodied, visually and vocally, and hence more autonomous and humanized—especially since Heinrich George's portrayal is a forceful and imposing one (**5**). Moreover, since George was a popular performer, the onscreen Biberkopf could be conflated with George's well-known film persona.[36] He was famous for depicting essentially good-hearted, but weak-minded and destructively impulsive men—much like Biberkopf. Yet George acted them in such a way that there was unity in the character; the impulsiveness was a "tragic flaw" in what was otherwise a vital and coherent personality. By the time that George played Biberkopf, his stage persona had become a stereotype. One critic noted in 1928 that George's figures were "colossi of strength, with childish emotions."[37] This aspect of his screen

5 Heinrich George as Franz Biberkopf in Piel Jutzi's *Berlin Alexanderplatz* (1931)

persona could even become tiresome, as a reviewer noted in 1929: "It is embarrassing that Heinrich George is not able to free himself from the cliché of good-natured brutality."[38]

George seems to have transferred the same cliché to his characterization of Biberkopf. According to one critic of the film, George portrayed "a Parsifal of the Alexanderplatz—massive, crude, and yet a pure fool. Violent but also gentle and tender."[39] In an interview at the time of the film's release, Jutzi essentially admitted that George was largely in control of his characterization of Biberkopf: "One of my most interesting tasks in the film was to allow such an exceptionally strong actor as Heinrich George, who portrays Franz Biberkopf, to move about freely, to avoid restraining the natural continuity of his movements, and yet to present only what was necessary for the cinematic production."[40] In other words, Jutzi provided only minimal direction for the star actor. Indeed, George's domination of the production was so great that several reviewers echoed Herbert Ihering's quip that the film should not be called *Berlin Alexanderplatz*, but rather *Heinrich George as Franz Biberkopf*.[41]

George's rendition of Biberkopf was not the only example of re-humanizing, re-integrating and simplifying Döblin's characters in the film. In an interview at the time of the premiere, Bernhard Minetti, who played the role of Reinhold, spoke of the challenge of "limiting the many-sidedness of this character, which Döblin had sketched so dramatically, in the interest of a clear plot development, without, however, depriving the figure of its enigmatical nature."[42] Thus even a newcomer to sound film like Minetti took it for granted that the medium required a simplification of character portrayal. This issue was addressed on a more general level by the film critic of *Vorwärts*, the Social Democratic daily, who wrote after the premiere: "What remains completely unrepresentable is the thought-world of Döblin's people, the purely associative manner whereby Döblin combines their ideas. A major attraction of the novel is thereby lost, since film has no means to represent visually or acoustically the unspoken feelings and thoughts of a human being."[43] Of course, that statement must be taken with a huge grain of salt, since silent films had developed by this time a whole range of optic effects—ranging from human gestures to symbolic use of objects—to represent "unspoken feelings."

The image of personal unity and coherence projected by Biberkopf/George,

Reinhold/Minetti, and the other characters is compounded by the fact that the *Berlin Alexanderplatz* film has a much more linear narration than the book. Indeed, a critic for the liberal *Vossische Zeitung* noted: "the plot is lifted out of Döblin's novel like bones from a fish."[44] Other reviewers, including Siegfried Kracauer, contended that Jutzi's presentation of the remaining story copied too closely the style and motifs of run-of-the-mill gangster films. Rudolf Arnheim expressed dismay that a director as talented as Jutzi should have resorted to "pub scenes such as we've seen *ad nauseam*, in which four men sit around a pub table in a conspiratorial manner, tough guys down shots of schnapps at the bar, and rakishly made-up women sashay through the joint as if they were models of iniquity."[45] As noted above, many critics expressed the view that something more like Ruttmann's *Berlin, The Symphony of a Great City* should have been produced. To be sure, Jutzi's film has a promising beginning: like the novel, it starts with Biberkopf's disorienting tram-ride into the city. The sequence consists of dynamic cuts among a dizzying variety of scenes: the tram in motion, the passing cityscape as seen from the tram, the conductor's view of traffic, close-ups of tracks in front of the speeding tram, and reaction shots of an increasingly nauseated Biberkopf. These sights are highlighted by a music track that underscores the speed and chaos of the journey. After that, however, the film falls into a fairly conventional narrative plot. The only truly advanced scenes are several montage sequences depicting the hustle and bustle of people and traffic around the Alexanderplatz, some of which clearly were inspired by Ruttmann's film. Many critics took note of those scenes, but also contended that they had a pasted-in quality. It seemed that Döblin's complex novel had been reduced to a conventional storyline, after which some Ruttmannesque scenes had been added in a futile attempt to evoke the montage aesthetic of the book. Kracauer described the problem most explicitly: "First to reduce a large-scale theme to a penny-dreadful story and then to try to bring it back to the level of the novel by adding decorative mock-ups: that is impossible."[46]

Even though Jutzi's film is entitled *Berlin Alexanderplatz*, the city itself hardly plays a commanding role. Döblin inadvertently admitted as much when he said, in an interview at the time of the film's release, that the shots of the Alexanderplatz milieu provided "local color."[47] Needless to say, the city provides much more than local color in the novel, where it is an active, shaping force. The fact that Jutzi's *Berlin Alexanderplatz* was an early sound film could have provided an opportunity for (quite literally) giving a voice to the city; it might have become a vehicle for the unique quality of Berlin dialect that played such a prominent role in the novel. Indeed, Walter Benjamin asserted that the book was born "from the spirit of Berlin's language."[48] A "talkie" film would have been an obvious medium in which to convey that aspect of the work, but once again, technical and commercial considerations conspired against it. On the one hand, the novelty of cinematic sound in 1931, along with its relatively poor acoustic quality, necessitated the use of dialogue coaches for actors accustomed to silent film. Pressburger hired the respected stage director Karl Heinz Martin as dialogue coach for *Berlin Alexanderplatz*. Martin succeeded in getting the actors to speak clearly and precisely, but in the process, the qualities that made the Berlin dialect unique—such as its rapid-fire speed—were lost. On the other hand, producers were being told by cinema owners not to make films in regional dialects, since audiences in other parts of Germany found them hard to understand: north German viewers did not like films with heavy Bavarian accents, and Berlin dialects did not play well in the south.[49] Consequently, the *Alexanderplatz* film employed a few well-known *berlinerisch* turns of phrase, but generally showed restraint in its use of the local argot. As a result, one Berlin critic noted that "the words don't sound genuine" and the audience heard only a "doctored dialect."[50]

In sum, neither visually nor acoustically was *Berlin Alexanderplatz* true to Berlin. There were several reasons why, in 1931, the "city" disappeared from what should have been a "city film." Censorship, reinforced by fear of the Nazis' mounting strength, precluded screening many of the discourses that made up the text of Döblin's Berlin: political clashes between Nazis and Communists, debates over social and economic conditions, and other controversial themes such as homosexuality. Beyond that, a combination of aesthetic prejudices and preconceptions about audience taste predisposed the filmmakers to be more conventional. The addition of sound eventuated in a widespread belief that film should be "realistic," now that human voices and other acoustic effects could be reproduced. At the time, the conventions of realism were still tied to nineteenth-century literary and dramatic modes of storytelling, wherein autonomous individuals followed linear plot lines—as does Biberkopf/George in the *Berlin Alexanderplatz* film. The use of conventionally "realistic" modes of characterization and narrative was a concession to what was perceived to be audience taste—a conscious and calculated choice during the Depression, when cinema attendance had dropped severely. Like many other critics, Kracauer sadly concluded: "Apparently in order to compromise with the supposed taste of the public, the virtues of Döblin's book—the very things that cry out for a cinematic treatment—are pushed aside."[51]

Perhaps the most obvious concession to cinematic convention was the film's conclusion. It sorely annoyed many reviewers, and it represents perhaps the greatest discrepancy from the novel. The book has a rather downbeat ending, as Biberkopf learns that he must integrate himself into society; he admits that his plan to stand alone on his own two feet had to fail, and he is last seen as a doorman in a midsize factory. The ending of the film's original script was quite different, but very striking. After suffering his final blow—the murder of his girlfriend by the gangster Reinhold—a dejected Biberkopf stands in front of a shop window on the Alexanderplatz and stares at his reflection. Suddenly, his mirrored image starts to speak to him. In the ensuing dialogue, Franz claims that he lacks any will to live, while his reflection tells him to pull himself together and integrate himself into the city around him. As the camera then circles away from the two and pans the Alexanderplatz, Franz exclaims "Yes!—I will!" The final shot was supposed to depict three machines, operating in rhythmic unity, while a speaking chorus proclaims with increasingly loud voices, "I will!"[52] That would have been, for the time, a highly innovative finale—one that would have optically presented the splitting of Biberkopf's persona and his integration with the city, and one that would have intoned the collectivist message at the conclusion of the novel.

The actual film, by contrast, culminates in a conventional "happy end": an upbeat Biberkopf stands again as a street vendor on the Alexanderplatz and hawks little figurines that bounce upright after being knocked down. He uses them to illustrate the maxim that if you have "metal in the right spot"—that is, if you are an intrinsically good person—then you will always bounce back, no matter how many times you fall. The very last shot of the film is a bird's-eye view of traffic on the Alexanderplatz, underscored by peppy, joyful music. As one critic noted: "It is grotesque that the film ends with the very type of 'have-sunshine-in-your-heart' that Döblin had made fun of in his novel."[53] But such happy endings had become *de rigueur* in the Great Depression. According to one tally, the number of German feature films with tragic endings dropped from 17.1 percent in 1930 to 4.7 percent the following year. Among box-office hits, the plunge was even more dramatic: while 40 percent of the most successful films of 1930 had tragic endings, there were none at all in 1931.[54]

Jutzi's *Berlin Alexanderplatz* not only had a happy ending, it also trumpeted notions of individuality and autonomy that had been radically undermined in the novel. Jutzi's *Berlin Alexanderplatz* told Depression-era viewers to "stand upright" and to persevere—much like many other, artistically less pretentious works of those years. But was that so bad? By the time the film was shot in the summer of 1931, calls for a collectivist subsuming of individuality into a higher cause were no longer primarily the purview of the left; they were being heard much more loudly and stridently on the extreme right. Wisely or not, the film replaced a call for collectivist integration with a classic liberal statement advocating self-reliance and self-worth. If that was indeed the message that the film-makers wanted to proclaim by the summer of 1931, then they were right (or at least consistent) to adopt more conventional forms of characterization and narrative, forms that traditionally showed how an autonomous individual sustains a series of setbacks but stands triumphant at the end. Faced with the growing clamor of right-wing collectivism, this throwback to an earlier liberal viewpoint—one that the novel *Berlin Alexanderplatz* had superseded—was understandable.

Unfortunately, it also was misplaced, since it was precisely the political liberals who, along with the nationalists, flocked to the Nazi Party in the early 1930s—and that slippage too can be seen in the conclusion of the film. Biberkopf/George begins his final monologue on the Alexanderplatz by pointing approvingly to the erect, upright stance of a nearby traffic cop. He then proceeds to say that "I and many of you" had faced grenades in the Great War; they had been cast down, but had always managed to rise to their feet again. To be sure, such references to policemen and to soldiers did not necessarily imply a right-wing ideology. The Berlin gendarmerie was still under Social Democratic leadership; it was they, after all, who had fought off the Nazi hordes protesting against *All Quiet on the Western Front* ten months earlier. Moreover, sympathetic portrayal of soldiers in the Great War was a trademark of pacifist literature,

Remarque's novel being the most obvious example. But all this having been said, it cannot be denied that appeals to soldierly virtues were much more a purview of nationalists and Nazis. Above all, unlike the novel, the film provided no leftist discourse to counterbalance the potentially right-wing rhetoric.

By combining classically liberal statements of individual autonomy with appreciative references to police and soldiers, the final monologue of *Berlin Alexanderplatz* reflected the political confusion of the final years of the Weimar Republic. Kracauer said as much in his review of the film when he asserted that its problems reflected the opacity of the times: "at the moment there is no social reality in Germany. [. . .] The space in which we live is confusing, the atmosphere is suffused with ideologies, and the ground under our feet is giving way."[55] But despite the all-pervasive murkiness, the general direction of the political march was clear. Just two days before the film's premiere, Chancellor Heinrich Brüning had issued his third emergency decree, which tightened film censorship even more. Herbert Ihering wrote in his review of Jutzi's work: "This is a film to grapple with. You also can learn from it (that includes learning how a film should not be made). But how much longer will such films be produced, if, in accordance with the new emergency decree, film censorship operates even more brutally than it has up till now?"[56] In 1931, pre-emptive fear of censorship, cautious assessments of audience expectations, and political uncertainty conspired to efface from the film the image of Berlin that Döblin had evoked in his novel—a city of socialists, Communists, anarchists, trade unionists, gays, lesbians, and Jews. Two years later, a regime came to power which aimed to erase those figures not only from the screen, but from the face of the earth.

NOTES

1 Alfred Döblin, "An Romanautoren und ihre Kritiker: Berliner Programm" (1913), in *Aufsätze zur Literatur*, Olten: Walter-Verlag, 1963, pp. 15–19.

2. Döblin, "Der Bau des epischen Werks," in Preussische Akademie der Künste, *Jahrbuch der Sektion für Dichtkunst 1929*, Berlin: S. Fischer Verlag, 1929, pp. 239, 262.

3. *Berliner Börsen-Courier*, December 19 1929.

4. Walter Benjamin, "Krisis des Romans: Zu Döblins 'Berlin Alexanderplatz'" (1930), in *Gesammelte Schriften*, 3, Frankfurt am Main: Suhrkamp, 1972, pp. 230–7.

5. W. Fiedler, "Heinrich George als Biberkopf," in *Deutsche Allgemeine Zeitung*, October 9 1931.

6. Ernst Jäger, "Berlin-Alexanderplatz," in *Film-Kurier*, October 9 1931.

7. Siegfried Kracauer, "'Berlin-Alexanderplatz' als Film," in *Frankfurter Zeitung*, October 13 1931.

8. Alfred Döblin, "'Ulysses' von Joyce" (1928), in *Aufsätze zur Literatur*, p. 288.

9. Alfred Döblin, *Berlin Alexanderplatz: Die Geschichte vom Franz Biberkopf*, Berlin: S. Fischer Verlag, 1929, p. 12.

10. Ibid., p. 13.

11. Ibid., p. 33.

12. Axel Eggebrecht, "Zu Döblins Erfolg," in *Die Weltbühne*, vol. 26, no. 6, February 4 1930, p. 210.

13. *Frankfurter Zeitung*, November 13 1927.

14. The most detailed account of film censorship during the Weimar era was written by the head of the appellate film review board: Ernst Seeger, *Reichslichtspielgesetz vom 12. Mai 1920: Für die Praxis erläutert*, Berlin: Heymann, 1932. For a critical contemporary assessment, see Wolfgang Petzet, *Verbotene Filme: Eine Streitschrift*, Frankfurt am Main: Societäts-Verlag, 1931. For recent surveys of film censorship in the Weimar era, see Klaus Petersen, *Zensur in der Weimarer Republik*, Stuttgart: Metzler, 1995, pp. 245–74; and Martin Loiperdinger, "Filmzensur und Selbstkontrolle," in Wolfgang Jacobsen, Anton Kaes, and Hans Helmut Prinzler, eds, *Geschichte des deutschen Films*, Stuttgart: Metzler, 1993, pp. 481–8.

15. See Gertraude Kühn et al., *Film und revolutionäre Arbeiterbewegung in Deutschland 1918–1932*, Berlin: Henschelverlag, 1975, 2, pp. 74–92.

16. Alexander Jason, *Handbuch des Films 1935/36*, Berlin: Hoppenstedt, 1935, p. 148.

17. "Der nächste Jannings-Film," *Film-Kurier*, May 17 1930.

18. Arnold Pressburger, "Die unabhängige Filmproduktion in Deutschland," in *Der Welt-Spiegel*, October 4 1931, special issue, "Tonfilm 1931," p. 6.

19. For example, see "Produktions-Optimismus bei der Südfilm," in *Film-Kurier*, and "Südfilm in weiterem Aufstieg," in *Lichtbildbühne*, both of December 24 1930.

20. "Heinrich Georges Tonfilmpläne," in *Film-Kurier*, October 3 1930.

21. "Piel Jutzi inszeniert 'Berlin-Alexanderplatz'," in *Film-Kurier*, March 30 1931.

22. For a short documentation of Jutzi's career, see Hans-Michael Bock and Wolfgang Jacobsen, *Piel Jutzi*, Hamburg: CineGraph, 1993.

23. For Döblin's attitude toward film, see Andrea Melcher, *Vom Schriftsteller zum Sprachsteller? Alfred Döblins Auseinandersetzung mit Film und Rundfunk, 1909–1932*, Frankfurt am Main: Peter Lang, 1996. For his work as a scriptwriter—which included drafting scenes for *Mrs. Miniver* and *Random Harvest* as an exile in California during the war—see Erich Kleinschmidt, "Alfred Döblin als Filmautor," in Alfred Döblin, *Drama Hörspiel Film*, Olten: Walter-Verlag, 1983, pp. 651–69.

24. *Berliner Börsen-Courier*, September 14 1922.

25. Alfred Döblin, "Literatur und Rundfunk," in Preussische Akademie der Künste and Reichs-Rundsfunk-Gesellschaft, *Dichtung und Rundfunk: Reden und Gegenreden*, Berlin: private printing of conference proceedings, 1930, p. 8.

26. "Nur der veränderte Autor kann den Film verändern," in *Film-Kurier*, August 16 1930.

27. The script of the radio play, entitled "Die Geschichte vom Franz Biberkopf," is reprinted in Döblin, *Drama Hörspiel Film*, pp. 273–317.

28. "Platz für den deutschen Film!," in *Völkischer Beobachter*, November 25 1930. The article was issued by the "Prop.-Abteilung Gau Gross-Berlin, Abtl. N. S.-Film-bühne," which was directly under Goebbels' authority.

29. See Modris Eksteins, "War, Memory, and Politics: The Fate of the Film *All Quiet on the Western Front*," in *Central European History* 13 (1980), pp. 60–82; and Bärbel Schrader, ed., *Der Fall Remarque: "Im Westen nichts Neues": Eine Dokumentation*, Leipzig: Reclam, 1992.

30. *Völkischer Beobachter*, December 20 1930.

31. *Deutsche Zeitung*, December 12 1930.

32. "Die unerträgliche Zensur: Rechtsunsicherheit der Filmindustrie," in *Film-Kurier*, April 25 1931.

33. *Film-Kurier*, May 9 1931.

34. *Berlin-Alexanderplatz: Drehbuch von Alfred Döblin und Hans Wilhelm zu Piel Jutzis Film von 1931*, Munich: edition text + kritik, 1996, p. 55. The script is analyzed in Eggo Müller, "Adaption als Medienreflexion: Das Drehbuch zu Piel Jutzis *Berlin Alexanderplatz* von Alfred Döblin und Hans Wilhelm," in Alexander Schwarz, ed., *Das Drehbuch: Geschichte, Theorie, Praxis*, Munich: diskurs film, 1992, pp. 91–115.

35. Compare Döblin, *Berlin Alexanderplatz*, pp. 96–108, with *Berlin-Alexanderplatz: Drehbuch*, pp. 66–75.

36. Two recent biographies of George are Peter Laregh, *Heinrich George: Komödiant seiner Zeit*, Munich: Langen Müller, 1992, and Werner Maser, *Heinrich George: Mensch aus Erde gemacht*, Berlin: edition q, 1998.

37. Alfred Mühr, *Kulturbankrott des Bürgertums*, Dresden: Sibyllen-Verlag, 1928, p. 83.

38. Hans Lustig, review of *Der Sträfling aus Stambul*, in *Tempo*, August 31 1929.

39. Hermann Sinsheimer, "Berlin Alexanderplatz," in *Berliner Tageblatt*, October 9 1931.

40. "Drei Tonfilm-Debütanten in 'Berlin-Alexanderplatz'," in *Lichtbildbühne*, October 8 1931.

41. Herbert Ihering, "Der Alexanderplatz-Film," in *Berliner Börsen-Courier*, October 9 1931.

42. "Drei Tonfilm-Debütanten in 'Berlin-Alexanderplatz'," in *Lichtbildbühne*, October 8 1931.

43. Felix Scherret, "Döblin: 'Berlin-Alexanderplatz'," in *Vorwärts*, October 9 1931.

44. O. A. Palitzsch, "Berlin-Alexanderplatz," in *Vossische Zeitung*, October 9 1931.

45. Rudolf Arnheim, "Zwei Filme," in *Weltbühne*, October 13 1931.

46. Siegfried Kracauer, "'Berlin-Alexanderplatz' als Film," in *Frankfurter Zeitung*, October 18 1931.

47. "Gespräch mit Alfred Döblin—Begegnungen mit Biberkopf," in *Lichtbildbühne*, October 7 1931.

48. Benjamin, "Krisis des Romans," p. 233.

49. See for example: "Theaterbesitzer schreiben: Berlinert nicht soviel! Norddeutschland versteht weder bayerisch noch wienerisch!," in *Film-Kurier*, July 18 1931.

50. Felix Scherret, "Döblin: 'Berlin-Alexanderplatz'," in *Vorwärts*, October 9 1931.

51. Siegfried Kracauer, "'Berlin-Alexanderplatz' als Film," in *Frankfurter Zeitung*, October 18 1931.

52. *Berlin-Alexanderplatz: Drehbuch*, pp. 205–208.

53. Ernst Jäger, "Berlin-Alexanderplatz," in *Film-Kurier*, October 9 1931.

54. Helmut Korte, *Der Spielfilm und das Ende der Weimarer Republik*, Göttingen: Vandenhoeck and Ruprecht, 1998, pp. 163–4.

55. Siegfried Kracauer, "'Berlin-Alexanderplatz' als Film," in *Frankfurter Zeitung*, October 18 1931.

56. Herbert Ihering, "Der Alexanderplatz-Film," in *Berliner Börsen-Courier*, October 9 1931.

4

"CUT OUT FROM LAST YEAR'S MOLDERING NEWSPAPERS": BRUNO SCHULZ AND THE BROTHERS QUAY ON *THE STREET OF CROCODILES*

TYRUS MILLER

FETISHISTIC URBANISM

And no face is Surrealistic in the same degree as the true face of a city.
Walter Benjamin, "Surrealism," 1929[1]

In 1986, the American-born animators Steven and Timothy Quay adapted the Polish writer Bruno Schulz's short story *The Street of Crocodiles*, originally published in 1933, into a dialogue-less, animated puppet film. But their film adaptation did not merely translate to another medium an essentially intact narrative structure from Schulz's story. Rather, it subjected the Polish novelist's text to the transformative force of time, working in several ways.

In their adaptation of *The Street of Crocodiles*, the Quays animate Schulz's figures, as if winding up their clockwork springs and setting them in motion. Taken out of the virtual realm of words, the puppets come to occupy a definite duration—twenty-one minutes—related to the materiality of the film and the calculated speed of its machinery. Yet the film also detours the text through a semiotic transposition and "projection" (from words to wordless pictures, from space to space): a process that Marcel Duchamp called, in relation to his *Large Glass*, "delay." By setting Schulz's prose in literal motion and by highlighting the systems of relays through which the literary text gives rise to a new filmic artwork, the Quays disclose physical and semiotic time as meaningful dimensions of their intertextual artistic efforts. They also, finally, foreground the historical gap between their animated film and Schulz's prose text through the device of a framing narrative. Literally a "framing device"—a seedy museum with a proto-cinematic viewing machine called "The Wooden Esophagus"—provides the narrative window onto Schulz's story. Cinematic preservation and physical extirpation of the East European Jewish communities that formed the substance of Schulz's flights of fancy thus appear, in the Quay Brothers' highly affecting film, as two facets of the same history that transpired between Schulz's story in 1933 and the Quays' own work in 1986 that shares its name and narrative premise.

Between the two works, which inscribe a single fictive and fantastic "street of crocodiles" in the incongruent spaces of text and moving image, there occurs a kind of double projection back and forth that allows the temporal gap that this projection bridges to signify, to "sign" itself in the margins of Schulz's narrative—indeed, to replace the determinate words of the verbal text with vaguer implications of a death, decay, and entropy that must engulf language and erode meanings. The Quay Brothers add their work to Schulz's across the partition of fifty years of history—including the Nazis' attempted extermination of the European Jews that claimed Schulz himself as one of its victims and the Soviet annexation of the part of Poland in which Schulz was born and died. With it their film constitutes a kind of "bachelor machine" of two partitioned elements, each occupying a different system of perspective and dimensionality. Through the looping delay of the Quays' film, Schulz's *The Street of Crocodiles* recurs an indefinite number of times, rehearsing once more that very compulsion to repeat that Schulz's text itself illustrates, and capturing its death drive within its mechanics to transmute it into a lyrical "art of dying."

Noteworthy in both Schulz's *The Street of Crocodiles* and the Quays' *The Street of Crocodiles* is an image of the city brought emphatically to light. The Quays reread Schulz's provincial dreamworld (based on his home town in southeastern Poland, Drohobycz) through the lens of dadaist and Surrealist automatism, through the prism of modernism's fascination with the mechanical body and the figures of the puppet, the insect, and the automaton. In their translation of Schulz into animated images, they also suggest the reference of these jointed, automatic figures, which populate the works of artists from Francis Picabia and Marcel Duchamp to Max Ernst and Hans Bellmer, to the urban landscape of the twentieth-century metropolis. They reveal both visible, perceptually apprehensible aspects of these relations and the invisible social dimension drawing things, spaces, and bodies together into the vortex of commodity time, subjecting each to a rapid cycle of creation, circulation, destruction, and re-creation in a new form.

Through the sightless eyes of their puppet figures, for whose life and perception their camera and editing stand in, the Quays present a subjectively apprehended image of the city as modern ruin. In his study of Surrealist art and literature, *Compulsive Beauty*, Hal Foster has suggested that modernist images of the automaton and the ruin can be understood against the background of capitalist modernization:

> these emblems . . . interested the Surrealists because they figured two uncanny changes wrought upon bodies and objects in the high capitalist epoch. On the one hand, the mannequin evokes the remaking of the body (especially the female body) as commodity, just as the automaton, its complement in the Surrealist image repertoire, evokes the reconfiguring of the body (especially the male body) as machine. On the other hand, the romantic ruin evokes the displacing of cultural forms by this regime of machine production and commodity consumption—not only archaic feudal forms but also "outmoded" capitalist ones.[2]

These images, which constitute the two basic poles of the Quays' *The Street of Crocodiles*, thus both register the forces of capitalist modernity and implicitly, by lingering on those objects and spaces that have been consigned to the scrapheap of history, interrupt them. The Quays conceive of the spaces of outmoded consumables as a labyrinth of delay, akin to the passage from image into language in Duchamp. The outmoded serves them as a language not separate from the commodity, from the circulation of money and goods, but one emerging from their oblique, even perverse way of occupying the commodity *erotically*:

But if we talk of language, we needn't talk objectively of just English, or Polish, or Portuguese: but rather more so of the language of things. Things of the senses which elude or resist classification, numbering, or cataloguing. A friend of ours once heard the sound of a voice counting out change in Polish and said it sounded like "rustling taffeta." This is a profoundly beautiful footnote to any language, to the innately mysterious texture of that language, and so you approach its hem with more trembling than you dare imagine.[3]

The urban landscape that the Quays depict is charged with a disquieting combination of stillness and agitation, suggesting a restless erotic desire hidden behind the banal inexpressiveness of its walls, windows, and doors (**6**). Underscoring the implicit blurring of the boundary between subjective and objective features of this represented space, I will call its basic mode "fetishistic urbanism," which I would characterize as having three major features. Firstly, it is ontologically indefinite: the spaces of this puppet-city and the objects inhabiting them confound oppositions of animated and dead, organic and inorganic, active and inert, real and imaginary, genuine and ersatz. Secondly, it is characterized by a reversibility of properties between the human body and inanimate objects, with bodies becoming rigid and jointed, while objects take on fleshly, pliable, and pulsate qualities. Finally, it is an essentially entropic mode, dominated by repetition and the dispersal of structured form in a spreading dilapidation and disorder.[4]

This mode of urbanism is not original to the film of the Surrealist animator, even though it has found its most faithful historian and archivist there. Rather, it was indigenous to the modern European metropolis itself, resulting from the spatial dynamics of capitalist accumulation, the movements of value through the built environment that marked the modernization of old European cities such as Paris in the successive implementations of Baron Haussmann's plans. The rapid development of zones of commerce, in which gerrybuilt façades quickly crumbled into strangely juxtaposed mixtures of newness and decrepitude, gave rise to a novel experience of temporal ambiguity embedded in the very spaces of everyday life.[5] The name for this experience was the "outmoded," which writers as varied as André Breton, Louis Aragon, and Walter Benjamin discovered hidden in the built remains of the previous epoch. Benjamin, for example, catalogued spaces and things saturated with this anachronistic

6 The Quay Brothers' *The Street of Crocodiles* (1986) (Copyright E. D. Distribution, 1986)

temporality of the once-and-no-longer new: "the first iron constructions, the first factory buildings, the earliest photos, the objects that have begun to be extinct, grand pianos, the dresses of five years ago, fashionable restaurants when the vogue has begun to ebb from them."[6] Exemplified by the new-old buildings of aging modern zones of the city, and equally by the commodified objects of dress or domesticity once invested with the gleam of fashionableness, they later, through the mere passage of time, came to carry the stigma of inauthenticity and destitution. But in their fall from newness, their qualities underwent a change of value.

In turn, the peculiar phenomenology of the outmoded spaces and objects of these zones facilitated their interfacing with perverse forms of erotic desire, fetishistic and masochistic, which displaced the erotic drive from a human object and extended it into the world of inanimate, partial objects. In their freshness and charm, before their decline into the grotesquerie of the out-of-date, such objects and places allowed the fetishism of the commodity to appear anything but perverse. Yielding oneself to the "sex appeal of the inorganic," as Benjamin characterized the commodity fetish of the fashionable object, became a public mode of gratification rather than something pursued in the shadows of the back room. In their decline, however, they became the material repositories of a desire fixated in the past, set on disavowing history, recapturing lost time, and preserving it in artificial suspension for periodic recall. Yet this paradoxical impulse, this attempt to arrest the ineluctable movement of the commodity on its circulatory course from fashionability to outmodedness, never really succeeds in re-animating a lost freshness. Instead, it produces a repetitive life-in-death and death-in-life, an uncanny circling in a narrow ambit among a diminishing selection of treasured things.

The ultimate image one derives from Schulz's and the Quays' works is that of the city as an intransitive and derisive machinery, in which the compulsive repetitions of fetishistic sexuality and the entropic movement of matter are complementary and mutually reinforcing aspects of the dynamics of urban space. Neither suggests anything either of the convulsive beauty that the Surrealists thought to discover in such spaces of the outmoded as the Passage de l'Opéra in Louis Aragon's *Paysan de Paris* or the flea market in André Breton's *Nadja*, nor of the "revolutionary nihilism" Walter Benjamin detected in the Surrealists' relation to the impoverished zones of the modern city:

> No one before these visionaries and augurs perceived how destitution—not only social but architectonic, the poverty of interiors, enslaved and enslaving objects—can be suddenly transformed into revolutionary nihilism . . . They bring the immense forces of "atmosphere" concealed in these things to the point of explosion.[7]

Rather, for Schulz and the Quays, it is as if a mutual regression gripped both the city and its human material. The decay of the urban world sets free the fragmentary objects of the fetishist's desire, while the fetishist's restless wandering from object to object drives forward the corruption, moral and material, of such zones of urban disintegration. Rather than dialectical, tending toward an intensification and reversal of urban decay into revolutionary destruction, the dynamics of fetishistic urbanism are *dissipative*—the entropic spiral progresses from repetition to repetition, gradually spreading from point to point; yet this very expansion of its bounds tends to limit it, slow its spread, and contain its virulence.

THE DIALECTICAL IMAGE

> People's weakness delivers their souls to us, makes them needy. That loss of an electron ionizes them and renders them suitable for chemical bonding. Without flaws they would stay locked inside themselves, not needing anything. It takes their vices to give them flavor and attraction.
>
> Bruno Schulz to Tadeusz and Zofia Breza, June 21 1934[8]

This confrontation of modernity and provinciality, childhood memory with rapid development and change, generates forms that are at once enigmatically fantastic and fragile, subject to appear and disappear without explanation of their epiphanic presence. It is, perhaps, in similar terms that one must describe Schulz's own unique *oeuvre* as a writer and artist, which is difficult to explain in typical literary and art historical terms of influence and affiliation. Schulz's life was one of quiet isolation, not only from international tendencies, but even with more metropolitan Polish ones. Though he had some experience of larger cities such as Lwów and Vienna in his aborted training as an architect and painter, he lived most of his life in his hometown of Drohobycz, hardly a cultural center, working as a drawing instructor in the same gymnasium he had attended in his youth. His first book *Cinnamon Shops* collected a series of vignettes originally conceived in his letters to another writer, Debrora Vogel; the timid Schulz only published it in 1933 upon the enthusiastic prompting of another friend, Zofia Nalkowska. Only after the strong reception of *Cinnamon Shops* did Schulz come in contact with other key literary-artistic figures of the interwar period in Poland, in particular the modernist writers Stanislaw Ignacy Witkiewicz and Witold Gombrowicz, for whose novel *Ferdydurke* Schulz provided the illustrations. Similarly, only after the publication of *Cinnamon Shops* did Schulz venture into the international literary field, with a translation of Franz Kafka's *The Trial*. Hence, though the relations of Schulz's work to the Polish avant garde, to German writers such as Kafka and Robert Walser, and to the poetics of Surrealism are retrospectively evident, we are compelled to see them in terms of analogies and "elective affinities" rather than in terms of influence. Ultimately, perhaps, the singular phenomenon of Schulz must be seen as an unlikely product of Central European historical and social conditions, which, glittering uncannily in the distorting mirror of his sensibility, enriched his narrow experience into fantastical works of art.

Bruno Schulz's *The Street of Crocodiles*—actually a single chapter from a book of interlinked stories from Schulz's childhood entitled in the Polish original *Cinnamon Shops*—explores a modernized section of an old, Central European provincial city. Though not identifying it explicitly, Schulz clearly based his fictive city on his hometown of Drohobycz, later incorporated as Drogobych into the Soviet Union (which has now itself been consumed by history). But even before the Nazi invasion and Soviet annexation had done its destructive work, the forces of decay had already taken hold on this far from cosmopolitan childhood city that, as Adam Zagajewski puts it, Schulz had imaginatively "transformed into some sort of eastern Baghdad" out of the *Arabian Nights*.[9] Schulz's *Cinnamon Shops* persists as a kind of fantastic ruin, or perhaps, given its author's more lurid imaginings, especially evident in his pen-and-ink drawings, a fetish of a lost object of love. As Zagajewski notes, "In transforming the cramped and dirty Drohobycz—in which probably only the half-wild gardens, orchards, cherry trees, sunflowers, and moldering fences were really beautiful—into an extraordinary, divine place, Schulz could say good-bye to it, he could leave it."[10]

Schulz's *The Street of Crocodiles* is an "industrial and commercial district," a zone of "pseudo-Americanism, grafted onto the old, crumbling core of the city."[11] At the same time, however, it is distinctly marked as an area of corruption. For example, it is a place in which the fetishist or masochist might look to find pictures and books to feed his imagination or even prostitutes willing to service his specialized tastes. Schulz subtly equivocates in his description of the relation of the area to the rest of the city, suggesting its compounding of repulsion and desire, its attraction and the need to disavow the basis of its attraction:

The old established inhabitants of the city kept away from that area where the scum, the lowest orders had settled—creatures without character, without background, moral dregs, that inferior species of human being which is born in such ephemeral communities. But on days of defeat, in hours of moral weakness, it would happen that one or another of the city dwellers would venture half by chance into that dubious district. The best among them were not entirely free from the temptation of voluntary degradation, of breaking down the barriers of hierarchy, of immersion in that shallow mud of companionship, of easy intimacy, of dirty interminglings.[12]

The Street of Crocodiles represents Schulz's provincial, Central European corollary to Louis Aragon's metropolitan Passage de l'Opéra, already fallen from past fashionability into seedy vice, in his Surrealist novel *Paysan de Paris*:

The great American passion for city planning, imported into Paris by a prefect of police during the Second Empire and now being applied to the task of redrawing the map of our capital in straight lines, will soon spell the doom of these human aquariums. Although the life that originally quickened them has drained away, they deserve, nevertheless, to be regarded as the secret repositories of several modern myths: it is only today, when the pickaxe menaces them, that they have at last become the true sanctuaries of a cult of the ephemeral, the ghostly landscape of damnable pleasures and professions. Places that were incomprehensible yesterday, and that tomorrow will never know.[13]

Aragon's text in turn inspired Walter Benjamin's extensive study of the historical rise and fall of the arcades as the architectural register of commodity time in the city, the *Passagenwerk*.[14] Schulz's text presents a "dialectical image" (to use Benjamin's term) of the impact of modernization on the small Central European city, offering a set of contradictory predicates for this ambiguous arcade-like zone: new yet rapidly rotting, metropolitanesque yet provincial, fetishistically arousing yet frustrating, bustling yet static.

Significantly, however, Schulz begins his story not with a direct approach to the zone, but rather through the detour of an outmoded domestic object possessed by his father, already revealed in earlier stories to be masochistically and fetishistically inclined and on the brink of psychotic disintegration into a delirium of communication with the material world of dust, insects, and tailors' dummies. The father's object is "an old and beautiful map" kept in the lower drawer of his desk, "a whole folio sheaf of parchment pages which, originally fastened with strips of linen, formed an enormous wall map, a bird's-eye panorama."[15] From the very outset, then, the city is eclipsed by a representation, but in turn a representation whose material support—the parchment and linen strips—threatens to exceed the significance of the lines printed upon it. *The Street of Crocodiles*, in contrast to other zones richly traced on this map, is marked by a disturbing absence:

> On that map, made in the style of baroque panoramas, the area of the Street of Crocodiles shone with the empty whiteness that usually marks polar regions or unexplored countries of which almost nothing is known. The lines of only a few streets were marked in black and their names given in simple, unadorned lettering, different from the noble script of the other captions.[16]

The reassuring perspicacity of the panoramic view is denied this space. The absence of any thickly textured weave of streets and names, the graphic image of the old European city's historical density, makes this neighborhood gape like an obscene view glimpsed through the otherwise intact fabric of the old city map.

The characteristic quality of this zone is its ambiguity, the same quality Benjamin identified as "dialectical" in his urban dream interpretation.[17] The oneiric ambiguity of *The Street of Crocodiles* is so strong as to undo the all-too-discrete categories of language in which some description of it might be tendered: "We spoke of the illusory character of that area, but these words have too precise and definite a meaning to describe its half-baked and undecided reality."[18] "Our language," Schulz continues, "has no definitions which would weigh, so to speak, the grade of reality, or define its suppleness. Let us say it bluntly: the misfortune of that area is that nothing ever succeeds there, nothing can ever reach a definite conclusion. Gestures hang in the air, movements are prematurely exhausted and cannot overcome a certain point of inertia."[19]

This inconclusiveness is the general corollary of the story's staging of erotic desire in an extendable series of displacements onto items of print, clothing, footwear, and other objects, which finally return us to the sheer facticity of the commodity, "outmoded" by its passage along the temporal chain of consumer desire and ultimately unsatisfying, leaving the desire that pushed it along progressively more enervated but never fully spent. The exemplary scene in this respect—made a central episode in the Quays' adaptation as well—is the tailor's shop, which remains deeply shrouded in ambiguity as to its true character. In the course of the story, the tailor's shop appears, perhaps in reality, perhaps only in the transfiguring light of day, to be a vendor of exotic pornography and a brothel specializing in the perverse. Yet after a narrative digression that explores the erotic scenario, it returns to being, after all, just a tailor's shop and nothing more.

Thus the space of the outmoded is a condensed image of commodity time, in which feverish fantasy and the nausea of the unadorned material are joined in unmediated proximity, through the trick of the collapse of the temporal interval between the fashionable and the no-longer-modish. When, through the passage of time, that vanished interval within the commodity is reconstituted, the result is a kind of Baudelairean spleen:

> Our hopes were a fallacy, the suspicious appearance of the premises and of the staff were a sham, the clothes were real clothes, and the salesman had no ulterior motives. . . . In that city of cheap human material, no instincts can flourish, no dark and unusual passions can be aroused.[20]

ENTROPIC ANIMATION

> I can't stand people laying claim to my time. They make the scrap they touch nauseating to me. I am incapable of sharing time, of feeding on somebody's leftovers.
> Bruno Schulz to Tadeusz Breza, December 2 1934[21]

In their adaptation of Schulz's complex literary text to a wordless, animated puppet film, the Quay Brothers pick up and intensify his close attention to the material textures and ambiguous qualities of this urban space. Their adaptation appears to draw iconographically not only on the short story entitled *The Street of Crocodiles*, but also on other sources from *Cinnamon Shops*. For instance, in their central use of animated puppets, automatons, and mannequins, they seem to allude strongly to the three-part story entitled "Tailors' Dummies," which also provides the images of sewing machines picked up in the bobbins and threads that run throughout the film and which offers an important interpretative context for the pervasive presence of incomplete, fragmentary, artificial bodies.

In this story, the narrator's mad father delivers a series of disquisitions on the tailor's dummy as a vehicle for philosophizing on the relation between creation, the human form, and the material world. In the second of his discourses, the father suggests that unlike the original Creator, who sought to hide matter under the guise of spirit, human beings must revel in matter's "creaking, its resistance, its clumsiness."[22]

The father would, surely, find his love gratified in the Quays' antique puppets, uncanny machines, and shoddy toys. He might himself be the designer of their mannequins with incomplete bodies, rollers for limbs, and hollow molded heads. Like a bizarrely misplaced Kurt Schwitters declaring the kingdom of Merz in a mid-sized Polish city at the turn of the century, Schulz's father issues a manifesto of the new creation:

> We openly admit: we shall not insist either on durability or solidity of workmanship; our creations will be temporary, to serve for a single occasion. If they be human beings, we shall give them, for example, only one profile, one hand, one leg, the one limb needed for their role. It would be pedantic to bother about the other, unnecessary, leg. Their backs can be made of canvas or simply white-washed . . . The Demiurge was in love with consummate, superb, and complicated materials; we shall give priority to trash. We are simply entranced and enchanted by the cheapness, shabbiness, and inferiority of material.[23]

Another story, "Cockroaches," in which the mad father believes himself to be metamorphosing into a bug, is alluded to through the furtive, cockroach-like movement of the Quays' adult puppet (to whom they refer in an interview as "The Stalker").

Although the Quays, like Schulz, also incorporate the device of the map to filter the depiction of *The Street of Crocodiles* through graphic representations and subjective fantasy, they also introduce a novel framing element not in Schulz's text: a black-and-white "prelude" section, entitled "The Wooden Esophagus," set in a run-down museum with a nickelodeon-like optical machine, through which the animated scene is set in motion. This adds one further layer of connotations to the ambiguous corruption of Schulz's *The Street of Crocodiles*, the "museal" quality that reflects not only Schulz's retrospective look at the city of his childhood, but also the Quay Brothers' perspective on a Central European

Jewish milieu largely destroyed by World War Two and the Holocaust. Within the narrative frame, this implication of museality is redoubled by a kind of pictorial icon in a panoramic shot of the street. In the upper foreground of the shot, stretched horizontally over the opening of the street on a ledge or in a case, is the skeleton of a crocodile. One is at once entering a kind of gaping mouth and a natural history museum, a curiosity cabinet full of dead fragments of nature. In his essay "Valéry Proust Museum," Theodor Adorno notes the association of "mausoleum" and "museum," arguing that "Museums are like the family sepulchres of works of art."[24] In this light, "the wooden esophagus" appears in a punning relation to a wooden sarcophagus, in which the corpse of the past is being placed in a flesh-eating coffin and digested into images. Schulz's memorial narrative, in the Quay Brothers' hands, thus becomes a self-reflexive commentary on our own museal relation to a history to which we "no longer have a vital relationship" and which only allows itself to be appropriated as a fetishized object, a heap of fragments artificially animated by our disavowal of history, by our desire to get past the dilapidated surfaces of artifacts and documents and to gain access to a throbbing, visceral inner life impervious to time's decay.

The keeper of this dim museum, peering as if at a peepshow, through some sort of primitive proto-cinematic machine, allows a drop of saliva to fall into it, starting its pulleys and bobbins moving. He cuts a thread to which one of the central puppets, representing Schulz's mad father, is tethered, thus allowing him to wander through the Street of Crocodiles. In light of Schulz's text, and also of the Quays' earlier film "Nocturna Artificiala (Those Who Desire Without End)" in which this same puppet was seen wandering through an East European city at night, we can interpret this cutting of the thread as the release of the puppet into the spiral of errant desire, an entry into the fetishistic bachelor machinery of the Street of Crocodiles within which his erotic-entropic quest will be played out. Notably, the spaces of the body and visual perspective are mapped onto the city in paradoxical ways. The wooden esophagus through which the museum keeper peers and into which he drops his saliva will open upon the scenography of *The Street of Crocodiles*, as if it were a dream-like figural translation of a digestion process going on within a slumbering puppet's body. The cutting of the thread might thus alternatively be interpreted as the snapping of the thread of consciousness and the passage of the subject into the rigidified state of sleep and dream. At the same time, however, the Street of Crocodiles is also an objectified space containing the wooden puppet bodies of the father, the child, and the various inhabitants of the Street. Analogously, at several points in the film, the perspective loses its panoramic character and is clearly focalized through the perspective of the father or child. Hence the ambiguities of this space: it both contains and is contained by wooden bodies; it is seen both from outside and from within, panoramically and through focalized views.

The space itself is characterized by what might be described as an entropic animation, a pseudomorphic life-likeness lent to inanimate material by the processes of breakdown and decay. One static image of this non-organic "life" is the dust that has rendered many of the shop windows in the Quays' film nearly opaque and that has gathered in a thick layer on the street.[25] As with Marcel Duchamp's temporal telescoping of movement into a still image by affixing the dust gathered on the surface of the *Large Glass* (Man Ray's famous photograph, *Dust Breeding*, documented Duchamp's glass with months of dust gathered on it), here the dust represents a negative imprint of crumbling façades and the drift of invisible particles in the air, once agitated by the passing of bodies and vehicles and now fallen all but still. While the images of dust are presented fairly unobtrusively in the Quays' film, Schulz's dedication of the father's third discourse on tailors' dummies to the pseudoflora and pseudofauna of dust that sprout in undisturbed rooms and that disintegrate upon their re-opening should alert us to its importance in the Quay Brothers' vision of the Street of Crocodiles as a sealed chamber of the East European urban past. Schulz recounts the "used-up atmospheres, rich in the specific ingredients of human dreams; rubbish heaps, abounding in the humus of memories, of nostalgia, and of sterile boredom." "On such a soil," he concludes, "this pseudovegetation sprouted abundantly yet ephemerally, brought forth short-lived generations which flourished suddenly and splendidly, only to wilt and perish."[26] In the Quays' film, dust is the index of just such an ephemeral life and rapid perishing in the city space as a whole, as well as a mark of the distance in time between their authorial present and the semi-fictional moment of Schulz's childhood.

Similarly, in close-up images of rainfall agitating fine grains of sand on the streets of the district, the Quays suggest that the dusty residues of urban life here now persist only in a minimal state of animation, a restless but aimless turbulence of matter at the threshold between motion and inert stillness. Yet at the same time, this minimal life is ambiguous, since it also suggests a pathetic reserve trapped in the very refuse generated by human labor and activity. In his third disquisition on tailors' dummies, following his account of the vegetative life of dust, Schulz's father rises to a mad pitch of mimetic empathy with a matter tortured into form by the work of unknowing men:

> "Who knows," he said, "how many suffering, crippled, fragmentary forms of life there are, such as the artificially created life of chests and tables quickly nailed together, crucified timbers, silent martyrs to cruel human inventiveness. The terrible transplantation of incompatible and hostile races of wood, their merging into one misbegotten personality.
>
> "How much ancient suffering is there in the varnished grain, in the veins and knots of our old familiar wardrobes? Who would recognize in them the old features, smiles, and glances, almost planed and polished out of all recognition?"
>
> My father's face, when he said that, dissolved into a thoughtful net of wrinkles, began to resemble an old plank full of knots and veins, from which all memories had been planed away.[27]

A second set of images of the spurious and uncanny life of the district can be found in the variety of automatons and machines that are the primary occupants of the shops lining the Street of Crocodiles. These include a monkey-doll with a set of cymbals, observed both by the father and son through the toy shop's dusty window and periodically shuddered by a paroxysm of mechanical agitation; the taffy machine in the candy shop window, repetitively jolting back to stretch the gray, amorphous gum and snapping back, while a mechanical finger juts up to extract a piece from the extended mass; seen through another window, a hammering craftsman figure made up of mechanical parts, a light bulb for his head and surrounded by other light bulbs scattered over the floor of the shop; the automaton tailor's assistants; and several other mechanical entities more indefinitely characterized. One should add that the Quays' representation of the city of Bruno Schulz's childhood is evoked by their signature use of antique Central European wooden puppets, which could very well have been seen in a toy store in Poland around the turn of the century. Thus even the central "characters" of the film, the puppet figures of Schulz's father and the child himself, have an obsolete, artifactual quality. Through these aging children's toys, Schulz's city is self-reflexively evoked as a space of aging, lifeless commodities brought artificially to life by the machinery of cinematic animation (note the implication of "anima," life and soul, in the term).

A third and symbolically rich icon of entropic animation is that of the repeated image of self-unscrewing and self-propelling wood screws. These not only clearly associate the deceptive appearance of life in the Street of Crocodiles with the process of decay and dilapidation undoing the neighborhood, which is almost literally coming apart at the seams; they also refer back self-reflexively to the process of cinematic animation. The incremental cranking of the animator's camera and the reverse running of the film by which the screws are made to unscrew themselves appear as the correlatives of the agentless undoing of the city's architectonic stability with the passage of time.

The screws, moreover, enter directly into the Quays' psychosexual narrative, both for the father and the child. The child, for example, is seen capturing a screw that is trying to escape by screwing itself, wormlike, into a piece of wood. The boy grabs its head and works it loose, and he is later seen playing with it, making it dance by reflecting light on it with a hand mirror. In case the masturbatory overtones of the image are missed, it is linked associatively to three other erotically charged scenes. First, the father is seen to pick up an errant screw and put it in a box that he is carrying around on his furtive wanderings through the Street of Crocodiles. The Quays allude, perhaps, to a similar container in Luis Buñuel's and Salvador Dali's classic Surrealist film *Un Chien andalou* (1929), in which such a box holds a severed hand. In a second scene in *Street of Crocodiles*, in the tailor's shop, this boxed screw is fetishistically replaced by a wooden shoe with a screw inset into it as a spike heel, which is put into the father's box and returned to him by the unctuous tailor assistant automatons. Finally, at the climax of the perverse and pornographic show given to the father at the back of the tailor's shop, he is invited to peer into a hidden space, as if upon a particularly obscene spectacle. What is revealed to his gaze, however, is the child, seated outside on the ground in the same posture he had been in when playing with the screws. Now, however, instead of his hand mirror casting a reflected light onto a dancing screw, he holds an illuminated light bulb on his lap and caresses it playfully. But soon the screws in the jackknife-shaped electrical circuit to which the bulb is attached by a thick wire unscrew themselves in the now-familiar manner, extinguishing the light.

When the light goes out, the boy covers the darkened bulb with a brown cloth sack.

The scene in the tailor's shop deserves special consideration because of its singular degree of narrative drama, reinforced by the scherzo quality of the music accompanying it up to the more somber ending. The basic narrative of this scene is that the father, wandering about and peering in the shop windows of the district, is drawn into the tailor's shop by the blandishment of its tailor and his glowing-eyed, automaton assistants. In a whirl of activity, the tailor and his helpers pull out and measure cloth, remove the wooden head of the father and replace it with a dummy head stuffed with cotton, and begin to refurbish the father's look, not merely by fabricating a new wardrobe for him, but by reconstructing his head and body. At the height of this activity, the tempo suddenly slackens, and the father is allowed to view anatomical drawings. He contemplates suggestively testicle-like pieces of meat with pins jutting out of them and caresses pieces of fur, cloth-covered shapes, and limply hanging, calves-leather gloves. In what appears to be the climax of this obscene spectacle, however, he is led to peer back out into the Street of Crocodiles, where his son is playing peacefully. The scene ends with the tailor's assistants having spent their charge of temporary life, with the camera sweeping past them, as their single arm gyrates erratically, like a burned-out machine.

As I have already suggested, the space of the tailor's shop offers a concentrated image of the contradictory qualities of the Street of Crocodiles as an urban district. In fact, it provides one more instance of the confounding of container-contained, microcosm–macrocosm relations that structure the film as a whole. Its reflective properties, produced through the shop's multiple mirrors and only partially transparent windows, project the inside of the space outside and open the internal vantages of the shop back out into the street. In the somber, long, leftward tracking shot that closes the tailor's shop episode, one passes through an extraordinary complex succession of fragmentary spaces in which outside and inside are literally indiscernible. Finally, even the outmost narrative frame—the museum of curiosities of "The Wooden Esophagus"—is redoubled within this scene in the shelf of fetish items, a strange miscellany of outmoded knick-knacks displayed briefly in the frame as the camera sweeps by.

Attentive viewing of this scene also reveals how closely the Quay Brothers associate the fragmentary organs and tissues of the body, the direct objects of fetishistic desire, with Schulz's original "fetish" of the map. In one shot, the assistants, having removed the father-puppet's wooden head, spread out a piece of liver upon a city map, covering it with the tailor's translucent sizing paper and attaching the blood-dampened paper to the raw flesh with pins. This shot conflates in a single disquieting image several contradictory meanings: the skin's attachment to the flesh and its painful separation from it; the skin's covering of the flesh and clothing's covering of naked skin; the utilitarian implements of the tailor's work and the extravagant instruments of inflicting masochistic pleasure-pain. In another, rapidly passing image, one sees that the eye of one of the tailor's assistants, gesturing toward a particularly lurid spectacle, appears "bloodshot" with crosshatched lines, as if the viewing of pornography in the Street of Crocodiles had etched its map into the very organ of seeing.

The map in both Schulz's text and the Quays' animated adaptation of it is an *aide-mémoire*, yet it is also strangely mobile in its reference, displaceable from the outer narrative frame into the visceral organs of characters at the deepest heart of its fictional space, the inner sanctum of the tailor's shop. This peculiar de-localization of the map follows from the fact that it corresponds only to a lost territory, memorializing an affectively charged fragment of a Drohobycz that no longer exists. It serves fetishistically to disavow, though not truly dispel, the melancholy knowledge of this district's essential ephemerality, its ultimate vacancy in the historical city's archive of experiences, the disconcertingly rapid slipping into oblivion of a space once so intensely invested with the aura of fantasy and perverse desire. Already by Schulz's time, and certainly for the Quays, the Street of Crocodiles designates nothing more than the errant imagi-nation's bringing to temporary, uncanny life a trace of ink on paper—the adult author's memory of his father's map and, derivatively, Schulz's printed text for the Brothers Quay. Obviously, we might say, retracing Schulz's concluding lines, "we were able to afford nothing better than this paper imitation, this montage of illustrations cut out from last year's moldering newspapers."[28]

NOTES

1. Walter Benjamin, "Surrealism, The Last Snapshot of the European Intelligentsia" (1929), in Peter Demetz, ed., *Reflections*, trans. Edmund Jephcott, New York: Schocken Books, 1978, p. 182.
2. Hal Foster, *Compulsive Beauty*, Cambridge, MA: MIT Press, 1993, pp. 125–6.
3. Timothy and Stephen Quay, quoted from Nick Wadley, "Interview with the Brothers Quay," March 1995, *Pix* 2, 1997, p. 136.
4. See Anthony Vidler, *The Architectural Uncanny: Essays in the Modern Unhomely*, Cambridge, MA: MIT Press, 1992.
5. For theoretical discussion of the spatial aspects of capitalist accumulation, see David Harvey, *The Limits to Capital*, Oxford: Basil Blackwell, 1982, and *The Urbanization of Capital: Studies in the History and Theory of Capitalist Urbanization*, Baltimore, MD: Johns Hopkins University Press, 1985.
6. Ibid., p. 181.
7. Ibid., pp. 181–2.
8. Bruno Schulz, in Jerzy Ficowski, ed., *Letters and Drawings of Bruno Schulz*, trans. Walter Arendt and Victoria Nelson, New York: Fromm International, 1988, p. 54.
9. Adam Zagajewski, "Preface to the American Edition" of *Letters and Drawings of Bruno Schulz*, p. 15.
10. Ibid., p. 17.
11. Bruno Schulz, *The Street of Crocodiles*, trans. Celina Wieniewska, New York: Penguin Books, 1963, pp. 100–101.
12. Ibid., p. 101.
13. Louis Aragon, *Paris Peasant*, trans. Simon Watson Taylor, London: Picador Books, 1971, pp. 28–9.
14. Walter Benjamin, *The Arcades Project*, trans. Howard Eiland and Kevin McLaughlin, Cambridge, MA: Belknap Press, 1999.
15. Schulz, *Street of Crocodiles*, p. 99.
16. Ibid., p. 100.
17. On Benjamin's dream theory, see my essay, "From City-Dreams to the Dreaming Collective: Walter Benjamin's Political Dream Interpretation," *Philosophy and Social Criticism*, vol. 22, no. 6, 1996, pp. 87–111.
18. Schulz, *Street of Crocodiles*, p. 108.
19. Ibid., p. 109.
20. Ibid., p. 110.
21. Schulz, *Letters and Drawings*, p. 56.
22. Schulz, *Street of Crocodiles*, p. 62.
23. Ibid., pp. 61–2.
24. Theodor W. Adorno, "Valéry Proust Museum" in *Prisms: Essays in Cultural*

Criticism, trans. Samuel and Shierry Weber, Cambridge, MA: MIT Press, 1967, p. 175.

25. I adopt the term "non-organic life" from Gilles Deleuze, who applies it to the cinema of expressionism: "[N]atural substances and artificial creations, candelabras and trees, turbine and sun are no longer any different. A wall which is alive is dreadful; but utensils, furniture, houses and their roofs also lean, crowd around, lie in wait, or pounce. Shadows of houses pursue the man running along the street. In all these cases, it is not the mechanical which is opposed to the organic: it is the vital as potent pre-organic germinality, common to the animate and the inanimate, to a matter which raises itself to the point of life, and to a life which spreads itself through all matter. The animal has lost the organic, as much as matter has gained life." Gilles Deleuze, *Cinema 1: The Movement-Image*, trans. Hugh Tomlinson and Barbara Habberjam, Minneapolis: University of Minnesota Press, 1986, p. 51. See Bruno Schulz's description of his book *Cinnamon Shops* in an essay that accompanied an interview with S. I. Witkiewicz: "*Cinnamon Shops* offers a certain recipe for reality, posits a certain special kind of substance. The substance of that reality exists in a state of constant fermentation, germination, hidden life. It contains no dead, hard, limited objects. Everything diffuses beyond its borders, remains in a given shape only momentarily, leaving this shape behind at the first opportunity. A principle of sorts appears in the habits, the modes of existence of this reality: universal masquerade. Reality takes on certain shapes merely for the sake of appearance, as a joke or form of play. One person is a human, another is a cockroach, but shape does not penetrate essence, it is only a role adopted for the moment, an outer skin soon to be shed. A certain extreme monism of the life substance is assumed here, for which specific objects are nothing more than masks." *Letters and Drawings of Bruno Schulz*, p. 113.

26. Schulz, *Street of Crocodiles*, p. 67.

27. Ibid., p. 69.

28. Ibid., p. 110.

5

ARCHITORTURE: JAN ŠVANKMAJER AND SURREALIST FILM

DAVID SORFA

Surrealism has always been associated with urban experience. Roger Cardinal and Robert Short's key introduction, *Surrealism: Permanent Revolution*, begins: "Surrealism is a collective adventure which began in Paris."[1] The large cities of Europe are vitally linked to the history of Surrealism and very often appear in the works of the Surrealists either as places of magical and often ruined wonder or as threatening and foreboding sites filled with lurking, unknowable desires.[2] The Surrealist is often seen as a jaded *flâneur*, whose sophisticated palate requires rather more titillating fare than that offered by the surface of the city—hence the celebrated interest in hidden or forgotten spaces, dead-end streets, sleazy bars and flea-markets filled with the signs of some other life going on elsewhere. Even when the Surrealist wanders into the country or the jungle it is only to discern a certain anthropomorphic exoticism that might reinvigorate the *ennui* of the urbane dweller.

More than individual countries, it is cities—Berlin, Paris, Prague, Geneva, London, Madrid, Chicago—that are associated with Surrealist activity. Although it may be enticing to imagine that there is something intrinsically Surrealist in the magnetic attraction of the city, it is more probable that those who have considered themselves "Surrealist" have usually been bourgeois intellectuals naturally given to traveling from city to city to attend universities, find work, or to participate in the group activity and artistic collaboration with like-minded colleagues which Surrealism has always considered to be central to its endeavors. The city, then, has long been both an imaginary and practical Surrealist space happily providing both the economic means for survival and the raw material for Surrealist exploration. From De Chirico's empty squares to Magritte's suburban conundrums, the Surrealist city embodies the central contradiction of urban life: the city as civilization and simultaneously as destroyer of the civilized. Sigmund Freud's evocation of the uncanny and the city seems to capture the romantic vertigo of the Surrealists:

> As I was walking, one hot summer afternoon, through the deserted streets of a provincial town in Italy which was unknown to me, I found myself in a quarter of whose character I could not long remain in doubt. Nothing but painted women were to be seen at the windows of the small houses, and I hastened to leave the narrow street at the next turning. But after having wandered about for a time without enquiring my way, I suddenly found myself back in the same street, where my presence was now beginning to excite attention. I hurried away once more, only to arrive by another *détour* at the same place yet a third time. Now, however, a feeling overcame me which I can only describe as uncanny, and I was glad enough to find myself back at the piazza I had left a short while before, without any further voyages of discovery.[3]

Although the paradigmatic Surrealist city must be Paris, there is no doubt that Prague, especially in the latter half of the twentieth century, had an equal if not greater resonance for Surrealist activity. André Breton, who visited the city with Paul Eluard in 1935, echoed Guillaume Apollinaire in calling Prague "the magical capital of Europe" (a phrase which, of course, is now the preferred cliché of travel guidebooks) and established close links with contemporary Czech Surrealists such as Toyen (Marie Cernunová), her partner, Jindrich Štýrský, and Karel Teige, "the very incarnation of intelligence, culture and the struggle for a better world, the founder and incomparable animator of the Surrealist group in Prague."[4] Breton goes on to eulogize Prague as that place of "intense and unparalleled seething of ideas and hopes, those impassioned exchanges at human level aspiring to wed poetry and revolution, while the gulls claimed the Vltava in every direction to make stars spurt out."[5]

The Surrealist group in Czechoslovakia developed out of the loose 1920s avant garde collective, *Devetsil* (The Nine Souls), and although officially established in 1934 by the poet Viteslav Nezval, it was Teige who soon became the group's "dominant figure."[6] Closely allied to the French group and taking Breton's Second Manifesto as its template, the group was briefly productive until 1938 when a combination of internal dissent (with Nezval attempting to dissolve the group) and the imminent Nazi occupation silenced the Surrealists throughout the war years. Unsuccessful attempts were made to revive the group after 1945, and in 1951 when Teige died of a heart attack the theorist Vratislav Effenberger took over leadership of the group. Many of the original Surrealists were either dead or had emigrated and, although the group now attracted new members, it was not until the political thaw of the 1960s that Surrealist activity became coherent and forceful once again. The Soviet invasion of Prague in 1968 did not at first affect Surrealist activity, but with the publication of the first issue of the journal *Analogon* in 1969 the group was effectively put into stasis until *Analogon*'s second issue could be published in 1990, almost as if the intervening twenty-one years had not occurred.[7]

In 1970, at the beginning of this "hidden" period, Jan Švankmajer and his wife, the painter-poet Eva, joined the Surrealist Group— Švankmajer himself coming from a background as a puppeteer at Prague's *Lanterna Magica* and an involvement with "trick" films. If it is through Švankmajer's films that the group's importance became established outside Czechoslovakia, perhaps Švankmajer's greatest contribution to the group in Czechoslovakia has been his interest in "Rudolfine Mannerism," characterized by the archival excesses of Rudolf II, who presided in Prague as the Holy Roman Emperor from 1576 until 1612, and in the composite paintings of his court painter, Arcimboldo (although these influences had been an earlier feature of the photography of Emila Medkova).[8] It is clear from many of his films that Švankmajer's fascination with Rudolf's bizarre and haphazard Kunstkammer collections of art and natural objects has contributed to the Surrealist destruction of the distinction between artifice and nature. For a long time now, Švankmajer has worked in a wide variety of media in addition to film, including ceramics, composite sculpture, printing, etching, and writing, reflecting the Prague Surrealist Group's insistence on heterogeneity and experimentation.[9]

For the Czech and Slovak Surrealists in general, and for Švankmajer in particular, Prague is central both to their physical existence and to their Surrealist practice. For example, *Analogon* 18 (III, 1996), entitled *"Praha Skrz Prsty*/Prague

Through Our Fingers," is dedicated to the experience of Prague, highlighting the notion that one can only ever approach the city obliquely, that the meaning of the city will always slip through one's grasp. In that issue, Krzysztof Fijalkowski comments on his experience as a tourist in Prague:

> Beneath the impression of an extraordinary poetic beauty that many of its native citizens have probably long since tired of hearing about from its visitors and tourist agencies, Prague also presents a city of pathways, of secret maps as knotted and inexorable as its network of tramlines; of half-erased painted signs and faces emerging from walls and torn posters; of invitations and admonitions that . . . make the whole metropolis a giant skein of palimpsests, from centre to suburb.[10]

It is possible to consider many of Švankmajer's films as explorations of this "secret map" which is used to undermine any sense of totalitarian explanation or understanding. Two of his four feature films, *Faust* (1994) and *Conspirators of Pleasure* (1996), are explicitly set in Prague. In a political sense the work of the Czech Surrealists in and on Prague can be seen as undermining the concept of a rational city that could be perfectly designed and planned. Paradoxically, both the programmed and the surreal city embody a certain experience of the sinister and occult: the threat of the rational city coming from a fear of external control and surveillance while the menace of the Surrealist city emerges from the unconscious of its inhabitants. It is this perilous nature of the city that I discuss in this chapter.

In *Discipline and Punish*, Michel Foucault writes that "At the beginning of the nineteenth century . . . the great spectacle of physical punishment disappeared; the tortured body was avoided; the theatrical representation of pain was excluded from punishment."[11] Leaving aside questions about the historical accuracy of this statement (and it must be remembered that Foucault is making quite a specific point about the history of punishment in France), I want to explore the idea that the "theatrical representation of pain" (pain in a very broad sense) has been again placed into the public domain through the agency of film, that most spectacular of twentieth-century media. Although this discussion is based mainly on Švankmajer's work, there is a much wider history to the representation of pain, suffering, and torture in the cinema that has been somewhat mapped in writings on horror and fantastic film: from the broadly psychoanalytic approach favored by Barbara Creed in her by now canonical *The*

7 The face of the goddess, after Arcimboldo, in Jan Švankmajer's *Flora* (1989) (Copyright MTV Productions, 1989)

Monstrous Feminine and by Carol Clover's *Men, Women and Chainsaws*, to Steven Shaviro's attempted post-structural valorization of the visceral in *The Cinematic Body*, and the exploitation academia of David Kerekes' and David Slater's *Killing for Culture*.[12] Most of these theorists are concerned either with explaining an audience's fascination with disturbing images and narratives or, in Kerekes and Slater's case, with providing a history of obscure and cult films. My interest here is less broad and examines a fairly small body of work produced by and surrounding Švankmajer in order to explore the ramifications of a single idea: what I call "architorture."

Švankmajer made *Flora*, a short 20 second film, in 1989 for that most mesmerizing of TV channels, MTV. Since the film is only available on video in the Czech edition of Švankmajer's complete short films, it will be useful to provide a shot by shot breakdown of the piece.[13] The central image of the film is the body of the goddess, Flora, made up of an Arcimboldo-esque collocation of vegetables and fruit tied with ropes to what resembles a metal hospital bed.[14] The head, hands, and feet are made of the smooth gray clay which features in many of Švankmajer's animations. Through the use of time-lapse photography, reminiscent of Peter Greenaway's *A Zed & Two Noughts* (1985), the organic matter rots throughout the duration of the film (**7** and **8**). The bed to which the figure is tied, perhaps playfully recalling Marcel Duchamp's *Apolinère enameled* (1916/17), is positioned in the corner of a room with dirty walls, and a glass of water stands on a small table next to the imprisoned figure:

Shot break-down
Black screen with "Flora" in generic white type in center
Black
[Soundtrack throughout: hissing of the outside urban world: traffic and occasional sirens. Palpable sound of rotting and disintegration. Squeaking of metal bed as the figure struggles]

1: C/U disintegrating tomato
2: C/U disintegrating cabbage
3: C/U disintegrating apple
4: C/U wide-open blue eyes staring to right of screen
5: C/U tied left hand, flexing against rope
    Track to left: arm composed of corn and other vegetables
6: M/S track down body to clay feet tied to bars at the foot of the bed. The feet flex
7: M/S from left of full figure on the bed, with a small table and glass of water in the right hand corner of the screen
    The vegetable body is decomposing
8: C/U of right hand tied to the bars of the head-board, testing the leather bond
9: C/U disintegrating cabbage
10: C/U disintegrating cauliflower
11: Medium C/U from the feet; torso and head in shot with the glass of water on extreme right

12:   C/U of vegetable matter (cauliflower?) erupting with maggots
13:   C/U of expressionless face surrounded by a head-dress of grapes, flowers, and
   cones—all disintegrating
   The face turns to look right toward the glass (unseen)
14:   C/U left hand flexing
   Pan to right, toward the table and glass
   Pause on glass, positioned slightly off-center toward the left of screen
15:   Extreme C/U of inside of glass and shimmering of clear water.

Fade to Black
No credits[15]

Although the reference to Flora as goddess of the spring is very clear in the film, there is also here a firm evocation of Flora, one of the underground Metro stations of Prague. While the film is claustrophobically concentrated on the bound figure, the city, like the glass of water, is tantalizingly close. So, as Flora lies tied to the bed, the sound of the traffic of Flora is heard from outside. Thus Flora is both inside and outside the room, both the antithesis of the city and the very heart of the city, both absolutely immobile and one of the nodes of mobility that allows movement within (but not out of) the city.

One of the few references to this film in the rather extensive commentary available on Švankmajer is in Michael O'Pray's essay "Jan Švankmajer: A Bohemian Surrealist," in which O'Pray writes that *Flora* "uses the natural corruption of flowers to reveal simultaneously a sexual sadism and a sarcastic comment on modern civilization's rape of the natural world."[16] Although Švankmajer's Flora is constituted mainly of vegetables and fruit and not flowers as O'Pray remembers, the film is easily read as this form of admonitory allegory: technological progress bringing about the inevitable destruction of an imagined pastoral harmony. Indeed, careful concentration on the *mise en scène* of this suitably short film shows how this particular representation of the urban environment as prison and as torture reverberates throughout Švankmajer's other work and in some other Surrealist film and literature. Of course, the Surrealist sensibility (and there seems to be a profound difficulty in understanding what Surrealism might actually be, a difficulty which is perhaps the core of Surrealism as such) constantly explores the idea of the "human" within the context of the city

8 The body as "organic matter," in *Flora* (1989) (Copyright MTV Productions, 1989)

and of the existence of a body in a room or on the street. The Surrealist fascination and hatred of the city is perhaps best expressed in Breton's famous explanation of Surrealism:

> The simplest Surrealist act consists of dashing down into the street, pistol in hand, and firing blindly, as fast as you can pull the trigger, into the crowd.[17]

In *Flora* there is no narrative to explain who the unfortunate goddess' gaoler might be or how long the figure has been tied to the grubby bed. The camera dissects the body both in space and in time, as hands, feet, and eyes are presented

for the audience's pornographic examination and the anthropomorphic vegetable body flowers into decay—an ironic and sterile blooming. The final cut to
the unreachable glass of water (with vague echoes of Travis Bickle's fizzing glass
in *Taxi Driver* (Martin Scorsese, 1976) and Jean-Luc Godard's coffee cup in *Two
or Three Things I Know About Her* (1967) emphasizes the helplessness of the animated figure and the sadism of the camera—a snuff movie with vegetables.
Rather than the fascinating figure tied to the bed, it is the room and the noise of
the city's traffic that are of interest. The room, if one is given to metaphoric
explication, may be seen as the city, and thus civilization, as a whole (this would
be O'Pray's reading) or may, on the other hand, be the virtual skull of any one of
that city's inhabitants—and in this reading the only countryside or natural
habitat that exists is already imprisoned within the psyche as a fantasy of the
possibility of escape—an escape which is only ever nostalgic. Rob Lapsley
writes:

> As real, the city is the city impossible of achievement. Although many people plainly
> prefer life in the city to any available alternative, for all inhabitants there is a non-
> coincidence between the actually existing city and their ideal, and consequently a
> sense of non-belonging. In the order of the real, therefore, the city is the impossibility
> of home; although there was no home prior to the city, a sense of homelessness is
> engendered by the city.[18]

It is this sense of homelessness that is at the center of *architorture*—a primal sense
of loss, a loss that has lost nothing, that has always already existed and that, like
Baudrillard's simulacrum, has no origin or original, but underpins the very possibility of existence. For Flora there is no escape since her existence is predicated
on her imprisonment and it is the very shortness of the film *Flora* that leaves an
image of constant, rather than teleological, decay. It is this paradoxically endless
disintegration that the film seems to encapsulate. Surrealism's relationship with
the city here is not one of antipathy or love, but one where both of these attitudes exist simultaneously and without contradiction. Breton, again, observes:

> Everything tends to make us believe that there exists a certain point of the mind at
> which life and death, the real and the imagined, past and future, the communicable
> and the incommunicable, high and low, cease to be perceived as contradictions. Now
> search as one may one will never find any other motivating force in the activities of

the Surrealists than the hope of finding and fixing this point. From this it becomes obvious how absurd it would be to define Surrealism solely as constructive or destructive: the point to which we are referring is *a fortiori* that point where construction and destruction can no longer be brandished one against the other.[19]

Christian Metz points out that "There is always a moment after the obvious observation that it is man who makes the symbol when it is also clear that the symbol makes man: this is one of the great lessons of psychoanalysis, anthropology and linguistics."[20] The significance of this for a consideration of the city and the subject is the insight that, in Anthony Easthope's words, "since subject and object are always produced together, the quality and design of city space will pose reciprocally a certain position and definition for the subject."[21] Flora does not exist without *Flora*. Jacques Derrida makes clear this imbrication of self in architecture and architecture in self:

> [The event] does not happen to a constituted *us*, to a human subjectivity whose essence would be arrested and which would *then* find itself affected by the history of this thing called architecture. We appear to ourselves only through an experience of spacing which is already marked by architecture. What happens through architecture both constructs and instructs this *us*. The latter *finds itself* engaged by architecture before it becomes the subject of it: master and possessor.[22]

Anthony Vidler makes a similar point when he refers to *Being and Nothingness*: "Sartre's body participates in a world within which it has to be immersed and to which it has to be subjected even before it can recognize itself as a body. It knows itself precisely because it is defined in relation to instrumental complexes that themselves are threatened by other instruments, understood as 'destructive devices.' . . . [Thus] in Sartrean terms the body is only seen to exist by virtue of the existence of the house: 'it is only in a world that there can be a body'."[23] It is this absolute and necessary relationship between self and architecture that, in denying any prior or privileged existence to the subject, underlies the sense of loss and lostness in Surrealist film. If we are no longer allowed to assume that humanity exists in some way before coming into its environment, we are left mourning for that which was never alive: the autonomous human subject. However, since grieving the loss of something that did not exist is patently ridiculous, this grief becomes humorous in the Surrealist world.

It is the comedy of life as a prison that animates Švankmajer's earlier comic film, *Byt* ("The Flat," 1968). In this film the protagonist (played by Ivan Kraus) is thrown into a dungeon-like flat only to find that normal physical rules no longer seem to apply: the tap drips stones, eggs have an astonishingly destructive power, and objects in general seem to have developed a wicked sense of humor. The flat and its objects tease their hapless victim with the possibility of food, sleep, and escape until a door collapses only to reveal a further wall covered with the signatures of past artists to which Kraus adds his name. The room itself is here mischievously malevolent but it is clear that nothing exists outside of it. Meanwhile, in Švankmajer's *Tma-světlo-tma* ("Darkness-Light-Darkness," 1989), a body assembles itself in a room as various body parts enter, only to find that the complete person is almost too big for the space. In both films the central figure finds itself within an architectural structure that both defines and confines that figure's existence but outside of which it is not able to exist.

Švankmajer uses the room and the city as a metaphor for the tragi-comedy of existence itself: a being-in-the-world which is always somehow not quite what it should be, and it is just such an uncomfortable existence that the city is often used to represent. David Clarke observes:

> The modern city was . . . the world as experienced by the stranger, and the experience of a world populated by strangers—a world in which a universal strangehood was coming to predominate.[24]

The individual in Surrealist film is always a stranger, like Kafka's bemused protagonists, wandering through a landscape that has no map and that seems unfathomably intent on doing the subject harm. It is this sense of dread, of *architorture*, that reflects the anxiety of the subject in the recognition of the misrecognition, *méconnaissance*, of its own autonomy. The very seriousness of this anxiety is so fundamental that it is laughable.

In this architorture of the Surrealist individual we find ourselves in the realm of the uncanny, the *unheimlich*, the unhomely, of *Hausangst*, which, while perhaps not being exactly homelessness is more of a homesickness without a hope of ever finding oneself at home. Perhaps the cinema of *architorture* and the oppressive buildings that do its bidding place the audience in a position of anxiety that forces the spectator to explore again Foucault's "theatrical representation of pain." The unsettling of the viewer is, for Švankmajer, part of the project that Andrew Benjamin has called for in a recent paper, a project for "developing an ontology of original displacement": a continuing reminder that there is no place like home.[25]

NOTES

1   Roger Cardinal and Robert Short, *Surrealism: Permanent Revelation*, London: Studio Vista, 1970, p. 9.

2. See Mary Ann Caws, "Décor: Desnos in Mourning," *The Surrealist Look: An Erotics of Encounter*, Cambridge, MA: MIT Press, 1997, pp. 151–67.

3. Sigmund Freud, "The Uncanny," in *The Standard Edition of the Complete Psychological Works of Sigmund Freud*, trans. James Strachey, vol. XVII, London: Hogarth, 1966, p. 237.

4. André Breton, *Surrealism and Painting*, trans. Simon Watson Taylor, London: MacDonald, 1975 (1965), p. 209.

5. Breton, *Surrealism and Painting*, p. 209. See also Michael O'Pray, "A Švankmajer Inventory," *Afterimage 13: Animating the Fantastic*, Autumn 1987, p. 10.

6. For a more detailed history of this period, see Krzysztof Fijalkowski and Michael Richardson, "Years of Long Days: Surrealism in Czechoslovakia," *Third Text* 36, Autumn 1996, pp. 15–28. A good overview of the group's activities is provided in Josef Janda's "On the Reverse Side of History," in *Invention/Imagination/Interpretation: A Retrospective Exhibition of the Group of Czech and Slovak Surrealists*, František Drye, ed., Jan Čap, Roman Dergam, and Kateřina Pińošova trans., Swansea Festival of Czech and Slovak Surrealism, City and County of Swansea, 1998.

7. The group was still active to some extent in the 1970s and 1980s. Alena Nádvorníková documents this period in *"Surrealistická Skupina v Československu* [The Surrealist Group in Czecholovakia]," *Zakázané Uměníi* [Forbidden Art], *Výtvarné Umění: The Magazine for Contemporary Art*, Milena Slavická and Marcela Pánková, eds, 3–4, 1995, pp. 114–23.

8. Interview with Švankmajer by František Drye, April 1997, *Evašvankmajerjan: Anima Animus Animation: Between Film and Free Expression*, Prague: Slovart, 1998, p. 33. See also Michael O'Pray, "Jan Švankmajer: a Mannerist Surrealist," in *Dark Alchemy: The Films of Jan Švankmajer*, Peter Hames, ed., Trowbridge: Flicks Books, 1995, pp. 48–77.

9. For a comprehensive overview of Švankmajer's work, see Michael Brooke's exhaustive website, *Jan Švankmajer: Alchemist of the Surreal* at www.illumin.co.uk/svank/index.html (April 1 1998).

10. "Red Work, Black Night, Remembered Maps," *Analogon* 18, III, 1996, p. 133.

11. Michel Foucault, *Discipline and Punish: The Birth of the Prison*, trans. Alan Sheridan, Harmondsworth: Penguin, 1991 (1975), p. 14.

12. Barbara Creed, *The Monstrous-Feminine: Film, Feminism, Psychoanalysis*, London and New York: Routledge, 1993; Carol J. Clover, *Men, Women and Chainsaws: Gender in the Modern Horror Film*, London: BFI, 1992; Steven Shaviro, *The Cinematic Body*, Minneapolis and London: University of Minnesota Press, 1993; David Kerekes and David Slater, *Killing for Culture: An Illustrated History of Death Film from Mondo to Snuff*, London: Creation Books, 1994.

13. *Jan Švankmajer: Krátké Filmy 1*, Prague: Krátké Film, 1993.

14. See Michael Brooke on "Flora (1989)" at www.illumin.co.uk/svank/films/flora/flora.html (April 1 1998).

15. The full credits are: written, directed, and produced by Jan Švankmajer; produced by Jaromír Kallista; photography by Svatopluk Malý; edited by Marie Zemanová; animated by Bedřich Glaser.

16. *Švankmajer in Wales: The Communication of Dreams/Švankmajer yng Nghymru: Cyfleu Breuddwydion*, Cardiff: Welsh Arts Council, 1992, p. 21.

17. "Second Manifesto of Surrealism" (1930), in *Manifestoes of Surrealism*, trans. Richard Seaver and Helen R. Lane, Ann Arbor, MI: University of Michigan Press, 1998 (1969), p. 125.

18. Rob Lapsley, "Mainly in Cities and at Night: Some Notes on Cities and Film," in David B. Clarke, ed., *The Cinematic City*, London and New York: Routledge, 1997, p. 192.

19. "Second Manifesto of Surrealism," pp. 123–4.

20. Christian Metz, *The Imaginary Signifier: Psychoanalysis and the Cinema*, trans. Celia Britton, Annwyl Williams, Ben Brewster, and Alfred Guzzetti, Bloomington, IN: Indiana University Press, 1982, p. 20.

21. Anthony Easthope, "Cinécities in the Sixties," in Clarke, *The Cinematic City*, p. 130.

22. Jacques Derrida, "Point de Folie—Maintenant L'Architecture," in Neil Leach, ed., *Rethinking Architecture: A Reader in Cultural Theory*, London and New York: Routledge, 1997, p. 322.

23. Anthony Vidler, *The Architectural Uncanny: Essays in the Modern Unhomely*, Cambridge, MA: MIT Press, 1992, pp. 82–3.

24. David B. Clarke, "Introduction: Previewing the Cinematic City," in *The Cinematic City*, p. 4.

25. Andrew Benjamin, address to Symposium on Subjectivity, Kent Institute for Advanced Studies in the Humanities, University of Kent at Canterbury, March 1 1999.

6

KIEŚLOWSKI'S *DEKALOG*, EVERYDAY LIFE, AND THE ART OF SOLIDARITY

JESSIE LABOV

> The art of Solidarity was . . . an effort to overstep the limits of the political horizon while remaining inside the same geographical borders.
> Irena Grudzinska Gross, *The Art of Solidarity*

In the few years since Krzysztof Kieślowski's untimely death in 1996, the shape of his filmography has already begun to change. In the early 1990s, the trilogy *Three Colors: Blue, White, Red* (1993–94) seemed to represent the peak of Kieślowski's career. These three films were by far the most widely distributed of his work, and had as high an international profile as any contemporary European film. In the last year or two, however, his earlier work *Dekalog* (1989) has found a wider audience, and some film critics have begun to turn to the series of ten films as the key to understanding Kieślowski's work as a whole.[1]

Dekalog was originally presented on Polish television in 1989 as a series of ten one-hour episodes about contemporary Polish life, loosely based on the Ten Commandments. As a condition of the initial funding of the film, Kieślowski adapted episodes 5 and 6 into 90-minute films intended for general distribution, respectively titled *A Short Film About Love* and *A Short Film About Killing*. During the following year, Kieślowski entered both the series and the feature-length films in several international festivals, where they were typically screened in five, two-hour segments. Also in 1990, *Dekalog* was subtitled in English and broadcast on the BBC, then made available on video throughout Europe. Meanwhile, on the other side of the Atlantic, video distribution of the series was held up until late 1999 and only periodically screened at art house cinemas and small festivals across the Americas. Due to this gradual transatlantic dissemination, *Dekalog* has only recently become a familiar part of Kieślowski's *oeuvre* to his wider viewing public.

As a director and a public figure, Kieślowski has occupied a variety of roles in the history of Polish cinema. His generation is usually associated with the "Cinema of Moral Anxiety" of the late 1970s and early 1980s, a movement that used both fiction and documentary films to convey a sense of moral crisis and the subsequent political reawakening in Polish society. Of course, the strong connection between oppositional politics and film throughout Eastern Europe, as well as the central role of film in Poland, would not have been possible without earlier movements such as the Polish School of filmmaking.[2] Led by directors such as Andrzej Munk, Kazimierz Kutz, and most prominently Andrzej Wajda, the Polish School formed in the mid-1950s with the momentum of a cultural thaw, a re-organized film studio system, and young, talented graduates of the new Łódź film school. In addition to its striking aesthetic contributions, the group is known for establishing a veiled dialogue with its audience about Polish nationalism and anti-totalitarianism, usually using literary adaptation or the then recent history of World War Two as a backdrop.[3] The Cinema of Moral Anxiety emerged gradually after the events of 1968, and included directors such as Ryszard Bugajski, Krzysztof Zanussi, and Wajda once again—their films held a more explicit conversation about current events and political opposition than that of the Polish School, often with documentary characteristics. (Kieślowski himself played a large part in this shift as he had earlier worked as a documentarist.) The movement perhaps reached its height during the Solidarity era with Wajda's *Man of Iron* when General Wojciech Jaruzelski declared martial law in December 1981. While Kieślowski's documentaries and feature films of the 1970s and early 1980s are an inextricable part of this film history, his experiences during martial law led him away from the direct political content of the Cinema of Moral Anxiety, as well as from the historical and literary codex of the Polish School.

For most of Kieślowski's interpreters, *Dekalog* marks a shift to an even more purely metaphysical concern. The adjective "metaphysical" is used liberally with Kieślowski's later works, sometimes to mark his disengagement from politics, and sometimes to distinguish films such as *Blind Chance* (1981), *No End* (1984), *The Double Life of Veronique* (1991), and *Three Colors: Blue, White, Red* (1993–94) from the strict documentary work which preceded it. Kieślowski himself described *Dekalog* as a turn away from politics after martial law:

> [Krzysztof Piesiewicz, co-writer of *Dekalog*, and I] knew from the beginning that the films would be contemporary. For a while, we considered setting them in the world of politics but, by the mid-1980s, politics had ceased to interest us.
>
> During martial law, I realized that politics aren't really important. In a way, of course, they define where we are and what we're allowed or aren't allowed to do, but they don't solve the really important human questions. They're not in a position to do anything about or to answer any of our fundamental human and humanistic questions.[4]

Kieślowski did not choose to explore this humanism in a completely abstract landscape, however. Central to the moral puzzles of *Dekalog* is the human crowd, the interchangeability of one face for another, and the coincidences and accidents of fate that lead to human exchanges and encounters. Here Kieślowski explains how the need for a crowd led him to set the films in a "large housing estate," a structure which is best described by the Polish word *blok*:

> We wanted to begin each film in a way which suggested that the main character had been picked by the camera as if at random. We thought of a huge stadium in which, from among the hundred thousand faces, we'd focus on one in particular. We also had an idea that the camera should pick somebody out from a crowded street and then follow him or her throughout the rest of the film. In the end we decided to locate the action in a large housing estate, with thousands of similar windows framed in the establishing shot. It's the most beautiful housing estate in Warsaw, which is why I chose it. It looks pretty awful so you can imagine what the others are like. The fact that the characters all live on one estate brings them together.[5](**9**)

Rows of windows take the place of rows of faces in a football stadium; the everyday lives that Kieślowski saw in Poland in 1987 could not be represented as a stadium full of people, unified behind one or two football teams. Instead, the *blok* allows us to observe parallel lives which take place simultaneously,

9 "The most beautiful housing estate in Warsaw," establishing shot of the *blok* from Krzysztof Kieślowski's *Dekalog 2* (1988) (Copyright New Yorker Films, 2000)

intersecting only when paths cross, and not for any larger, ideological (or even sporting) goal.

In this, I argue that the choice of the Soviet-era *blok* as a setting, as opposed to a stadium or a street, effectively re-politicizes this film, in three distinct ways. Firstly, the images of the *blok* are perceived differently in Poland and Eastern Europe than they are by Western critics. Kieślowski marks that difference in the passage above, when he refers to the *blok* as "the most beautiful housing estate in Warsaw," although he freely acknowledges the absurdity of the category itself—in another interview he dubs it "the least ugly housing estate in Warsaw."[6] Secondly, by declining to show overt political practices, and focusing instead on the practice of everyday life, *Dekalog* indirectly reflects the philosophy of the Solidarity movement. From its earliest incarnation as a committee to defend striking shipyard workers and political prisoners, Solidarity represented a different method of resisting totalitarianism than the opposition movements that had come before it. Its philosophy advocated living daily life "as if" it took place in a fair and open society, investing everyday rituals and events with a new, political meaning. Finally, by reflecting this philosophy onto television, Kieślowski reclaimed a medium that had been dominated by government propaganda during the period of martial law and largely distrusted by the Polish public ever since. His gesture heralded a new possibility for communication—between different voices within Poland, and also from the West—through the medium of television.

THE MOST BEAUTIFUL *BLOK* IN WARSAW

"What is special about Kieślowski's work?" asked Charles Eidsvik in *Film Quarterly*: "First, his starting point: a near total despair about the everyday realities of housing-project Poland."[7] In an otherwise positive review, Eidsvik refers to the buildings of the *blok* as "drab concrete silos"—"drab" being a word used also in the *Variety* review of *Dekalog*: "All 10 stories are placed in the same gray and depressing block of new concrete buildings in a Warsaw suburb where university professors and taxi drivers live side by side. It's a drab and unattractive solution offered by the Socialist regime to growing housing problems."[8] Both reviews understand the depiction of life in the *blok* as specific to Poland, even Warsaw. Eidsvik's word "housing-project" evokes an urban landscape, while the *Variety* review identifies these structures as suburban, perhaps reminiscent of the housing complexes of the *banlieues* of Paris. In both cases, however, the atmosphere is not urban in the sense that a Western city of that era might be— dynamic, thrilling, even dangerous in its diversity—but "drab," "gray," and identifiably Socialist and homogenous.

Kieślowski and Piesiewicz offer their own description of the *blok* in the first words of the opening sequence of *Dekalog I*:

> Springtime, a gray morning. The great slab of a huge *blok* which, at times like these, looks depressing. A few dogs run after a mongrel bitch. The owners of cars parked along the street bring batteries and industriously install them in the engines. The drivers and dogs startle a flock of freezing pigeons, which take off for a short flight, and then immediately settle down again. One of the birds glides higher, chooses one of the several hundred windowsills of the *blok*, settles down on it and looks into the apartment.[9]

Immediately, the authors qualify the drabness of the building: "a huge *blok* which, *at times like these*, looks depressing" (my emphasis). The grayness of the façade of the building is the effect of early morning light, a feature of the morning routine, as people walk to their cars to leave for work. The goal is not one of depressing the viewer, or of producing despair; in fact, Kieślowski was careful to keep the harsher realities of Polish life (bread lines, ration cards, "anything as horrible as politics") in the background.[10]

After an establishing shot of the grounds of the housing estate, there is a long, slow pan, which follows the pigeon up the face of a building until it arrives at the window. The *blok* seen as a whole illustrates Kieślowski's original vision of thousands of windows from which to choose a protagonist. The slow pan, which travels up the building, is more mundane, seemingly endless; the surface of the building is *drab*. The frame seems too small to take in the entire building, and as a result the image is abstracted to the point of illegibility, as the camera travels across granite and glass with no figures to lend perspective or context. There are sequences like this throughout the ten parts of *Dekalog*, where the building is magnified to such an extent that the viewer must wait patiently for a point of reference. One of the most notable occurs toward the end of *Dekalog 2*.

From the way the following sequence in *Dekalog 2* is described in the script, the most obvious way of realizing it would be in three discrete takes, cutting from one face to another.

> Twilight. Dorota stands in the window of her apartment. She looks into space. Behind her is the darkness of an unlit apartment.
>
> The doctor looks out the window of his greenhouse, lit by an electric, red heater, and like Dorota, looks forward.
>
> Andrzej's face is pale. The sound of a delicate ringing? a hum? a buzz? Andrzej

lifts an eyelid. A bee is struggling in circles in a glass half-filled with compote. At a certain moment the ringing stops. The bee slowly climbs to the rim of the glass. It pauses on the edge, shakes off its wings, and flies away.[11]

Instead, for several minutes, as the camera travels from the lit window of one character to that of another, its gaze rests on the granite surface of the building in almost complete, grainy darkness.

Dorota is linked to the doctor by the granite between their windows; the doctor is linked to Dorota's husband Andrzej first by several meters of granite, and then by a blurred traveling pan which continues in the same direction and comes to rest on Andrzej's face as he lies in a hospital several blocks away. The traveling motion is repeated as the camera follows Andrzej's gaze to the glass with a bee. Only after the bee has made its escape does Kieślowski insert a distinct cut. In this sequence, the granite building material that separates Dorota from the doctor is indistinguishable from that which separates the doctor and Andrzej. The surface of the *blok* plays the same interstitial role as the music, the other device which binds this sequence together (first in the background, and then in the foreground with a cut to Dorota in the orchestra as the series' theme music is performed). Kieślowski is thoroughly self-conscious here about what is arbitrary and what is logical in the conventions of film language, using a material surface to rest between images where there would normally be a cut. The result is that the boundaries of space and time become less certain: we seem on the one hand to be following the gaze of someone observing the building and on the other to be following the characters' mental associations. Kieślowski is similarly aware that the ten episodes of *Dekalog* are held together as much by their common location and opening music as by their thematic connection to a religious text.

Furthermore, the chain of images which sets *Dekalog 2* in motion—dogs, drivers, pigeons, window—is constructed as a set of coincidences, so that it seems an accident (or perhaps the enigmatic choice of a pigeon) that we arrive at a particular window and follow that particular story. There is a limit to human agency in all ten of these parables, a fact made palpable by Kieślowski's and Piesiewicz's use of coincidence to determine the narrative. The gesture of coincidence is found in every one of Kieślowski's feature films, and it simulates the effect of his documentary work.[12] When the camera travels across a room from surface to surface, or across a building from window to window, it records what falls within the frame in a quasi-documentary mode. The objects that lie in the camera's path then acquire either a narrative or symbolic significance, ostensibly through coincidence. The result is that the fictional mode is infused with a documentary aesthetic, a combination that produces the perceived quality of "drabness" as seen from the West, and at the same time familiar, almost stereotypical mornings and evenings for those viewers of the original series on Polish television.

THE ART OF SOLIDARITY

It is the aesthetic texture lent by the *blok*, and its omnipresence in everyday life, which connects the superficially apolitical films of the Dekalog to the political philosophy of Solidarity. Furthermore, there is a strong political resonance in Kieślowski's references to his own documentary career. In order to see these correspondences more clearly, we must first reach a definition of "the practice of everyday life"—in this case through the work of the French cultural theorist and philosopher Henri Lefebvre—before tracing the relevance of the concept to the history of Solidarity and the history of Polish film.

When Lefebvre began to develop his critique of everyday life in post-World War Two France, it was already a politicized concept. With the totalitarian application of Marxism in the Soviet Union and China, and the explosion of a consuming capitalism in France, intellectuals with a commitment to the principles of Marxism were searching for a way to negotiate between the two extremes. In Lefebvre's own words, his *Critique of Everyday Life* "contains an interpretation of Marxist thought which . . . challenges both philosophism and economism, refusing to admit that Marx's legacy can be reduced to a philosophical system (dialectical materialism) or to a theory of political economy."[13] Instead, Lefebvre uses a Marxist analysis of contemporary France to examine the conditions of reproduction of labor and consumption, a "*praxis* and *poesis* [which] does not take place in the higher spheres of society (state, scholarship, "culture") but in everyday life."[14]

Lefebvre's theorization of "everyday life" was specific to postwar France. He cautioned against any broad comparative study of everyday life for fear that a lack of depth of familiarity with a culture could lead to a superficial race-psychology, content to "scan the horizon, knowing that it is out of reach."[15] Yet for the same reason that Lefebvre's critique of everyday life remained active and relevant for decades after the moment that it described, its reach also extended beyond the borders of France. Because the critique of everyday life was "what remained after all specialized structured activities had been singled out by analysis," it not only could be applied to other contexts and milieux, but informed work in other fields that attempted to theorize daily social interaction. One such example is the political and social theory that developed in dissident circles in Poland in the late 1960s, initiated by figures such as Adam Michnik and Jacek Kuron, and practiced as a form of resistance to authoritarianism.

According to Czeslaw Milosz, the difference between authoritarian rule such as nineteenth-century colonialism—British India, for example—and the Polish situation is that "the modern totalitarian or police state does not recognize any bounds to the exercise of its power."[16] After 1968, when dissidents throughout the Soviet Bloc came to understand that traditional methods of resisting authoritarian power had little or no effect, they began to search for a different kind of non-violent resistance. Michnik, one of the Warsaw University student protesters arrested repeatedly during this period, was among the first to find a new way—what Jonathan Schell called "a revolution in revolution." If the Communist authorities insisted that every moment of civic life was inherently political, Michnik argued, then one could resist that authority on the level of individual, everyday choices:

> Abandoning, for the time being, all hope of a jailbreak, the members of the Polish opposition began to examine more closely the cell in which, it appeared, it was the country's fate to live for an indefinite period; that is, realizing that there was no salvation for Poland in our time in the movements of armies, they began to scrutinize the minutiae of their local environment.[17]

Michnik and fellow student protester Kuron founded the Committee for the Defense of Workers (KOR) in 1976, beginning a campaign of self-defined "social work," as opposed to political work. This could mean supporting the families of workers who were fired, arrested, or even killed during strikes and violent confrontations at shipyards and coal mines throughout Poland, or raising money for the legal defense of these workers and for other political prisoners.

Michnik readily admitted that both the work and its guiding principles were "banality incarnate," but that this was a time when even acting with banality in everyday life required courage and was, therefore, a significant radical gesture:

> [W]hat in the eyes of KOR might be considered social was considered by the government definitely political, for in a totalitarian system every aspect of collective existence is supposed to originate with the government and be under its management. In this deep reach of totalitarian government into daily life, which is usually seen as a source of its strength, KOR discovered a point of weakness: precisely because totalitarian governments politicize daily life, daily life becomes a vast terrain on which totalitarianism can be opposed.[18]

Much like Lefebvre's everyday life, KOR acted in the public sphere which was left over when "specialized structured activities" (striking, petitioning, appealing in court) had been ruled out. The proof that KOR was something external to the political system, a power "created where there was none instead of wrenched from the existing authority," was that when a true political party—*Solidarność*—came along in 1980, KOR dissolved without incident.[19] It had not acquired the status of a (resistant) ideological state apparatus, it was simply the collective force of several thousand everyday lives. While the practice of living an individual life was recovered as a potential site of resistance, the representation of the everyday became its own battleground.

From the beginning of Soviet occupation, Polish film had succeeded in articulating an oppositional voice where the more traditional medium of print had failed, or was at least hidden deeply underground. As described above, during the 1950s and 1960s, this conversation between filmmakers and the Polish public took place largely in fictional films; documentaries went almost unnoticed by the public when they were shown either on television or before a feature film at the local cinema, being limited as they usually were to vehicles for government slogans.[20] But in the early 1970s, a new documentary trend emerged among the recent graduates of Łódź. With new films like *Workers '71*, which realistically captured the views and expressions of Polish workers after the December strikes of 1970, the public began to turn to documentaries for an unofficial newscast that could provide a counter-narrative to the official Party version of events. *Workers '71* was a collective effort by Kieślowski and several of his colleagues. They wrote a "manifesto of documentary realism" to describe their intentions, which were not always carried out because of the censor's re-editing of the films that they submitted.[21]

The shift in emphasis from feature films to documentary as a means of providing a counter-cultural subtext to Polish politics was simultaneous with the political movements that brought about Solidarity. After years of feature films staging and re-staging the great tragedies of Polish history, the story of everyday life took over. The previous generation (Wajda, Ford, and Zanussi) was profoundly disillusioned by the events of 1968, and it took several years for the two strains of filmmaking to reconcile. They did finally in Wajda's *Man of Marble* (1977), which chronicles a young film student's attempts to make a documentary about a Stakhanovite hero, the subject of a propaganda campaign from the 1950s. Wajda's film demonstrates that the very act of researching a documentary, of filming people in their homes and workplaces, of asking very basic questions about what did or did not happen had become a political gesture in 1970s Poland. At the same time, *Man of Marble* continues the tradition of the Polish School by encoding a reference to contemporary politics in the story. We discover by the end of the film, and the end of the documentarist's search, that the fallen Stakhanovite hero has died. There are several references, comprehensible only to someone familiar with contemporary Polish politics and culture, which imply that the hero was killed during a strikers' demonstration at a shipyard (this implication is made explicit in Wajda's 1981 sequel, *Man of Iron*). *Man of Marble* simultaneously comments on and participates in the legacy of feature and documentary films.

Kieślowski had been making both documentaries and features throughout the 1970s; two years after *Man of Marble*, Kieślowski's answer to Wajda appeared in *Camera Buff* (1979).[22] His most famous film from this period, *Camera Buff* is also a fiction piece about the art of the documentary. A white-collar worker, Filip Mosz, buys an 8mm camera to film the birth of his first child, and then finds himself filming the world around him almost compulsively. He is commissioned by his manager to make a documentary about the factory, but is unable to produce anything that does not reveal some unpalatable truth. Filip is drawn to the trashy backyards of housing projects, construction sites that are left incomplete, and an exemplary worker at the factory who happens to be a dwarf (and is, therefore, unacceptable as an official representative of the Polish worker). With *Camera Buff*, the act of documentary filmmaking itself is drawn into the sphere of everyday life—away from film schools and artists' cafés—where it is still truthful, dangerous, censored, and inherently political.

The last chapter of this convergence between fiction, reality, documentary film, and politics took place in Gdansk in 1980. Two weeks after the shipyard strikes led by Lech Wałęsa, the moment of the strike was re-lived and projected into epic dimensions at the 1980 Festival of Polish Feature Films, September 8–15. At midnight on the 15th, two hours of barely edited footage of the shipyard strike (titled *Workers '80*) were screened in the reconstructed Old Town of Gdansk. This footage included the negotiations between Wałęsa and Premier Mieczysław Jagielski and inspired cheers from the viewing audience for every government concession leading to the final settlement. This scene was also foreshadowed earlier in the Festival week, when Andrzej Wajda sat across from the Vice Minister of Culture at a press conference and accused him directly of fraud in reporting box office statistics. But in the audience of the midnight screening, all of the players were mixed in with the viewers, as Wałęsa, Wajda, Jagielski, and the Vice Minister of Culture watched, listened, and signed autographs.

During the next year, millions of Poles joined the Solidarity Party, the first glimpse of a successful, oppositional, political movement. The imposition of martial law, in December 1981, came as a complete shock to the artists and leaders of Solidarity—almost as much of a shock as their initial success was to the Polish government. As Jonathan Schell suggests:

> [i]t may be that the two sides underestimated each other's strength so drastically because they possessed different *kinds* of strength, and each side judged the other on the basis of its own kind: to the government the opposition looked weak because it lacked military and police power, while to the opposition the government looked weak because it lacked public support. According to the "realistic" laws of the government, the Solidarity movement was an impossibility, but equally, according to the "idealistic" laws of Solidarity's existence, martial law was impossible.[23]

An incident during the filming of Kieślowski's *Dworzec* (*Station*) in 1981 forced the director to confront this misrecognition, and caused him to move from documentary filmmaking to fiction.

Station was to be a documentary about people waiting and/or sleeping in a train station in Warsaw. At some point Kieślowski decided to use the camera as a blatant "spectator" to tie the segments together and produce a stronger narrative. In addition to overhead "spy" cameras, the crew began to work with concealed or half-concealed cameras on the station floor. One night, Kieślowski and his crew were filming people's reaction to new storage lockers installed in the station. In the morning, the police appeared, seized the film, and brought Kieślowski in for a blind interrogation, repeatedly asking him about the events of the evening without any hint as to why. Many weeks later, after the film was returned and edited, Kieślowski found out that the police had been pursuing a murder suspect that night—a young girl who allegedly "killed her mother, cut her into pieces, packed her into two suitcases, and put her into a locker at the train station."[24] Kieślowski was horrified, not just by the crime, but by the fact that his cameras had been used as instruments of the government.

> Right, so we didn't film the girl. But what if we had, by chance? . . . I'd have become a police collaborator. And that was the moment I realized that I didn't want to make any more documentaries . . . All this made me aware again of what a small cog I am in a wheel which is being turned by somebody else for reasons unknown to me.[25]

Because the relationship between the government and its subjects had changed during the height of Solidarity, description of everyday life, of the way things "really" were, began to serve a different purpose. In the 1970s, everyday life was shown to an audience by documentarists to confirm popular suspicion that official histories were distorted. Now, the police were looking back through the documentarist's camera lens to pinpoint the areas of everyday life in need of control under martial law.

With politics and film so thoroughly entangled, it was no coincidence that the imposition of martial law in December 1981 included a virtual ban on film production. After fourteen months had passed and "stabilization" was proclaimed by General Jaruzelski, some film production projects submitted to the state-run production house were considered, among them Kieślowski's proposal for a documentary about the court system.[26] Here, filming court trials, Kieślowski met Krzysztof Piesiewicz, a defense lawyer for oppositional causes who would become a co-author on several scripts. The courtroom documentary was supposed to expose the harsh sentencing of Solidarity supporters for minor infractions, but in front of the camera the judges would not perform their roles "correctly." In every trial that Kieślowski filmed, the sentence would be deferred, or dismissed. When word of this got out, defense lawyers began to request the camera crew at their trials, even trying to bribe Kieślowski to appear. He stopped putting film in the cameras, realizing that his purpose was no longer one of documenting facts. Eventually, after several months of this, the filmmaker withdrew from the project, and began filming *Bez Końca* (*No End*, 1984) instead. This feature covered similar ground, but more explicitly: because of its fictional status, Kieślowski could control the situation, the actors, and the verdict, if necessary. Kieślowski's second encounter with the law and documentary filmmaking left him firmly convinced that filming actual events was not the road to autonomy—without some control over the purpose of his films, he could not expect to find any creative control.

Kieślowski began work with Piesiewicz in 1987 on a series of screenplays formally based on the Ten Commandments (as they are listed in the Catholic tradition). Originally, they were to serve as ten debut short films for young directors working for the TOR Production House, but as the screenplays took shape, Kieślowski changed his mind and decided to direct them all himself, using different cinematographers for each episode.[27] The episodes were extremely tightly scripted, and while some correspond more literally to their respective Commandment than others, the purpose of the series could be easily understood as a spiritual one, hardly subject to censorship or other uses for political ends. The stories, settings, and professional occupations of the characters were all chosen for their perceived universality, so that Kieślowski could be free to direct without answering to a controlling authority. Truly recognizing this motive means distinguishing between the influence of a documentary aesthetic referred to above and the mere attempt to record quotidian details, a technique that Kieślowski had come to look upon with horror as "banality incarnate." *Dekalog* is genuinely concerned with its *minima moralia*. It is the *blok* which stands in the place of the quotidian, linking characters through physical proximity and co-incidental encounter, thereby releasing them from being the subjects of an anthropological study.

KIEŚLOWSKI ON TELEVISION

This level of creative autonomy in Poland in 1987, however, had to be earned with even more creative financing. The bulk of support came from Polish Television; TOR bought options for the two expanded feature-length films (*A Short Film About Killing* and *A Short Film About Love*), and a German production company provided the means to film in 35mm instead of 16mm.[28] As *perestroika* began to take effect in the Soviet Union and its satellites, Kieślowski was one of the first Polish artists to admit that "the freedom we've achieved in Poland now doesn't really bring us anything, because we can't satisfy it . . . There simply isn't any money to spare for culture."[29] When he went to Polish state television, Kieślowski was stepping outside of the accepted arena for cultural production, in order to gain access to the artistic freedom that the late 1980s promised. Since martial law, television had been used almost exclusively by the government for propaganda purposes.[30] The public was suspicious of the truthfulness and the politics of the medium itself.

Kieślowski did more toward re-investing television with a new counter-cultural power than just present his movie on a small screen. The distinction that he made between his work for film and that for television was never one of quality—of an elite, cinematic aesthetic as opposed to a low-end, disposable televisual one:[31]

> I don't think the television viewer is less intelligent than the cinema audience. The reason why television is the way it is isn't because viewers are slow-witted but because editors think they are.[32]

In writing the script of *Dekalog*, Kieślowski and Piesiewicz worked to meet the medium halfway, taking into account several conventions of "drama on television" that distinguish it from feature films. Some differences, he went on to explain, were closely linked to financial and time constraints: for example, "shots are closer rather than wider because in a wider shot you'd have to set up more scenery."[33] Another element is habit, Kieślowski concedes: the way people have become accustomed to watching television. Consequently, *Dekalog* is written for a viewer who is alone, who has been seeing the characters once a week ("like their family visiting on Sundays"), and who might have to get up and stir something

on the stove. The intermittent viewing that Kieślowski points to in his delineation of television and film invokes partial or blocked vision, a reliance on audi-
tory signals, or distracted attention (intermittent viewers, busy in the practice of
everyday life, do not always devote their entire attention to the screen).[34] Often
the characters of *Dekalog* have a similarly obstructed view of the scene in front of
them: the young boy in *Dekalog 1* watches his father lecture from behind a slide
projector; the murderer in *Dekalog 5* frames the street behind him through the
crook of his arm; Roman, the husband in *Dekalog 9*, watches a meeting between
his wife and her lover through a crack in a closet door.

 The other major character that is obstructed from view is the city of Warsaw
itself. As seen on the television screen in Poland, the setting of *Dekalog* is in
many ways a neutral space. There is no skyline of Warsaw in the series, so there
is no reminder of the Soviet presence in Poland in the form of the Palace of
Culture and Science (a tower built by Soviet authorities that until recently completely dominated the cityscape). Because the *blok* is located in a suburb, and
because of its self-contained design, it is free from the views of Warsaw that are
already historically overdetermined. It is its own universe; in the scenes that
take place at the *blok*, there is not even one glimpse of the city itself. To
Kieślowski, this was yet another attractive feature of "the least ugly housing
estate" in Warsaw: "What's more, it has the advantage of always suggesting
closed spaces. The ways in which the buildings are constructed and arranged
fence in the field of view, which leads me to some interesting compositions with
the camera."[35]

As Warsaw was virtually razed by the end of World War Two, each of its
neighborhoods came to contain a slightly different layer of historical meaning,
depending on its path to reconstruction. The Old Town, for example, is a simulacrum, reconstructed from photographs to look exactly as it did before the war.
It has become a symbol of the covering over of Polish national martyrdom (particularly of the Warsaw Uprising) by the postwar Communist state. Żoliborz, a
neighborhood to the north, contains several streets that were not destroyed by
the end of Nazi occupation, and is treasured by many natives of Warsaw for its
postwar continuity. The Palace of Culture and Science is recognized first and
foremost as a "gift" from Stalin to the People's Republic of Poland, and therefore
universally detested. In this case, memories of the remarkable prewar vistas of

downtown Warsaw—of Pilsudksi Square and Złota (Gold) Street where the Palace now stands—have given way to a symbol of Soviet oppression, and to its demonization. Any of these historical narratives would overshadow the individual stories that Kieślowski contains within the *blok*.

This is remarkably illustrated in *Dekalog 8*, the one episode that submerges itself in the history of Warsaw, as well as the history of Polish film. Elźbieta, a Jewish scholar who lives in New York, is sitting in on an ethics class at the university. She is in Poland looking for clues about her childhood during the war. As Elźbieta approaches the professor of ethics, she realizes that this is the same woman who had refused her shelter from the Nazis as a young girl. The two women visit the apartment in downtown Warsaw where they met during the war, and Elźbieta gets lost in the shadows and is overwhelmed by memories. The desire to get beyond these forces of history is spoken by another character in *Dekalog 8*, a tailor (played by Tadeusz Łomnicki, the lead actor from the first movie of Wajda's war trilogy, *A Generation*). Elźbieta visits the tailor to try and learn more about what happened during the war, possibly about his role in rescuing her. He responds very simply:

> I don't want to talk about what happened during the war. I don't want to talk about what happened after the war. I don't want to talk about what's happening right now.

The tailor's refusal to participate in the conversation begun by *Dekalog 8* is symptomatic of life in Warsaw proper—particularly for those of Wajda's generation. This is a life lived in the shadow of the Palace of Culture and Science, where discussions of the past must take place in a coded setting—in this case Łomnicki's presence, and his role in Wajda's first major film is a piece of that code. The tailor is subsumed into the narrative of *Dekalog*, however, by his next action: he watches the two women on the sidewalk outside of his shop through the curtain and bars on his front window (**10**).

This is the last sequence of *Dekalog 8*, as the camera rests on the tailor's obstructed perspective and on his own measured expression of observation. Once again, the partially blocked field of vision makes reference to the television viewer, who is momentarily allied with the tailor in a shared history and perhaps a shared reticence in the face of such difficult questions. It is not necessary to recognize Łomnicki's face, or to be aware of his significance to Polish film in order

10 The tailor watches through a curtained window in *Dekalog 8* (Copyright New Yorker Films, 2000)

to understand *Dekalog 8*; the series succeeds in its claim to universality, or meta-physicality. At the same time, Kieślowski uses Łomnicki as a bridge to his Polish audience, to demonstrate a familiar perspective from within the city of Warsaw, with all of its overwhelming history. His recommendation to the viewer is simply to watch.

BEYOND THE QUOTIDIAN

While there is unquestionably a documentary aesthetic running throughout Kieślowski's feature films, its presence in *Dekalog* is very carefully circumscribed as a means of connecting people's individual stories. This hierarchy is established by the *blok*, the object *par excellence* in Kieślowski's object-centered dramaturgy. By grounding his documenting eye in these interstitial materials, the director is free to explore the metaphysical, the universal confusions that arise from a text as seemingly straightforward as the Ten Commandments. The contrast between the two modes of storytelling is what allows the viewer to recognize the everyday life of the *blok* as it is depicted on television, while deliberating over an end-game of moral reasoning, and all the while "stirring something on the stove."

This is not an art corresponding to the early years of Solidarity, nor belonging to the Cinema of Moral Anxiety. Even though *Dekalog* was made before 1989, there is nothing in it that suggests the continuing existence of a Communist regime, just the souvenirs of one that remains even now in everyday life. As Tony Rayns comments, in tracing Kieślowski's path from Polish filmmaker to European filmmaker, "Kieślowski was obviously ahead of the game when he started treating the state, totalitarian or otherwise, as an irrelevance to the lives of most people."[36]

This is the fundamental reason why the skyline of Warsaw does not appear in *Dekalog*: Kieślowski, like his colleagues who joined Solidarity in the late 1980s, came to realize that their shared goal was to get beyond that particular historical horizon. By restoring an image of contemporary life to a medium that had lost its currency, *Dekalog* marks a transition from pallid government programming to the deluge of images from the West that would soon fill this televisual space. The combination of a still-extant Socialist architecture with an outlook that had already superseded it marks *Dekalog* as belonging to a very specific historical moment, and Kieślowski as anticipating the future that would follow. The skyline of Warsaw has already changed again, and Stalin's Palace will soon be a small part of a much bigger picture.

NOTES

1. See Christopher Garbowski, *Krzysztof Kieślowski's* Dekalog *Series*, New York: Columbia University Press, 1996; Janina Fałkowska, "The Political in the Films of Andrzej Wajda and Krzysztof Kieślowski's," *Cinema Journal*, vol. 34, no. 2, 1995; Stanisław Zawiślinski, *Kieślowski's bez końca*, Warszawa: Wydawnictwo Skorpion, 1994; Fałkowska's essay can also be found along with several insightful essays in Paul Coates, ed., *Lucid Dreams: The Films of Krzysztof Kieślowski*, Trowbridge: Flicks Books, 1999.

2. The most thorough English-language source on this period in Polish cinema remains Bolesław Michałek and Frank Turaj, *The Modern Cinema of Poland*, Bloomington, IN: Indiana University Press, 1988. On pre-1989 Polish film and politics, see also Frank Turaj, "The Cinema of Moral Concern," in Daniel J. Goulding, ed., *Post New Wave Cinema in the Soviet Union and Eastern Europe*, Bloomington, IN: Indiana University Press, 1989, pp. 143–71; David Paul, ed., *Politics, Art, and Commitment in the East European Cinema*, New York: St Martin's Press, 1983; and Michael Jon Stoil, "Cinema as Critic: Eastern Europe, 1955–1971," in *Cinema Beyond the Danube*, Metuchen, NJ: Scarecrow Press, 1974, pp. 127–59.

3. Michałek, p. 18.

4. Danuta Stok, ed., *Kieślowski on Kieślowski*, London; Boston: Faber and Faber, 1993, p. 144.

5. Ibid., p. 146.

6. "[C]'est le moins laid des quartiers nouveaux de Varsovie," Michel Ciment and Hubert Niogret, "Le Décalogue: entretien avec Krzysztof Kieślowski," *Positif*, 346, p. 37.

7. Charles Eidsvik, "Kieślowski's 'Short Films'," *Film Quarterly*, vol. 44, no. 1, 1990, pp. 50–5.

8. "Venice Film Fest Reviews: *Dekalog*," *Variety*, September 27 1989, p. 36.

9. "Późna jesień, szary ranek. Wielka płyta ogromnego bloku wygląda o takiej porze zniechęcająco. Kilka psów ugania się za skundloną suką. Właściciele samochodów, parkujących w alejkach, wynoszą akumulatory i montują je w silnikach aut. Kierowcy i psy płoszą stadko zmarzniętych gołębi, które podrywają się do krótkiego lotu i zaraz opadają. Jeden z ptaków ślizgowym lotem opada z góry, wybiera jeden z kilkuset parapetów bloku, siada na nim i zagląda do mieszkania." Krzysztof Kieślowski and Krzysztof Piesiewicz, *Dekalog*, Warsaw: Jacek Santorski, 7, author's translation.

10. Stok, p. 144.

11. "Zmierzch. Dorota stoi w oknie swego mieszkania. Patrzy w przesztreń. Za nią ciemność nie oświetlonego mieszkania. Przez okno swojej szklarni, oświetlony czerwienią maszynki elektrycznej, ogrzewającej wnętrze, wygląda ordynator i, jak

Dorota, patrzy przed siebie. Twarz Andrzeja jest blada. Słychać delikatny brzęk? szum? bzyczenie? Andrzej unosi powieki. W szklance napełnionej do połowy kompotem kręci sie w kólko pszczoła. W pewnym momencie brzęk cichnie. Pszczoła powoli wspina się na brzeg szklanki. Staje na krawędzi, otrzepuje skrzydełka i odlatuje." Kieślowski and Piesiewicz, p. 51.

12. Several recent essays have focused on the "symbiotic connection of Kieślowski the documentarist to Kieślowski the filmmaker"—see Christopher Garbowski, "*Double Lives* and *Lucid Dreams*: Two takes on Kieślowski," *Polish Review*, vol. 45, no. 3, 2000, p. 370; and Coates, *Lucid Dreams*.

13. Henri Lefebvre, *Everyday Life in the Modern World*, trans. Sacha Rabinovitch, New Brunswick, NJ and London: Transaction, 1994, p. 30.

14. Lefebvre, p. 31.

15. Ibid., p. 26.

16. Quoted in Adam Michnik, *Letters from Prison*, trans. Maya Latynski, Berkeley, CA: University of California Press, 1987, p. ix.

17. Michnik, p. xxiii.

18. Ibid., p. xxvii.

19. Ibid., p. 26.

20. A notable exception to this rule was the so-called "Black Series," and other experiments of critical realism in Łódź in the late 1950s.

21. When *Workers '71* was finally shown on television, it was almost unrecognizable as the original film that this group had made. Kieślowski did not go back to it in more liberal times, however, to re-edit it or any other film because he believed that they should stand as a record of what was possible at the time they were made.

22. "Amateur" would be a more literal translation of the Polish title, *Amator*.

23. Michnik, p. xxxii.

24. Stok, p. 81.

25. Ibid., p. 81.

26. "This was after *Station* so . . . I didn't want to make any more documentaries but there was no question of making features at the time." Stok, p. 125.

27. TOR was technically Zanussi's production house, which Kieślowski was running while Zanussi worked abroad. Kieślowski and Piesiewicz, p. 144.

28. Tony Rayns, "Kieślowski Crossing Over," *Sight and Sound*, vol. 1, no. 11, 1992, p. 22.

29. Stok, p. 151.

30. This was not necessarily the case before 1981, and not exclusively the case afterward: throughout the 1960s and 1970s, television had provided real opportunities for young directors of theater and film to try out their ideas in a lower-risk setting than feature-length funding. Even Grotowski and Kantor's theatrical experiments occasionally found their way onto TV. See A. Simonov, "I Live in a Provincial

Town," Yevgeni Dugin, ed., *Perestroika and the Development of Culture: Literature, Theatre and Cinema*, New Delhi: Sterling, 1989.

31. In contrast, the reaction to the series' original medium as it traveled around the festival circuit was dismissive of television as a site of high cultural activity. *Variety* reported that "after the Venice screenings, the general opinion was that in spite of its being produced for TV, the cycle should be given theatrical exposure first. With judicious handling it could fit perfectly in slots that accommodated earlier film events of the same scope, like *Berlin Alexanderplatz*, *Heimat* and *Shoah*." *Variety*, September 27, 1989, p. 36. Tony Rayns, writing in *Sight and Sound*, suggested that Kieślowski was "coming to terms with some of the main tenets of television soap opera." See Rayns, "Glowing in the Dark," *Sight and Sound*, vol. 4, no. 6, 1994, pp. 8–10.

32. Stok, p. 153.

33. Ibid., p. 154. See also Ciment and Niogret, p. 39.

34. Kieślowski's descriptions of his hypothetical viewer resonate strongly with attempts to theorize a televisual aesthetic in cultural studies, particularly David Morley, *Television, Audiences and Cultural Studies*, London and New York: Routledge, 1992; David Gauntlett and Annette Hill, *TV Living: Television, Culture, and Everyday Life*, London and New York: Routledge, 1999; and Horace Newcomb, "Toward a Television Aesthetic," in Horace Newcomb, ed., *Television: the Critical View*, New York: Oxford, 6th edition, 2000.

35. "De plus, il a l'avantage de proposer toujours les espaces fermés. La façon dont les maisons sont construites et disposées clôt le champ de vision et cela me permet des compositions intéressantes avec la caméra." Ciment and Niogret, p. 37.

36. Rayns, pp. 22–3.

PART II

THE POSTMODERN CITY: NORTH AMERICA

7

AFTER THE SIXTIES: CHANGING PARADIGMS IN THE REPRESENTATION OF URBAN SPACE

ALLAN SIEGEL

There is no place left where people can discuss the realities which concern
them, because they can never lastingly free themselves from the crushing
presence of media discourse and of the various forces organized to relay it.
Guy Debord[1]

PERSPECTIVE

During the twentieth century, the cinema, as a site of spectatorship and medium
of communication and entertainment, became a primary means of cultural
expression for representing the realities of urban life. In its earliest forms, the
cinema appropriated the city both as metaphorical canvas and as figurative backdrop. Whether in *Berlin, The Symphony of a Great City* (Ruttmann, 1927) or
Strike (Eisenstein, 1925), as artistic subject or place of ideological conflict, the
cinema provided the public with distinct images and ideas. In this context, and
throughout its evolution, the cinema has influenced political, economic, and
cultural reality and transformed our perception and reading of the urban environment. The processes of cinema specify representations of the city, refract
memory, and shape perspectives of history that engender the formulation and
reading of social space—re-generating processes of spectatorship—and thereby
changing a society's cultural vocabulary. Through its delineation of social space

the cinema becomes a significant element in the social dynamics that Henri Lefebvre suggests contribute to "a materialization of 'social being.'"[2]

The production, distribution, and viewing processes of the cinema form a paradigm that influences the interpretation and representation of social space. In the United States, until the years just following World War Two, the paradigm was built upon three primary factors: the production and distribution of film as commodity; artistic mediations as employed by specific directors within the Hollywood studio system; and the experiences of the audience—the interpretive vocabulary and cultural perspective of the spectator. At particular historical moments these elements have been more or less visible and malleable.

The 1960s was one moment when the 'structural integrity' of the paradigm that dominated postwar cinema became both apparent as an ideological marker and debatable in its relationship to everyday reality.[3] The 1960s was also a period in which the paradigm was momentarily ruptured. It was a time of frenetic, spasmodic activity. Political and cultural energy agitated the popular imagination. Critiques called to task the ideological assumptions that lay behind the practices of liberal democracy and endeavored to unearth, explain, and rectify a shopping list of social inequities. The baby boomer 'youth culture' that emerged in conjunction with the civil rights and anti-war movements opened up and popularized new areas of cultural expression that challenged the boundaries of the existing structures of production, distribution, and exhibition.

For Jesus Martín-Barbero, the 1960s is particularly significant because it foregrounds the role of culture as an arena of conflict. In seeking to comprehend the turbulent forces at play he draws upon Edgar Morin's essays, *L'Esprit du Temps II*, and Morin's description of a

> socio-political crisis. The crisis marks a rediscovery of the "event"—that is, culture as the historical dimension and action of different protagonists who are creating culture, discarding a concept of culture limited to code and structure. [The crisis] revealed the "eruption of the fermenting enzymes at the margins of society"—blacks, women, crazies, gays, the Third World—bringing to the surface their conflictiveness, throwing into crisis a conception of culture incapable of understanding their movements and their transformations of social meaning . . . The crisis undermined an art separated from life and a culture abstracted from everyday existence, a culture that attempted to rebaptize bourgeois materialism as a kind of spirituality.[4]

Morin's crisis suggests the 1960s as a moment of asynchronization in which the various institutions, social forces, and political priorities that had shaped capitalist development in the postwar years were out of alignment. Momentarily, for the era's "protagonists" the character and design of civic and political structures were unveiled and became indefensible. Their transformation appeared both imminent and possible. The historically shaped paradigms of the media could not contain "events" such as the massing of thousands of people at the Lincoln Memorial in Washington, DC in support of civil rights, the use of police dogs in a public park to terrorize demonstrators in Birmingham, Alabama, protests against the Pentagon and the Vietnam War or, for GIs, the circumstances and trauma of Vietnam. These, and countless other resonant cultural significations, outbursts of political upheaval that physically and psychologically transformed the urban topography of the city, forced a reconfiguration of dominant filmic representations.

Emanating from deep-rooted social imbalances, the effect of Morin's "sociopolitical crisis" has been persistent. On the material plane, within the United States, the crisis has profoundly altered urban reality and caused massive demographic shifts (the growth of sprawling suburban communities), dislocated economies (the decline of a community-based urban manufacturing sector), and reconfigured—in some cases destroying—those public spheres (local, community-based media) that were discursive sites within the urban world. This particular moment thus becomes a pivotal point for an examination of two worlds: the abstractions of cultural representation and the actualities of lived experience.[5]

What draws our attention is the aftershock of the "crisis," the fault-lines in the paradigm. The ruptures that altered social geography illustrate what Meaghan Morris identifies as:

> a contradiction which is over familiar as both a theoretical dilemma and an everyday experience. It is the contradiction between one's pleasure, fascination, thrill and sense of "life," even birth, in popular culture, and the deathly shadows of war, invasion, emergency, crisis and terror that perpetually haunt the networks.[6]

The loosely associated media of the 1960s revealed an array of contradictions that shaped the city. The moment also reaffirmed utopian notions that the social space of the city was a contested space, a living space, not necessarily immutable but subject to innovation and design.[7] At People's Park in Berkeley, California, on the pages of countless "underground" newspapers, in the streets of Paris, Chicago, or Mexico City, cities were reconfigured to expose social conditions and present new ideas which previously were invisible or rendered marginal.

As a filmmaker in the 1960s, I was part of a filmmaking "collective" called Newsreel. 9 produced documentary films about such issues as the student rebellion at Columbia University, the Black Panthers and Young Lords, the women's movement, housing conditions and the anti-war movement. Within three years of its founding in 1968, Newsreel had branches in six US cities and had produced close to forty films; in addition, it was distributing films from Europe, Asia, and Latin America. Regardless of the shifts in its theoretical underpinnings, Newsreel saw production and distribution as inseparable and interdependent aspects of a creative process. We envisioned, and constantly discussed, the dynamic relationship between the way a film was conceived and produced and the manner in which it was shown. The audience was viewed as a potential social agent—an actor in a social drama whose script was in constant gestation. Each film was perceived as a possible catalyst which might provoke and facilitate discussion. Collectively, Newsreel grappled with the cinema's ability to represent social conflict and act as a bridge between the audience and processes of social transformation. The ongoing debate which surrounded these questions compelled each film to be grounded in its own stylistic and thematic possibilities.

Collective discourse became an inherent element of the production process and in this context the film—a film—was viewed as a flexible instrument for decoding sites of struggle or change: a navigational aid into an undefined or misrepresented territory such as the Vietnam War, student struggles, the Black Panthers or the women's movement. Films were seen as compasses that enabled the audience to situate themselves within an arena of events—frequently distant and unfamiliar—that could be seen as intimate and immediate. In retrospect, this rather rough-hewn paradigm that Newsreel formulated facilitated processes of legitimation for communities of people, cultures, and social issues that had been historically misrepresented and marginalized.[8] The fragile model that we constantly tinkered with fostered and validated new sites of discussion and social activity and fractured hegemonic concepts of the public sphere. The new sites, or spheres, of cultural activity that emerged gave voice to and validated an "alternative" vision of social reality and helped expose the dominant production/distribution paradigm of mainstream cinema.[9]

Using this locus of historical and institutional activity as a point of departure, a realm in which practical considerations and theoretical assumptions were in constant tension, I would suggest that present discursive practices surrounding the medium of film tend to exaggerate the decoding, deconstructing, and dissecting of the film text at the expense of those quotidian media creating experiences that elucidate and alter social space. In the 1960s new cinematic languages in Europe, the Third World, and the United States emerged from critiques of the calcified production and distribution practices of studio-based film industries. When most successful, these critical discourses were bridges across areas of cultural theory, film production, and the audience. Today, discursive practices relating to media criticism and production have become ensconced within the academic world. Ironically, these practices, crammed with thorough analyses and trenchant observations, often seem marginal to the realities of a rapidly consolidating global media environment.

THE REALMS OF CRITICAL THEORY

Certainly, the viability of this perspective rests upon the critical examination of particular films and production practices. But it is equally dependent upon untangling the social space that sustains filmic reality.[10] These two are inseparable and rely upon an ability to demystify vocabularies shaped by the imploding critical languages of media theory, cultural studies, or film criticism (to name just a few of the domains). How can we prevent ourselves from being suffocated within an inwardly spiraling vocabulary that threatens to nullify the possibilities of discourse? Tentatively, as an alternative route toward other discursive possibilities, I will follow in this chapter the trajectory formed from representations of urban social space reflected in a cross-section of films from the 1960s to the present day.[11]

Within the confusing reality of this cultural upheaval—what Morris describes as an ensuing "theoretical dilemma"—it seems possible only to describe bridges between fragments, pieces of dreams, splinters of possibilities in which potentialities of social space have only a tenuous, shifting sense of coherence. But perhaps attempting to describe the nature of this tenuousness is more useful than falsely portraying a theoretical cohesiveness that somehow seems easier to come by when film is cut off from the social spaces within which its *meanings* are created.

Since the 1960s a considerable body of literature has focused on film as an art form and as a component of popular culture. Unfortunately, the discourses that have circumscribed this anatomization of the cinema have tended more toward analysis of filmic reality as a "fetishized abstract space"[12] as opposed to cinema as a social space with accompanying strategic and ideological implications.[13] It is not the intensity or depth of these theoretical categories that is at issue here nor even the precision of a particular perspective, but rather an insularity that has dulled their critical edge. As a result, these discourses have proved to be inadequate tools for working in a media environment that is multi-dimensional and in which codes and signs of communication constantly overlap, intersect, and mutate as they pass through urbanized global nodes of cultural and commercial activity.

There is an accelerating slippage between the life-world that nourishes popular culture and the academic milieus that thrive on criticism of its component elements. Like a shift in weather patterns, there seems to be a portentous gulf that separates these two areas of activity. The implications are grievous considering that from its earliest years the cinema's economic, representational, and architectural characteristics were woven into twentieth-century urban reality. Tom Gunning's study of D. W. Griffith and American narrative film solidly situates the earliest movie theaters (nickelodeons) and audiences within the social space of the city. Early cinema is filled with countless examples of films that represent the city and urban space—films that elaborate upon practices of spatialization at a particular historical moment. But the symptomatic ghettoization of discourse, its academic insularity, fosters boundaries and areas of study that take us far afield from those arenas where there is a vital interplay between the city and the cinema. In part, as Kristin Ross states, the problem stems from a critical bias in which space was thought of as an autonomous determinant, separate from the structure of social relations and class conflict—a theoretical confusion deemed somewhat akin to technological determinism. But space, as a social fact, as a social factor and as an instance of society, is always political and strategic.[14]

The way to cut through this "theoretical confusion" is not to discard or toss aside modes of analysis, but rather to view them from another perspective—not as self-contained conceptual tools, but as guideposts, historical markers on a broadly textured map. The goal, therefore, is not to arrive at a specific point of comprehension (if indeed such a place exists) but to perform "a quite different task," as Michel Foucault has suggested:

> a task that consists of not—no longer—treating discourses as groups of signs (signifying elements referring to contents or representations) but as practices that systematically form the objects of which they speak.[15]

A cinematic praxis indicates a process of spatialization because it emanates from the exchange taking place between the film text and the spectator. These exchanges reveal discursive practices and also map urban social/political geographies which articulate relationships between the city and the cinema.[16]

THE CITY AND "SPATIAL REPRESENTATION"

It would be erroneous to talk of the city as a singular, unified social reality that we have all experienced, participated in, or have an understanding of. Such a city does not exist. More appropriate to this discussion are images of a city, a multi-faceted city that represents ideological concepts, economic forces, and social spaces that reflect a diversity of cultural, historical, and geographical markers.

Throughout the twentieth century, the forces of modern capitalism, social revolutions, imperial conflagrations, colonial upheavals, and Nature itself have built, destroyed, and rebuilt the urban landscape. Any one of the causes that propel these transformations would be a suitable point of analysis, and any one major city would be a productive site of investigation. However, my concern is with the imbrications of daily urban experiences with the cinematic imaginary, and the dissonance that arises when landscapes of illusion become enmeshed with everyday banalities: the fission that initiates a flow of meanings, the nuanced movement between spheres of social activity and their representation. These exchanges indicate a topography and bring into focus what Henri Lefebvre calls *the problematic of space*

> which subsumes the problems of the urban sphere (the city and its extensions) and of everyday life (programmed consumption), [which] has displaced the problematic of industrialization.[17]

This topography provides a discernible index of the qualities of what Lefebvre calls "everyday life." These qualities designate a social geography marked with clues that clarify cinematic paradigms linked to the reproduction of social space. In this context, social space is both the filmic representation of urban reality and the site (or arena) within which the cinematic spectacle takes place—the home, the movie theater, or the cineplex.

THE MOVIE THEATER AND URBAN SPACE

The cinema, as commodity and art form, has been inextricably linked to the cultural and economic realities of the city. At the beginning of the twentieth century, the movie theater, quickly and with great fanfare, established itself as a profitable site of cultural activity: an embryonic public sphere, a pre-eminent urban social space and, as Tom Gunning has stated, a place of "social discourse."[18] In the tumultuous polyglot world of the flourishing modern American city, "The new nickelodeon audience was part of a broader transformation in American entertainment, the commercialization of the newly won leisure time of the working class . . . [in which] film very early formed a relation to female and family audiences."[19] In this "broader context," a film's social space emerged as a result of the tension that exists between the cinematic experience (and all that this entails) and the social reality of the spectator.[20]

Today, the spatial reality of contemporary cinema forms around a multiplicity of public and private sites of spectatorship: movie theaters, television, and "home entertainment centers," or the Internet. The alterations and variations in the spaces within which film viewing takes place indicate an evolving discursive reality that challenges traditional definitions of how the film text works. They also delineate the diversity of social spaces that define and give substance to a multi-layered paradigm, an intertextual paradigm different from its predecessors at the turn of the century and those aberrations that appeared briefly during the 1960s and early 1970s.

In the interdependent realms of cultural production, the cinema, as Julian Murphet asserts, is now simply one element

> Within our global space of instantaneous exchange and incessant circulation, [where] cultural forms undergo an unprecedented degree of reconfiguration according to site-specific contingencies and the absence of a viable universal. Forms once meant to respond to specific national or urban problems (and destined for a limited export market), now circulate around an incalculable web of interpretative communities.[21]

Therefore, while the cinema is certainly a prominent medium of culture, it no longer maintains its governing position as the central elocutionist of iconographies and *voices* shaping popular culture. As both a medium that articulates and represents social space and as commodity, the filmic system circulates hypostatized realities that are valorized and conflated within Murphet's "interpretive communities." The resilience of these spatializations, their resonance, gives meaning to a film's discursive attributes. The filmic material that marked, for example, Jules Dassin's *The Naked City* (1948) or, later, Gordon Parks' *Shaft* (1971) are inseparable from the viewing environment and the interpretative language of the spectator. These intertwined perspectives add substance and dimension to filmic discourse. Gunning states that:

> A particular narrative discourse addresses a spectator in a particular way, eliciting specific sorts of activities . . . Along with a new sort of filmic narrator, Griffith's transformation of filmic discourse constructs a new sort of spectator for film . . . [or] the spectator constructs a new sort of film experience as cued by Griffith's narrative discourse.[22]

Spectators today shape cinematic experiences based on Murphet's "site-specific contingencies"—contingencies that alter the nature of filmic discourse and resonate with the economic, technological, and aesthetic factors that define a particular cinematic paradigm. Finding ourselves immersed within these shifting patterns of mediation, the nature of discourse takes on an allusive quality. Its substance is buried beneath the gloss of hyperbole that coats the surface of popular culture. Within the matrix of factors that define filmic discourse, where historical threads are often obscured by a stylistic sheaf, space is hidden behind a residue of glittering isolated alliterations. How easy it is then to find ourselves buried under what Guy Debord called "the crushing presence of media discourse," wandering within a labyrinth of streetscapes of simulacra or lost inside the dystopic police state of Kathryn Bigelow's *Strange Days* (1995). Confounded by the nothingness of hyper-mediated urban life, the penultimate escape, the ultimate high, is into an illusionary digitized identity: a journey within a shopping mall of sensations and events driven by a global corporate feeding-frenzy that promises—always—to fulfill an expanding recurrent quest for the "stuff you can't have."

THE POSTWAR URBAN LANDSCAPE

In the post-World War Two period three major urban realities influence the cinematic landscape. Firstly, the economically unstable North American city contending with the repercussions of white flight and the concurrent conflicts that emanate from the civil rights movement. Secondly, the physically and psychologically scarred re-emerging European city. Thirdly, the city of the Other: the metropoles of Africa, Asia, and Latin America: the urban centers of the colonial and post-colonial world.

These are the urban realities that nurtured a cinematic geography from which we can identify the characteristics of cities in transition, in a state of ferment. Upon visions of Algiers, Athens, Buenos Aires, Chicago, Paris or Saigon are embossed social spaces of "a city" that both traverses and defines national boundaries. A city rooted in the specifics of its own locale yet illuminated by the ideological, economic, and political dynamics of a global reality.

What began to materialize in the 1960s in such disparate films as *Battle of Algiers* (Pontecorvo, 1967), *Z* (Costa-Gavras, 1969), *Blow-Up* (Antonioni, 1966),

Weekend (Godard, 1967), *Hour of the Furnaces* (Solanas, 1968) or *Medium Cool* (Wexler, 1969) was the transnational coordinates of an inter-urban *gestalt*. These films designated the contested terrain of private and public space, illuminated political struggles and highlighted new forces of consumerism and commodification. Thematically, these films challenged traditional social and economic relationships and narrativized a visual and psychological geography that was both specific to particular locales but also symptomatic of a larger global complexity. These films presented us with a series of compacted urban representations which strategically examined destabilized social relations and the ambivalent nature of social space. They alluded to what Rob Shields has called a

> discursive sphere [that] offers complex re-coded and even de-coded versions of lived spatializations, veiled criticism of dominant social orders and of the categories of social thought often expressed in aesthetic terms as symbolic resistance.[23]

In Elia Kazan's *On the Waterfront* (1954), the iconographic skyline of Manhattan—viewed from the rooftop of a Brooklyn tenement—looms in the background and serves as an ascendant, totalizing image of an urban ideological reality. In contrast, *Blow-Up*, *Weekend* or *Battle of Algiers* delineated new spheres of discourse which attempted to politically and/or sociologically deconstruct the abstract totality of the city. These films struggled against a paradigm in which the spectator existed in a state of self-containment and inertia. In this transitional period from the 1950s to the late 1960s the urban realities of societies in ferment, combined with new cinematic forms emerging from the Third World, brought about new levels of engagement between filmmaker and audience.

URBAN SPACE AND *FILM NOIR*

A film's social space arises via the positing of representations.[24] These representations are an hypostatized filmic reality and take on meaning because of their relationship to the real world of the spectator. But, as Margaret Morse indicates, the two realities are conflated:

> The late twentieth century has witnessed the growing dominance of a differently constituted kind of space, a *nonspace* of both experience and representation, an *elsewhere* that inhabits the everyday . . . This ground is without locus, a partially derealized realm from which a new quotidian emanates.[25]

This "derealized realm" that Morse describes emerges at those points where filmic reality overlaps with a commodified social reality. This "nonspace" circulates within and "inhabits the everyday." In contrast to the space of derealization are moments when the cinematic experience engages the perceptual capacities of the spectator in another manner.[26] Within these moments the boundary between filmic reality and the lived reality of the spectator is traversed. Tom Gunning defines this process as one where

> The film text's address to its spectator meshes with the industrial processes of production, distribution and exhibition. Both rest upon a definition of the film experience and together define that experience.[27]

Thus, the social space of cinema is not defined by the particularities of a film's text, from the decoding of frozen moments, but rather emerges from its experience. Its social space flows from the unleashing of the discursive contingencies of the moment. Spatialization takes place at that moment when representations extend themselves, reach beyond all the physical qualities of their construction. What becomes visible at the intersection of the filmic with the quotidian, at the place where these two realities are intertwined and seem to nourish one another, is a space that "has strange effects," as Lefebvre said, a space that "unleashes desire":

> It presents desire with a "transparency" which encourages it to surge forth in an attempt to lay claim to an apparently clear field. Searching in vain for plenitude, desire must make do with words, with the rhetoric of desire.[28]

Within this context, *film noir* forms the filmic narrative of urban social space—not that every film about or taking place within a city emulates that genre—but the narrative codes of *film noir* form a persistent urban cultural topography. *Noir*'s easily identifiable landmarks (free floating, intertextual signifiers) are reference points that mediate, assemble, and in general decode a flow of meanings. These narrative codes are indices that ground and stabilize meaning within a consistent ideological framework. They situate the city—urban people and events—and form a bridge between the sensory world of everyday reality (the quotidian) and its representation.

Film noir charts both a yearning and its displacement/absence. It posits a paradox that appears to be both self-sustaining and yet on the verge of disintegration.[29] Raymond Chandler's Phillip Marlowe or Dashiel Hammett's Sam Spade are characters who are endurable because they embody explicitness within a corruptible world in which people are too often evasive and misleading. These archetypes and their counterparts are plunged into a narrative framework which is derived from

> the chronotope of a particular social grouping at a pivotal moment in the production of US urban space, responding symptomatically but originally to the very juncture at which the great US cities were being disarticulated by a logic of suburbanization and consumerism.[30]

Against the ascendant values of "suburbanization and consumerism," *noir*, even in its most extreme configurations, grounds the representation of urban space within a system of signs that strive to maintain a semblance of coherence. Through either hyper-realistic or nostalgic configurations—as, for example, in *Blade Runner* (Scott, 1982) and *LA Confidential* (Hanson, 1997), respectively—it can suggest a logic to neutralize the dislocations of the spectator. *Noir* then presents a distinct urban chronotope—a point at which the social spaces of the city crystallize to form representations that extend the specificity of the moment.[31] This is a place in which, in Julian Murphet's Bakhtinian terms, space "becomes charged and responsive to the movements of time, plot, and history." What the *noir* chronotope allegorizes for us is the privatization of public life. The opposition between a perilous, alluring commercial space and a staid, static domestic space.[32]

What happens to this chronotope in the 1960s is its inversion: *noir*, with its easily recognizable archetypes and narratives of urban America, reappears within a much broader social perspective. The city, its boundaries only alluded to in classical *noir*, is more diverse and complex. Migratory, invidious archetypes spill out onto a broad urban space. The genre breaks free from what Murphet calls the "nocturnally shot urban corridors which organize the *noir* chronotope into a new system of spaces and flows of time."[33]

An early example of this inversion is *Bullitt* (Peter Yates, 1968). Set in San Francisco, the once claustrophobic city is transposed into a shifting backdrop for Steve McQueen's Ford Mustang. McQueen's car, not simply a sign of class or upward mobility, seems to embody the impending chaos of an emerging post-industrial urban reality.[34] Though this reality evolves via a series of disconnected, emblematic social spaces, it is now shaped and defined by an archetype who has broken free from a "nocturnal" world. McQueen is not constrained by the formalities of genre or representational taboos. Nor is he driven by the same sense of existential anomie that underlies the classic anti-heroes of the genre. He is not outside the system but within it; though implicitly the system is corruptible, Bullitt is not. He is that uniquely American actualization of the post-World War Two urban cowboy who has traded in his horse for a squad car and—in Bullitt's case—one with considerable cachet.

The colorful motif that pervades the design of *Point Blank* (John Boorman, 1967) proclaims and revels in the inversions of *noir*'s narrative conventions. The film's extreme dislocations of traditional spatial and temporal motifs parallel an abstract world of white-collar crime—symbolized by the "multiplex corporation"—and a corporate crime world in which cash and the criminal are invisible. The film's story is built around Walker (Lee Marvin), who in the expository opening sequence, stumbles, injured, out of Alcatraz prison—now a vacant island—and into San Francisco Bay (**11**). Left for dead by his former partners, he swims back to the city to claim his share of stolen money. Searching for the men who betrayed him he navigates the hierarchy of a new criminal syndicate. In vain, he invokes traditional codes of criminal behavior only to find that they have been discarded for the more abstract economics of the "multiplex corporation." Walker's disassembling archetype engages in a fruitless struggle with a moral universe that is beyond his grasp.

Noir's traditional narrative universe is built upon an urban space consisting of an established social geography and moral order. The genre's resonance builds upon these historically constituted markers to maintain the form's transgressive capacities. *Point Blank* describes the disintegration of those parameters and the futility of their renewal. It is a transitional piece that heralds an urban post-industrial new world order.

11 Walker (Lee Marvin) stumbles into San Francisco Bay in John Boorman's *Point Blank* (1967) (Copyright MGM, 1967)

"BECAUSE SOMETHING IS HAPPENING, BUT YOU DON'T KNOW WHAT IT IS, DO YOU, MISTER JONES?"[35]

With the appearance of the iconic rogue cop in *Madigan* (Don Siegel, 1968), the dystopic reality of *Point Blank* is approached from another less surreal angle. This new access point is finally personified by Clint Eastwood in the character of Lt Harry Callahan in *Dirty Harry* (Don Siegel, 1971). In order to apprehend a serial killer terrorizing the city of San Francisco, Callahan flaunts the restraints of normative police procedures. He mocks the impotence of liberal civility and its corporate façades. Although in the film's conclusion Callahan eliminates the threat to social stability, he is unable to resolve his frustration with the city's inherent moral disorder. Callahan's confusion stems from a confrontation with what Kristin Ross calls the illusion of "evenness" in which

> The process of development in the West has been completed; what comes now is already in existence: the confused syncretism of all styles, futures, and possibilities.

12, 13 "What a city, if only we could see it," Ray (Gabriel Byrne) in Wim Wenders' *The End of Violence* (1997) (Copyright Road Movies Filmproduktion, 1997)

> Modernization promises a perfect reconciliation of past and future in an endless present, a world where all sedimentation of social experience has been leveled or smoothed away.[36]

The archetype of the rogue cop, the urban misfit, and similar new filmic representations do not displace the narrative devices of *noir*. Rather their use situates the spectator within a reconfigured urban space, a layered social space in which conflicts are played out on a more nuanced canvas. Similarly, in *The Conversation* (Francis Ford Coppola, 1974), *Taxi Driver* (Martin Scorsese, 1976) and *Chinatown* (Roman Polanski, 1974), the ideological interventions that define social space appear with momentary clarity. In these films, not only are the coordinates of modern metropolitan reality marked, but the dimensions of the corporate/political ethos that underlie assumptions about American progress and prosperity are also calculated.

Toward the conclusion of *The End of Violence* (Wim Wenders, 1997), Ray, played by Gabriel Byrne, peers out into a fog-enshrouded Los Angeles landscape and says, "what a city, if only we could see it" (**12, 13**). Moments later he is killed by an unseen assassin. Ray, a scientist, has been hired by a secret government agency to design a massive city-wide video surveillance system. He scans and calibrates a seemingly infinite array of TV cameras and peers into the public and private spaces that lie beneath the urban haze. Ensconced in an observatory that also scans the heavens, Ray surveys interstates, streets, and rooms to penetrate and quantify reality—to totalize, the city's metaphoric invisibility. His job is part of a quest "to end violence as we know it."

Coming moments before his death, Ray's observation is an ironic reflection on the powers that lie beyond his technological universe. It is counterbalanced by the *invisibility* of the Mexicans that inhabit the city and who become both the figurative and literal saviors of Michael Max, a film producer whose film career has been built upon representations of violence. With his current production in financial crisis, Max is forced to submit to the "sudden attack" he has been expecting all his life. Under the shadows of the commercial arteries that convey the life-blood of the city, in a scene visible only to Ray's hidden cameras and satellites, Max himself is confronted with an arbitrary act of violence and, in a Hollywood epiphany, his life is transformed.

The End of Violence charts a geography of social spaces—some clinging to tradition and others encapsulated in illusion, pretense, and power—spaces that can morph effortlessly according to the dictates of global finance.[37] Linked only by a vague commonality of place, the film charts disconnected public and private social space. Only in the quotidian realities of the interactions between Ray and his father (Sam Fuller), between Mike and his extended Mexican family, between a police detective and an actress, does life suggest any continuity or meaning.

Within these relationships there is a sense of the past, and a tangible present defined by a longing for (the possibility of) love, family, and a sense of history.

As a thinly veiled (though inverted) homage to Nicholas Ray and *Rebel Without a Cause* (1956) the film balances micro- and macro-representations of social space. Cultural underpinnings of private worlds are contrasted with constructed façades that define the public sphere. The film's paradigmatic qualities lie in the manner in which it strives to narrativize social space and the self-consciousness (even the awkwardness) of its undertaking. Its resonance rests upon its quest for historical moorings that might somehow momentarily stabilize the contradictions that fill its vision. Within the urban reality of *The End of Violence* the social space of the city appears as dislocated tableaux and the machinery of surveillance, technological siphons that turn quotidian realities into data, becomes a trope for exigencies of the New World information order. Within this urban nebula, human relationships appear like ephemeral arcs of light streaming across a vast horizon and then disappearing into an anonymous mass of people.

Whereas *The End of Violence* tackles the implications of observation, Krzysztof Kieślowski's *Three Colors: Red* (1994) approaches surveillance from another vantage point. While *The End of Violence* charts the implications of constructed and invisible realities, *Red* seeks to decipher the nuances and emotional topography of communication and the human voice. Thus, the two films are linked by a determination to chart an urban landscape which thrives below the surface of visible and listened-to daily reality.

In the opening moments of *Red* the viewer is rapidly propelled along underwater cables. The sequence simulates the high speed flow of communications, the spanning of distances, and the impact of instantaneous invisible technologies that facilitate a phone call. The film contrasts these miracles of design and rationality with the randomness of forces of nature and unforeseen circumstances which bring people together and rip apart the illusions and seductive surfaces that add *color* to the highly mediated life world of the modern metropolis. Using telephone conversations and messages exchanged between Valentine (Irène Jacob) and her unseen lover, the prologue of *Red* alludes to the levels of intimacy and emotion that are revealed in human conversation. Returning his injured dog to him, Valentine discovers Jean-Louis Trintignant, a retired judge, sitting in his disheveled home blissfully absorbed in eavesdropping his neighbors' conversations on the phone. The fragility of domestic space, the temporality of the home as a social institution, indicates, as Linda McDowell states, a contemporary reality in which

> the scale and magnitude of dislocation and movement is such that it is argued that we are entering a new era . . . the transnational attenuation of "local" space, and this breaking of space into "discontinuous realities" which alters our sense of ourselves as individuals, members of various groups and communities, as citizens of a nation state.[38]

Within McDowell's "attenuated local space" and "discontinuous realities" lie the indices that can continue to aid us in decoding processes of spatialization. These provide the landmarks that enable us to situate ourselves not in an abstract geography but within the social spaces that correlate to McDowell's "new era."

"LET US NOT TALK FALSELY NOW, THE HOUR'S GETTING LATE . . . "[39]

Whereas in the 1960s we witnessed upheavals that provoked social transformations, today the crisis is of a different nature, but no less profound. Rapidly, what continues to evolve in the developed world is not only a dramatic shift in the socio-economic realities of the urban lifeworld but also alterations in the cultural prisms and media networks that refract and re-construct our image of the world. The globe is being refashioned as a vast media playground of criss-crossing currents and priorities and the city is being mapped with a new sociological topography: warehouses and factories are gentrified, new immigrants are ghettoized or expelled, and entertainment districts are homogenized and codified. The once distinctive local movie theater has been replaced by corporate cineplexes imbued with all the architectural distinctiveness of the globe-straddling yellow arch of McDonald's. Within this kinetic media environment traditional paradigms built around the cinema of yester-year strain under the weight of a transnational economic order.

In the wake of this media maelstrom appear new forms and vehicles of expressive possibility. Low-cost digital video production techniques and new forms of distribution on the Internet are fostering media flows that can color the life-world of the city and give voice to publics that are ordinarily marginalized or invisible. These eddies of cultural activity contain not only the seeds of new cinematic languages but also the potential to counterbalance the corporate homogenization of urban reality. Though often only transitional, localized centers of production and distribution, these alternative social spaces can affect the cultural tide from below. And while at the moment their impact may seem inconsequential, they do suggest the possibility of a future, contrary to Guy Debord's expectations, in which "people can discuss the realities that concern them."

NOTES

1. Guy Debord, *Comments on the Society of the Spectacle*, London and New York: Verso, 1990.
2. "Social space *per se* is at once *work* and *product*—a materialization of 'social being'," Henri Lefebvre, *The Production of Space*, trans. Donald Nicholson-Smith, Oxford: Blackwell Publishers, 1991, p. 102.
3. This is not to say that many of these paradigms did not exist before World War Two; what I am pointing at is their reformulation and evolution within the context of a new domestic and global social reality after World War Two: the Cold War, the Hollywood witch hunts, the McCarthy hearings, the Civil Rights movement, the anti-colonial struggles of the 1950s and 1960s—these historical perturbations often ruptured pre-existing models.
4. Jesus Martín-Barbero, *The Culture Industry: Capitalism and Legitimacy*, New York: Sage Publications, 1993, p. 56.
5. At this moment then, according to Lefebvre, "Social space, and especially urban space, emerged in all its diversity—and with a structure far more reminiscent of flaky mille-feuille pastry than of the homogenous and isotropic space of classical (Euclidean/Cartesian) mathematics. Social Spaces interpenetrate one another. They are not things, which have mutually limiting boundaries and which collide because of their contours or as a result of inertia." Lefebvre, pp. 86–7.
6. Meaghan Morris and Patricia Mellencamp, eds, *Banality in Cultural Studies*, in *Logics of Television*, London: BFI Publishing, 1990, p. 18.
7. Films such as Chris Marker's *Le Joli mai* (1963) and Newsreel's *Columbia Revolt* (1968) or *People's Park* (1969) brought some of these events and ideas to a new global audience.

8. Many aspects of this particular model were not necessarily new. One might even say that it was simply a replication of the Kino Pravda model of Dziga Vertov or the extensive audience interactions that accompanied *The Hour of the Furnaces* (Octavio Getino, Fernando Solanas, Santiago Alvarez, 1968) when it was shown clandestinely throughout Argentina. Perhaps all that was new in our conception was an ignorance of the other models that we were building upon or the lineage we shared. Although we did not know it at the time, this was a paradigm related to the "cinema of attractions" that, as Tom Gunning defines it, "rather than telling stories, bases itself on a film's ability to show something . . . a cinema that displays its visibility, willing to rupture a self-enclosed fictional world to solicit the attention of the spectator." Tom Gunning, *D. W. Griffith and the Origins of American Narrative Film: The Early Biograph Years*, Chicago, IL: University of Illinois Press, 1991, p. 41.

9. In the United States these "sites" were grouped around various labels or organizations such as the New American Cinema or the "underground" cinema associated with Jonas Mekas and other experimental filmmakers; the "alternative" vision of social reality gave rise to Newsreel and other specialized organizations during the 1970s and 1980s such as the Black Filmmakers Foundation, Women Make Movies, and the Independent Feature Project. Many of these organizations still exist and give credence to and validate the idea of an "alternative" media.

10. By this I mean the reality that nourishes the growth of the cinema as a creative tool and as a medium that engages audiences.

11. In pursuing this, I am admittedly stymied by the limitations of those instruments of navigation that increasingly contain the landscape of film criticism and bind it within a language that insinuates a theoretical paint-by-numbers. I find myself searching for the critical tools that can make this project conceptually possible.

12. This "fetishized abstract space" implies "'users' who cannot recognize themselves within it, and a thought which cannot conceive of adopting a critical stance toward it." Lefebvre, p. 93.

13. For Lefebvre, *strategic space* is space that "seeks to impose itself as reality despite the fact that it is an abstraction," Lefebvre, p. 94.

14. Kristin Ross, *The Emergence of Social Space: Rimbaud and the Paris Commune*, Minneapolis: University of Minnesota Press, 1988, p. 9.

15. Michel Foucault, *The Archaeology of Knowledge*, trans. A. M. Sheridan Smith, New York: Pantheon Books, 1981, p. 49.

16. "After its fashion the image kills. In this it is like all signs. Occasionally, however, an artist's tenderness or cruelty transgresses the limits of the image. Something else altogether may then emerge, a truth and a reality answering to criteria quite different from those of exactitude, clarity, readability and plasticity." Lefebvre, p. 97.

17. Lefebvre, p. 89.

18. Historically, the architecture of the movie theater, its position on the street, its

location within a neighborhood or district designated both a physical focal point defining or shaping a visual panorama and a center of cultural activity. The movie theater marquee was emblematic of the social reality of a particular street or avenue. It attracted other ancillary forms of commercial activity. The visual redundancy of theatre marquees defined the scale of social space: whether in the spectacular vision of Broadway with its proliferation of marquees and lights or as the visual center of Main Street USA. As a marker of social space, the marquee represents a metaphor for one of three poles of social activity: the church, the civic, and the social; whereas civic and religious architecture embodied their own particular sets of philosophical perspectives, characteristics, and signs, the movie theater marquee became a symbol of popular culture and mass entertainment. See also Miriam Hansen, foreword to *Alexander Kluge: Theoretical Writings, Stories and an Interview*, Cambridge, MA: MIT Press: *October*, no. 46, Fall 1988, p. 186.

19. Gunning, pp. 86–7.
20. "An understanding of film in relation to social and ideological history can be seen as a movement from the filmic discourse of an individual text to the economic and ideological discourse that penetrates it. Opening up a filmic text to a broader context does not necessarily move from representation to reality or from cause to effect. Rather, it traces relations between, as Raymond Williams puts it, different signifying systems of a culture." Gunning, p. 11.
21. Julian Murphet, "*Film Noir* and the Racial Unconscious," *Screen*, vol. 39, no. 1, Spring 1998, p. 33.
22. Gunning, p. 23.
23. Rob Shields, *Places on the Margin: Alternative Geographies of Modernity*, London: Routledge, 1991, p. 54.
24. Among its other qualities, a "social space" is not static. Lefebvre, pp. 16–17. Thus, a film's social space is a construction that evolves during the process of viewing. While watching a film we take apart, "decode" what we see and we simultaneously reconstruct space based on the meanings we attach to cinematic representations.
25. Margaret Morse, *Virtualities: Television, Media Art and Cyberculture*, Bloomington, IN: Indiana University Press, 1998, p. 196.
26. A filmic space forms around the Text. It simultaneously carries the weight of its ideological and cultural baggage and also embodies the fecund representational realities of the present moment. "The Text is not a co-existence of meanings but a passage, an overcrossing; thus it answers not to an interpretation, even a liberal one, but to an explosion, a dissemination . . . [It] is that space where no language has a hold over any other, where languages circulate." Using Roland Barthes' description, then, I see the Text as an element that elucidates filmic paradigms for it implies "space" as a fluid zone, an area where meanings both congeal and evaporate; it is a space that forms between the film and the spectator. Roland Barthes, *Image, Music,*

Text, selected essays, trans. Stephen Heath, New York: Hill and Wang, 1977, pp. 159, 164.

27. Gunning, p. 12.

28. Lefebvre, p. 97.

29. "Spaces are strange: homogenous, rationalized and as such constraining; yet, at the same time utterly dislocated." Lefebvre, p. 97.

30. Murphet, "*Film Noir* and the Racial Unconscious," p. 30.

31. Murphet, p. 25.

32. Ibid., pp. 25–6.

33. Ibid., p. 26.

34. As Kristin Ross describes the process, "the car had become a project: what one was going to buy next. And it is at this point, when the car stands on the verge of becoming a universal accessory, that the cinema no longer represents the car as a fabulous or wondrous item." Ross, *Fast Cars, Clean Bodies: Decolonization and the Reordering of French Culture*, Cambridge, MA: MIT Press, 1995, p. 29.

35. Bob Dylan, "Ballad of a Thin Man," from the album *Highway 61 Revisited* (1965), Columbia Records #09189.

36. Ross, p. 11.

37. The film draws upon stylistic elements of the *noir* canon as well as such icons of urban topography as Edward Hopper's painting, *Nighthawks* (1942).

38. Linda McDowell, "Spatializing Feminism: Geographical Perspectives," in Nancy Duncan, ed., *Body Space: Destabilizing Geographies of Gender and Sexuality*, London, Routledge, 1996, p. 44.

39. Bob Dylan, "All Along the Watchtower," from the album *John Wesley Harding* (1968), Columbia Records #09064.

8

A NOSTALGIA FOR MODERNITY: NEW YORK, LOS ANGELES, AND AMERICAN CINEMA IN THE 1970s

MARK SHIEL

This essay aims to demonstrate some of the ways in which examination of Hollywood cinematic representations of the city over the past thirty years can shed light on the decisive emergence in society, economics, and culture since the 1960s of what is now commonly known as "postmodernity." In particular, I am interested in examining how the distinctive spatial geographies which characterize certain Hollywood representations of the cities of New York and Los Angeles may be understood as allegories of the actual objective relationship between those two cities as acknowledged paradigmatic city types—New York as the ultimate modern urban environment, Los Angeles as the ultimate postmodern urban environment.

A discussion of two particular films which actually incorporate the relationship between NY and LA as thematic content will form the core of my investigation—the two films being *Annie Hall* (Woody Allen, 1977) and *Network* (Sidney Lumet, 1976). Both were made at a historical moment generally agreed upon as pivotal by those historians and theorists who point to an all-embracing shift from modernity to postmodernity in the last third of the twentieth century.[1]

In discussing these two films, my approach will be underpinned by a firm belief that, in the final analysis, all cinema—especially Hollywood cinema, which generally tends to be exclusively entertaining and consumable—is most fruitfully examined in terms of a dynamic and integral relationship between culture and society. To use the phraseology of Raymond Williams, cinema exists as part of a "lived social reality," or a "whole social process," in relation to which it operates both as an articulation and an intervention.[2] I hope to suggest here that Hollywood cinema in the past thirty years has not only "reflected" the shift from modernity to postmodernity, but has been instrumental in the pace, manner, and degree of that shift from the outset.

THREE STAGES OF CAPITALISM

Here, of course, I am indebted to that historiographical model which views Western history, and more recently world history, as the history of the development of capitalism through a series of three particular "stages," not predetermined or leading to a teleologically identifiable end, but recognizable nonetheless as key social, economic, and cultural stages, each connected to and overlapping with its predecessor and its successor, but sufficiently distinct to deserve its own specific nomenclature.

Fredric Jameson and David Harvey best elaborate upon this model of history, which is worth outlining here briefly in order to lay the ground for my discussion of Hollywood in the 1970s.[3] Jameson views the history of Western society since the Renaissance as a lengthy and often intangible process of development from "market capitalism" to "imperialist capitalism" to today's "multinational capitalism." Each stage is accompanied by its own distinctive and historically appropriate and determined philosophical, political, and cultural discourses and economic practices in a long process of gradual change. All of these are punctuated occasionally by huge "paradigm shifts" or moments of "cultural revolution" in which the philosophical, political, cultural, and economic ground shifts seismically as capitalism, the fundamental reality underpinning all others, moves inexorably (perhaps, perhaps not?) forward through time.[4]

According to this persuasive historical model, classical market capitalism, underpinned by artisan production, and free trade and commerce between a large number of roughly equal kingdoms and early nation states, dominated from the early fifteenth century to the turn of the nineteenth century. Characterized by an essential positivism, rationalism, and a secularizing humanism, it was given, in cultural representation, to a preference for Cartesian geometry and verisimilitude—to classical realism in other words.[5] Imperialist capitalism succeeded market capitalism, underpinned by a second wave of aggressive capitalist expansion based upon industrialization and the rule of a small number of strong and internationally powerful mature nation states over most of the peoples of the rest of the world. As Marshall Berman has explained, this first age of modernity, from the early nineteenth century, was accompanied by a profound cultural split.[6] An increasingly assertive and authoritarian use of classical realism by imperialist powers was opposed with mounting bitterness by an eventually almost fatal attack upon classical realism by that cultural explosion generally known as "modernism." This modernism arose out of an increasing discrepancy between the individual self, on the one hand, and the vast geographical scale, authoritarian reach, and instrumentalist logic of imperialism as a world system, on the other. In this climate it became increasingly difficult for artists, writers, and intellectuals to understand their relation to the social reality in which they lived, let alone to identify with it. Further, it was a social reality with which they became increasingly disillusioned and disgusted as the twentieth century opened and then progressed through catastrophe after catastrophe. This economic, social, and cultural reality dominated from the early nineteenth century to somewhere near the middle of the twentieth century until the next "paradigm shift," this time from modernity to postmodernity—for most historians and theorists who subscribe to the term, sometime in the late 1960s or early 1970s.[7]

MODERNITY AND POSTMODERNITY

"Multinational capitalism," "late capitalism," or "advanced capitalism" (a variety of terminologies exist) succeeded imperial capitalism in that turbulent and violent era known as the Sixties. Today it is underpinned by a qualitatively new degree of capitalist expansion on a truly global scale. This expansion is driven by a relative decline in the power of individual nation states as such and by a proportionate rise in the power and status of corporations and a newly emergent transnational capitalist class, based, as Saskia Sassen has demonstrated, in a relatively small number of particular world cities which operate as command and control centers for corporate function and global reach.[8] In this new global system, not only has there been a significant shift in the center of power, but there has been a perhaps even more significant modification in the ways in which power is exercised and the ways in which power represents itself—a shift identified by David Harvey, from the centralized, hierarchical, and rigid order of imperialism and production-driven capital in modernity to the decentralized, modular, and flexible order of consumption-driven global capitalism and post-modernity today.[9]

In this relatively new postmodern global capitalist order, moreover, much of the utopian antagonistic conviction which underpinned modernist culture is once again lost, neutralized by what Colin MacCabe has called "the full entry of art into the world of commodity production."[10] Modernism has given way instead to a very ill-defined and enigmatically heterogeneous postmodernism in which consumerism, and its characteristic brand of individualism, has become, in Jameson's words, "the very linchpin of our economic system, and also the mode of daily life in which all our mass culture and entertainment industries train us ceaselessly day after day, in an image and media barrage quite unparalleled in human history."[11] However, this postmodernism, while perhaps excitingly and often disorientingly fluid and enigmatic in cultural terms—one thinks here of Charles Jencks' celebration of the architectural playfulness of present-day Los Angeles—evades apprehension and understanding as a world system to an extent even greater than that encountered by those with the inclination to consider such questions during the second stage of imperialism and modernity.[12]

At least modern imperialist capitalism manifested itself, and could be recognized, for better or worse, in the solidity and permanence of monumental architecture or urban planning—from Haussmann's Paris of the 1870s, to Robert Moses' New York of the 1940s—urban environments whose geometrical, centralized spatial organization on the ground and monolithic building projects commanding the skyline articulated the expansionist arrogance of their commissioning powers—France of the Third Empire, the United States of the post-World War Two Pax Americana. As the examples of Paris and New York suggest, the historical development from market capitalism and classical realism, to imperialist capitalism and modernism, to global capitalism and postmodernism, has always been easiest to apprehend on the ground as a spatial development—in the development of urban spaces as articulations of a current world system *at a given moment in time*, and (less often attended to) the development of particular cities over other cities as the articulation of the succession of one world system over another *through time*.

Specifically, the historical relationship between modernity and postmodernity has actually played itself out most clearly in spatial terms—both in an objective sense in terms of complex series of social and economic developments felt most acutely in major world cities, and in a mediated sense, in the representation of such cities by cinema. Thus, for example, the historical development from modernity to postmodernity may be apprehended most clearly as a process of succession in which the dominance of the archetypal early modern European cities of Paris, Berlin, and London—whose heyday from the 1890s to the 1930s was filmed by, for example, Louis Lumière, Walter Ruttmann, and Alfred Hitchcock—were shaded into second place by the dominance of archetypal late modern American cities such as New York, Chicago, or Pittsburgh—whose heyday from the 1920s to the 1960s was filmed by, for example, Vincente Minnelli, Howard Hawks, and John Huston.[13] This is a process of historical migration which the art historian Serge Guilbaut has described, in his book *How New York Stole Modern Art*, in terms of the eclipse of Paris by New York as the world center of modern art after World War Two. The eclipse took place on foot of the now legendary wave of forced migration imposed upon European modernist artists—most famously, the Surrealists—by the rise of fascism in their home countries, and their influential and energizing sojourn during and after the war itself at the heart of a burgeoning and increasingly sophisticated New York art scene dominated by the Abstract Expressionism of the New York School.[14]

But the next step in this historical development has not yet been sufficiently documented in terms of cinema or visual culture more generally. It comprised the subsequent paradigm shift from modernity to postmodernity manifest in the rise to prominence during the 1960s, in both the domestic US and international spheres, of what would soon come to be labeled as key postmodern cities. These included less celebrated cities such as Phoenix, Houston, or Las Vegas—featuring in *Psycho* (Alfred Hitchcock, 1960), *The Right Stuff* (Philip Kaufman, 1978), and *Casino* (Martin Scorsese, 1995), respectively—and the quintessential postmodern urban environment, Los Angeles, which appeared with increasing frequency and self-confidence in Hollywood cinema after World War Two from *Rebel Without a*

Cause (Nicholas Ray, 1955), to *The Graduate* (Mike Nichols, 1967), *Chinatown* (Roman Polanski, 1974), *The Terminator* (James Cameron, 1989), *Short Cuts* (Robert Altman, 1994), and *LA Confidential* (Curtis Hanson, 1997).[15]

In this rise to prominence, we see the cinematic articulation of a movement encapsulated by Kirkpatrick Sale in the title of his book, *Power Shift*, first published in 1976. Famous in its time, Sale's book documented the decisive "power shift" of the 1960s and 1970s from the long-established dominance of so-called "Yankee" economic power or "old money" in major cities in the northeastern United States (New York, Boston, Philadelphia, Detroit, Pittsburgh, or in the Midwest, Chicago) to an aggressive, upstart brand of so-called "Cowboy" capitalism based around key power blocs and cities in the southwestern United States—Dallas, Houston, Santa Fe, Albuquerque, Phoenix, Las Vegas, San Diego, and Los Angeles. This was a rise to prominence integrally related to the increasing "post-industrialization" of the US economy, and not coincidentally linked to the preponderance since the 1960s of presidential administrations with strong links to that part of the country—from Lyndon Johnson to Richard Nixon, Ronald Reagan, and, today, George Bush I and II—as suggested by Oliver Stone's *JFK* (1993).[16]

This move extends a generally westward historical migration from the metropoles of Western Europe in the nineteenth century to those of the northeastern United States in the first two-thirds of the twentieth century to those of the southwestern United States in the latter part of the twentieth century and into the twenty-first. In this process, though no city type erases any other and all today come to co-exist in an increasingly compounded state of uneven development, each city type—for example, Paris, New York, Los Angeles—becomes iconic of the dominant social, economic, and cultural realities of its respective historical stage.

NEW YORK AS PARADIGM OF MODERNITY

For Douglas Tallack, the emergence of New York as paradigmatic of a distinctive American modernity was effectively ensured in 1898 with the consolidation of the five boroughs (Manhattan, the Bronx, Queens, Brooklyn, Staten Island) into one city, New York City.[17] The ten years on either side of the turn of the century, of course, were witness to tides of immigration greater than any other single city has ever encountered, a burgeoning economy energized by the nation's emergence as a world power (especially after the 1892 Spanish-American War), and a cataclysmic urban expansion comprising a revolution both in mass transportation (bridges, tunnels, subways) and in architecture and the design of public space for unprecedented levels of high-density living. This was the era of the emergence of New York as a skyscraper city, a field of monumental or iconic structures and spaces—Central Park, the Brooklyn Bridge, the Statue of Liberty, Coney Island, the Empire State Building, Times Square, Madison Avenue, Fifth Avenue, and Broadway—or, to borrow from Marshall Berman, "a Baudelairean forest of symbols" which was "conceived and executed not merely to serve immediate economic and political needs" but as a form of "symbolic action" which might "demonstrate to the whole world what modern men can build and how modern life can be imagined and lived."[18]

As Douglas Tallack has explained, this larger-than-life New York presented new problems and challenges of conceptualization for American artists who sought to respond to a profound need for a new epistemology of the city—a way of visualizing the novelty, activity, labor, speed, chaos, routine, density, and intensity of the metropolis of metropolises. This is the New York captured with a romantic touch, for example, by the avant garde film classic *Manhatta*, made by the painter Charles Sheeler and the photographer Paul Strand in 1920.[19] This is the New York of opportunity and expansive optimism idealized in Hollywood musicals from *42nd Street* (1933) to *On the Town* (1949), and, in a harsher though ultimately no less sentimental way, *West Side Story* (1962). And this is also essentially the New York of Woody Allen's 1979 feature *Manhattan* in which a particularly touristic version of the city—comprising sunset shots of the Brooklyn Bridge, the Empire State Building, or Central Park—serves as the bitter but then sweet setting for human interaction, emotion, expression, and romance.

But if the celebration of New York by Sheeler and Strand or by the classical Hollywood musical makes sense as so many articulations of a modern city in its noisy and brash heyday, Allen's eulogization of the city distinguishes itself as anomalous in the 1970s, for by then the cinematic representation of New York had long since degraded into dystopian projections of that particular city as the purest distillation of urban nightmare. As Marshall Berman explains with regard to post-World War Two urban planning in New York, the city's ascendant trajectory from the 1930s to the 1960s—epitomized by the gargantuan public works of the legendary though often vilified planner and developer Robert Moses (responsible, for example, for Kennedy Airport and the Cross-Bronx Expressway)—collapsed in the notorious abyss of racial conflict, rising crime, urban dilapidation, brutalist architecture, and financial ruin into which the city fell in the later 1960s and 1970s.[20] This was the "new" urban reality pointed to with such influence, of course, by Jane Jacobs in her seminal *The Death and Life of Great American Cities* (1960), and subsequently documented on screen through twenty years of urban decay in such films as *Midnight Cowboy* (1969), *Dog Day Afternoon* (1975), *Taxi Driver* (1976), *The Warriors* (1978), and *Escape from New York* (1981). New York, first and foremost of all cities, as Will Straw has neatly phrased it, came to appear in social commentary and popular culture as the most telling "barometer" of "a generalized social rot."[21]

ANNIE HALL

Los Angeles, meanwhile—at least if one were to believe the portrait of the city given in Woody Allen's *Annie Hall* (1977)—had long since laminated itself as the ultimate space of affluence, comfort, health, control, superficiality, and consumerist pleasure which so disgusted and yet fascinated Jean Baudrillard in his postmodern travelogue, *America* (1984). The film tells the life-story of stand-up comic and B-celebrity Alvy Singer (Woody Allen) and his constant quest for the right woman despite his typically long list of neurotic complaints and psycho-sexual complexes, and a resultant twenty year string of abortive romances all set against the backdrop of upper middle class life in New York City's Upper West Side, and weekends in the Hamptons, in the hedonistic so-called "Me decade" of the 1970s.

Like most Woody Allen films, *Annie Hall* is a film about the difficulty of human relationships—in a philosophical sense, particularly the relationship between the self (Woody Allen) and other people (mostly women) as an addictive source of both pleasure and pain. But, again like many Woody Allen films, *Annie*

Hall is also a film about the relationship between the self (Woody Allen) and the city of New York which functions much as another person—sometimes hostile, sometimes as a source of irritation, an engine of neurosis, almost as if a softer and comic version of the psychotic relationship between Travis Bickle and New York City in Scorsese's *Taxi Driver* of the previous year. For despite their obvious differences, what *Taxi Driver* and *Annie Hall* fundamentally share is a belief in the city, New York City, as a deep well of authentic personal experience, a source of self, of tangible subjectivity, and of intense emotion, action, and human interaction. As in many of the films of Scorsese and Spike Lee, and in occasional film adaptations of the work of Paul Auster like *Smoke* and *Blue in the Face*, as well as in his own *Radio Days* and the collaborative *New York Stories*, Allen's New York is a site of personal memory and the forging of identity, and of a characteristic (though often self-deprecating) nostalgia—in the case of *Annie Hall*, for a tough-though-idyllic working class 1940s childhood in Coney Island. The New York of Allen's memory is, of course, the quintessential modern and modernist New York of the first half of the twentieth century, not simply in its visual iconography (the strategic deployment of a romantic kiss between Allen and leading lady, Diane Keaton, under the Brooklyn Bridge) but in its typically modernist insistence upon an intrinsic relationship between place, self, and emotion (**14**).

Thus, one of Alvy Singer's favorite pursuits in the film is precisely to stroll through the city and its parks (as did Walter Benjamin's *flâneur* in late-nineteenth-century Paris), enjoying a human pedestrian environment in which the *flâneur* is afforded the simple pleasure of watching other people in the park, deriving interest from their eccentricities and weaknesses and in which, through such urban exploration, the self draws inspiration for self-commentary and self-awareness through constant talking, description, explanation of himself, others, the city, the meaning of life itself. For better or worse, then, New York appears in the film not just as a place but as an icon of a certain historically definable relationship between oneself, one's past, and one's place in the world—as a source of self and deeper meaning in life. Moreover, this is an emotional authenticity which Alvy Singer insists upon experiencing, despite the pain it often entails, refusing to take drugs when they are offered at parties (smoking dope, taking acid), and showing a general impatience with other "artificial" subjective states such as transcendental meditation as desensitizing and dehumanizing.

14 "Place, self, and emotion" in New York City, Woody Allen's *Annie Hall* (1977)
(Copyright MGM-UA, 1977)

Because if human relationships are difficult in New York City, they are at least
meaningful, having an emotional tangibility akin to the physical tangibility of
the city's monumental architecture and public spaces. On the other hand, when
Alvy Singer flies to Los Angeles in pursuit of his lover Annie Hall who has been
seduced away from New York by the promise of a successful music recording
career, that city—LA—lacks all depth or authenticity. Instead, it is the home of
the brightly lit, soft-focus Beverly Hills garden party where groupies fawn over
overweight pampered music industry executives whose interpersonal communication consists almost entirely of making arrangements for business meetings.
Here, Allen deploys LA as the ultimate non-intellectual environment where New
York's association with sophisticated high culture (jazz, classical music, and
European art house cinema, especially Bergman) is replaced by a postmodern pro-
clivity for pop music and the consumer-oriented "fad"—in this case, 1970s
vogues for health food, yoga, self-awareness therapy, and environmentalism.[22]

Where in New York, Alvy Singer makes a living as a stand-up comic dealing with the vagaries and frequent abuse of a live audience, in LA, his best friend and fellow comic Max has taken up work as a TV comedian, dubbing canned laughter onto insipid taped sitcoms. This opposition of synthetic and authentic culture appears immediately on Alvy's arrival on the West Coast at Christmas time where the festive strains of "We Wish You a Merry Christmas" are met by the blazing heat of a Pacific sun. Indeed, not only is the total automobile dependency of LA entirely antipathetic to the pedestrian, to the direct human interaction and experience of the *flâneur*, but LA lacks even seasons and, thus, the emotional meaning of "Autumn in New York," "New York in June," or even, "Paris in the Springtime." After a failed attempt to persuade Annie Hall to return to New York with him, Alvy Singer leaves with characteristic disillusion to return to his true love, New York City, where he famously explains in the final moments of the film that, despite the emotional hardships of his search for the right woman, he keeps on looking for love (as we all do) because "I need the eggs." "The eggs" of Allen's final joke, of course, is not only shorthand for the addiction to romantic love, but for the constant trials and dangers of life in the modern metropolis which Allen cannot do without. This is precisely the problem he identifies with the excessive ease of life in LA: "You know, it's important to make a little effort once in a while."

The portrayal of LA in *Annie Hall*, therefore, stands as an early articulation of motifs and general characteristics of that city now widely recognized and theorized in urban studies and film studies, but many years before the more obvious manifestations of LA's postmodern urbanism in such 1990s *überwerks* as *Terminator II* (Cameron, 1991), *Boyz N the Hood* (Singleton, 1991), *Falling Down* (Schumacher, 1993), *Pulp Fiction* (Tarantino, 1994), and *Heat* (Mann, 1995). Allen's LA is a comically stereotypical place drawing equally on the two common myths which have historically surrounded the city. On the one hand, there is LA's legendary promotion of itself from the turn of the twentieth century as the opposite of urban modernity, an escape from the social ills, environmental hazards, and physical confines of cities such as New York. On the other hand, there is LA as historically lacking in any sophisticated artistic, musical, literary or intellectual endeavor of its own, despite, as Mike Davis has explained, the city's actual cultural complexity even in the modern era from F. Scott Fitzgerald, Bertolt Brecht, and Raymond Chandler in the 1930s and 1940s, to Kenneth Anger, Ed Ruscha, and Ed Kienholz in the 1960s.[23] Allen's LA, therefore, is both prescient and yet missing something—an extra ingredient which, I would suggest, only begins to accumulate through the 1980s and 1990s, in such cinematic complications of LA's urban typology as *Blade Runner* (Scott, 1982), such seminal cultural studies of the city as Davis' *City of Quartz*, and such important social-scientific exposition of LA's economic importance and emergence as a world city as Edward Soja's *Postmodern Geographies*.

NETWORK

In this respect, a film which provides a harder portrait of LA, closer in spirit to that of the now familiar popular cultural conception of the city as an apocalyptic "Fortress LA," to use Mike Davis' evocative term, is the contemporaneous *Network* (Sidney Lumet, 1976).[24] Where Allen's portrayal of LA was bound by the generic requirements of romantic comedy to remain at the level of light-hearted social satire, Lumet's film goes for the jugular of the then emergent global capitalist regime. Of course, in the 1970s, Lumet was a filmmaker perhaps more than any other identified with projections of New York as bankrupt dystopia, thanks to the success of such features as *Serpico* (1973), *Dog Day Afternoon* (1975), and *Prince of the City* (1979), and New York also features strongly in *Network*. But here New York appears with its gloves off, as it were, not as a place for hapless romantics, but as a major nodal point in the world system of transnational capitalism, in a narrative which focuses on a struggle for control of a fictional though typical television network, UBS, between the competing forces of an ascendant diversified corporation, CCA (the Communications Corporation of America), on the one hand, and a morally principled though increasingly obsolete group of television news journalists and administrators, on the other. These people are intent on maintaining the traditional integrity of their profession against the debasing, dehumanizing logic of corporate takeover and control.

In contrast to *Annie Hall*, New York in *Network* is the stomping ground of media conglomerates and not much else. Its central narrative portrays the acceleration of corporate capital into every nook and cranny of personal life, and, particularly, the incorporation of culture by global capital characteristic of post-modernity—in this case, in the insistence that the dedication to truth and human interest of television news journalism should submit to the inexorable logic of corporate profit and audience ratings, on the one hand, and in the consequent blurring of the line between hard news and entertainment, on the other. In a manner very much in keeping with the popularity of conspiracy narratives in 1970s American cinema, which Jameson explains as a reaction to the increasing un-mappability of postmodern global capital itself in those days (especially in light of Watergate), control in *Network* takes place entirely behind the scenes. Power is exercised among senior executives of the corporate board, at shareholders' general meetings, and is entirely lacking in any moral principle, instead destroying age-old notions of ethics—not only among journalists, but even in inter-personal relationships, between best friends, between lovers.[25]

Against this backdrop of corporate greed and brutalization, scenes of human warmth or intimacy do occur in the film. For example the world-weary Chief of the News Division at UBS, Max Schumacher (played by William Holden) and the news anchor on the verge of a nervous breakdown, Howard Beale (played by Peter Finch), share whiskies-on-the-rocks and swap stories about the old days, at some faintly glamorous downtown hotel; and between Schumacher/Holden and the upwardly mobile programming executive, Diana Christensen (played by Faye Dunaway) who share dinner by candlelight at a plush restaurant. But such scenes seem profoundly dated in the film, resembling the scattered sentimental remnants of some older, more elegant and genteel classical Hollywood melodrama. Indeed, the film plays upon a contrast between cultural forms in a manner akin to the contrast in *Annie Hall* between stand-up comedy and the TV sitcom, but on a deeper and more persistent level. In *Network*, that is, in addition to the diegetic conflict between TV news and entertainment, one can detect an extra-diegetic tension between three entire cultural forms—theater, cinema, and television. Theater is an unannounced presence, so to speak, throughout the film in the wordy and pacy script by playwright Paddy Chayefsky, and in the intensely emotional, declamatory, not to say Method acting of William Holden and Peter Finch. This theatricality—indeed, a characteristically postwar New York theatricality—sits uneasily with the lavish cinematic form and big-budget

Hollywood credentials of the film itself. And, finally, both the theater and the cinema seem threatened by television in the film—a profoundly bleak, instrumental, Marshall McLuhanite portrait of television as an upstart medium, more spontaneous and yet more vulgar and irrational than its relatively traditional predecessors.

Indeed, it is on this note that Los Angeles makes its entrance into the film. For LA appears in *Network*, as it does in *Annie Hall*, as the home of the creative talent which is the backbone of the new postmodern "culture industry." If corporate management and the programming of television content takes place in New York, the actual content itself originates in Los Angeles—a bizarre soup of pulp television dramas, soap operas, sitcoms, cartoons, commercials, and infomercials—anodyne, superficial, and lacking in any human meaning. The corruption of television news in the film by the logic of entertainment and profit, indeed, is explicitly presented as the contamination of the reality of New York by the fiction of Los Angeles in an inevitably corrupting bargain in which what Max Schumacher desperately refers. to as "simple human decency" is destroyed by its West Coast opposite—TV.

Network, then, like *Annie Hall*, plays out the transcontinental divide between New York and LA, signified occasionally by the ubiquitous and characteristically 1970s shot of the shining aluminum underbelly of a landing Boeing 747, tires screeching on asphalt, icon of the first great age of mass transcontinental and intercontinental jet travel. *Network* too suggests this divide as a contrast between New York as human emotion and deeper meaning, for better or worse, and LA as synthetic comfort, numbness, and spiritual void. But where Allen's film nonetheless maintained a belief in the importance of emotion and human contact, as well as a muted optimism that it would always be out there for discovery, *Network* seems to despair of even such faint hope. For its main social motif is an insistence on the atomization of the television audience and, by extension, of the American public in the regressively privatized, anti-collective, 1970s. If the new priority of the corporation is elevated in the film almost to the level of corporate theology and mysticism, the complete absence of orthodox political power, or of any sense of the power of the people, in *Network* lies in the film's parody of popular political participation in the famous catchphrase of the pop evangelical Howard Beale Show, "I'm mad as hell and I'm not going to take it any more!"—and, thereby, in the film's general despondency *vis à vis* the recent end of the 1960s (**15**).

One of the more perverse contributions made by Los Angeles to UBS' news programming in the film comes in the form of real-time documentary footage of real-life bank robberies in progress, shot with a hand-held camera by the so-called Ecumenical Liberation Army as a record of their revolutionary exploits— an obvious fictionalization by Chayefsky and Lumet of the real-life 1970s Symbionese Liberation Army, a Maoist group famous for kidnapping the multi-millionaire heiress Patty Hearst. In the film, the footage is flown in to New York from LA each week to boost the television news hour's poor ratings by adding an element of drama and sensationalism. Any Utopian hopes which the 1960s might have held are here represented as debased, co-opted, and deformed by global capitalism itself, such that not only does the corporation come to sleep with the enemy in the name of profit, but the corporation becomes in the eyes of the law a co-conspirator in its crimes, and the Maoist guerillas themselves lose sight of any revolutionary agenda or commitment to the oppressed and become wholly taken up with the negotiation with UBS of contracts, distribution deals and "subsidiary rights."

Network, in 1976, thus provides us with a dispiriting lesson in the end of politics as such in postmodernity—or, more precisely, the replacement of the vanguard utopianism and radical politics of the 1960s by a postmodern micropolitics of disassociated lone individuals—as if as an epilog to the revolutionary defiance of another famous representation of LA's emergence as postmodern paradigm, Michelangelo Antonioni's *Zabriskie Point* (1969), which featured the real-life Black Panther Party in their heyday. For if the onset of postmodernity had particularly debilitating effects on political practice in general, it was precisely those communities who could least afford it who were worst hit. As Mike Davis and other commentators have explained with reference to the city's social and political devastation in the post-Civil Rights, post-1960s era, Los Angeles, characterized by extremes of luxury and poverty, and repressive law and order, more or less unparalleled in the United States, spent the subsequent three decades spiraling deeper and deeper into crime, racial conflict, urban decay, and social meltdown.

But this is not the end of *Network*'s mapping of the specific socio-political

15 "Corporate theology and mysticism" in Sidney Lumet's *Network* (1976) (Copyright MGM-UA, 1976)

tragedies of postmodern LA. The final stage in the deciphering of the film's allegory of the traumatic transition from modernity to postmodernity requires that we relate this discussion of the film's content back to the original historical process which formed the starting point of this chapter. The paradigm shift from modern monopoly capitalism to postmodern global capitalism was particularly evident in the Hollywood motion picture industry itself for which the 1970s was a period of post-traumatic resettlement and restabilization at least as crucial as it was for the rest of the United States socially, politically, and economically.

This restabilization was especially dependent, as film historians such as Tino Balio and Janet Wasko have explained, upon a dual process.[26] Firstly, it involved the consolidation of the actual relationship between New York banking and financial power, and West Coast creative and services power, but now as competitor world cities, rather than big city and little city. And, secondly and more importantly, it involved the integration of the Hollywood film industry in a new postmodern production regime. In this, the centralized oligarchy and national economy of the classical studio system was replaced by the relative polycentrism, devolved authority, and global multinational diversification of the contemporary

American media and entertainment industry, an industry which today has further integrated itself inextricably with the information technology and communications industries worldwide, as the recent merger of AOL and Time-Warner demonstrates.[27] Thus, the Hollywood film industry played a key role in the now noted rise of Los Angeles as a world city on the Pacific Rim since the 1970s, as the apotheosis of the postmodern, post-Fordist urban economy based upon what David Harvey calls "flexible accumulation"—that is, a complex set of social and economic changes including social polarization, decentralization, and vertical disintegration of industry, the rise of services and of low-paid unskilled labor, and the relocation of much industrial production either to Third World immigrant populations based in First World cities or to Third World cities *tout court*.[28]

NOSTALGIA

But all of these developments appear only on the distant horizon in *Network*, not yet hardened into cliché as they will become in the formulaic contrast between the honest and tough New York cop and the corrupt glitz and emasculating glamour of Los Angeles in a film such as *Die Hard* (McTiernan, 1988), or in the reconfiguration in a film such as *Speed* (de Bont, 1994) of 1960s non-conformism and 1990s neo-liberal world order in the figure of the disgruntled lone terrorist (played in an ironic, if not outrightly cynical, casting move by ex-countercultural icon, Dennis Hopper). In both *Annie Hall* and *Network*, though in different ways, the changes and traumas engendered by the paradigm shift from modernity to postmodernity are felt to have real, decisive, and not altogether positive impacts upon individual and social life. Both films demonstrate what Jameson has characterized as the postmodern predicament, one step more acute than that of modernity, which "involves our insertion as individual subjects into a multidimensional set of radically discontinuous realities, whose frames range from the still surviving spaces of bourgeois private life all the way to the unimaginable de-centering of global capital itself."[29]

Both films are underpinned by a strong sense of uncertainty about the future, and nostalgia for the past, though neither film—unlike, for example, the much more recent *Sleepless in Seattle* (1994)—is naive enough to believe in the past either as some ideal place or time. Rather, both films look upon the past as a valuable era of authentic human experience and emotion—pleasure and pain, associated not with just any space but with New York City as icon of modernity. In this, both films are best understood as akin to, though not the same as, the "nostalgia film" identified by Fredric Jameson as the articulation of both the sense of vertiginous disorientation and loss of history which postmodernism entails and the simultaneous recognition that "the way back to the modern is sealed for good."[30] In this respect, perhaps the clearest object lesson in the cultural contradictions of capitalism such films provide is in the manner in which the traumatic social reality of one generation often becomes the comforting myth of the next.

NOTES

1. See David Harvey, *The Condition of Postmodernity: An Enquiry Into the Origins of Cultural Change*, Cambridge, MA, and Oxford, UK: Blackwell Publishing, 1989, pp. 39–65.
2. Raymond Williams, *Marxism and Literature*, Oxford: Oxford University Press, 1990, pp. 11–20.
3. Fredric Jameson, *The Political Unconscious: Narrative as a Socially Symbolic Act*, London: Methuen, 1981, pp. 89–102; Harvey, *The Condition of Postmodernity*, pp. 3–118.
4. Jameson, *The Political Unconscious*, pp. 93–8. While arguing for an understanding of history in terms of identifiable historical stages ("modes of production") and intervening paradigm shifts, Jameson importantly acknowledges the methodological and ideological dangers which overly schematic applications of such thinking can entail—pointing, for example, to some of the work of Max Weber, Michel Foucault, Jean Baudrillard, and Daniel Bell. In cultural analysis, Jameson particularly warns against "the temptation to use the various modes of production for a classifying or typologizing operation, in which cultural texts are simply dropped into so many compartments." Jameson, *Political Unconscious*, p. 90. See also Jameson, *Signatures of the Visible*, New York and London: Routledge, 1992, pp. 155–62; and Harvey, *The Condition of Postmodernity*, p. 42.
5. Fredric Jameson, "Cognitive Mapping," in Cary Nelson and Lawrence Grossberg, eds, *Marxism and the Interpretation of Culture*, Urbana and Chicago, IL: University of Chicago Press, 1988, pp. 347–57.

6. Marshall Berman, *All That Is Solid Melts Into Air: The Experience of Modernity*, London: Verso, 1993 (1983).

7. See Harvey, *The Condition of Postmodernity*; and Jameson's description of the so-called "third, multinational stage of capitalism, of which globalization is an intrinsic feature and which we now largely tend, whether we like it or not, to associate with that thing called postmodernity," in Jameson, "Notes on Globalization as a Philosophical Issue," in Fredric Jameson and Masao Miyoshi, eds, *Cultures of Globalization*, Durham, NC: Duke University Press, 1998, p. 54.

8. Saskia Sassen, *Cities in a World Economy*, Thousand Oaks, CA: Pine Forge Press, 2000.

9. Harvey, *The Condition of Postmodernity*, pp. 141–72.

10. Colin MacCabe, Preface to Jameson, *The Geopolitical Aesthetic: Cinema and Space in the World System*, Bloomington, IN, and London: Indiana University Press and British Film Institute, 1992, p. xii.

11. Jameson, "Notes on Globalization as a Philosophical Issue," p. 64.

12. Charles Jencks, *Heteropolis: Los Angeles, the Riots and the Strange Beauty of Hetero-architecture*, London: Academy Editions, 1993.

13. One thinks here, for example, of Lumière's *La Tour Eiffel* (1900), Ruttmann's *Berlin, The Symphony of a Great City* (1927), Hitchcock's *Sabotage* (1936); and Minnelli's *Bells Are Ringing* (1960), Hawks' *Scarface* (1932), and Huston's *The Asphalt Jungle* (1950; though some commentators argue Huston's film is set in Cincinnati).

14. Serge Guilbaut, *How New York Stole Modern Art: Abstract Expressionism, Freedom, and the Cold War*, Chicago, IL, and London: University of Chicago Press, 1983.

15. In addition to the burgeoning critical discourse on Los Angeles, these smaller Southwestern cities have also been receiving increasing attention in recent years as, for example, in M. Gottdiener, Claudia C. Collins, and David R. Dickens, *Las Vegas: The Social Production of an All-American City*, Oxford and Malden, MA: Blackwell Publishing, 1999; and James Hay, "Shamrock: Houston's Green Promise," in Mark Shiel and Tony Fitzmaurice, eds, *Cinema and the City: Film and Urban Societies in a Global Context*, Oxford and Malden, MA: Blackwell Publishing, 2001, pp. 75–87.

16. Kirkpatrick Sale, *Power Shift: The Rise of the Southern Rim and its Challenge to the Eastern Establishment*, New York: Vintage Books, 1976.

17. Douglas Tallack, "City Sights: Mapping and Representing New York City," in Maria Balshaw and Liam Kennedy, eds, *Urban Space and Representation*, London: Pluto Press, 2000, pp. 25–38.

18. Berman, *All That Is Solid Melts Into Air*, pp. 288–9.

19. For more on Sheeler and Strand's *Manhatta*, see Jan-Christopher Horak, ed., *Lovers of Cinema: The First American Film Avant-garde, 1919–1945*, Madison, WI: University of Wisconsin Press, 1995.

20. Berman, *All That Is Solid Melts Into Air*, pp. 287–348.

21. Will Straw, "Urban Confidential: The Lurid City in the 1950s," in David Clarke, ed., *The Cinematic City*, London and New York: Routledge, 1997, p. 115.

22. Of course, if Allen is condescending toward LA's lack of an intellectual culture, in other scenes he is intolerant of New York's intellectual pretension.

23. Mike Davis, *City of Quartz: Excavating the Future in Los Angeles*, London: Vintage, 1992, pp. 46–54, 62–8.

24. Ibid., pp. 223–63.

25. On conspiracy films, see Jameson, *The Geopolitical Aesthetic*, pp. 9–84.

26. Tino Balio, "Part IV: Introduction: Retrenchment, Reappraisal, and Reorganization, 1948–," in Balio, ed., *The American Film Industry*, Madison: University of Wisconsin Press, 1985, pp. 439–47; Janet Wasko, *Movies and Money: Financing the American Film Industry*, Norwood, NJ: Ablex Publ. Corp., 1982.

27. See Colin Hoskins, Stuart McFadyen, and Adam Finn, *Global Television and Film: An Introduction to the Economics of the Business*, Oxford: Oxford University Press, 1998; Mark Balnaves, James Donald, and Stephanie Hemelryk Donald, *The Global Media Atlas*, London: British Film Institute, 2001, pp. 62–3; Toby Miller, Nitin Govil, John McMurria, and Richard Maxwell, *Global Hollywood*, London: BFI Publishing, 2001, pp. 44–82.

28. Harvey, *The Condition of Postmodernity*, p. 124. See also Mike Savage and Alan Ward, "Cities and Uneven Economic Development," in Richard T. LeGates and Frederic Stout, eds, *Urban Sociology, Capitalism and Modernity*, London and New York: Routledge, 2000, pp. 312–27; Michael Storper and Susan Christopherson, *The Changing Organization and Location of the Motion Picture Industry: Interregional Shifts in the United States*, Los Angeles: UCLA Graduate School of Architecture and Urban Planning, 1985; Susan Christopherson and Michael Storper, *Flexible Specialization: A Critique and Case Study* [of the motion picture industry], Los Angeles: UCLA Graduate School of Architecture and Urban Planning, 1986.

29. Jameson, "Cognitive Mapping," p. 351.

30. Jameson, *The Geopolitical Aesthetic*, p. 197.

9

THE AFFECTIVE CITY: URBAN BLACK BODIES AND MILIEU IN *MENACE II SOCIETY* AND *PULP FICTION*

PAUL GORMLEY

I want to begin this chapter by focusing on Spike Lee's comments and criticisms of Quentin Tarantino. Following the release of *Jackie Brown* (1997), Lee implied that Tarantino is a "wannabe" black filmmaker who has appropriated the language and aesthetics of contemporary African-American culture to produce a kind of exploitative shock in the audience.[1]

Lee's major criticisms center around the liberal use of the word "nigger" in all of Tarantino's screenplays and particularly in *Jackie Brown*. His implicit critique is that it is impossible for a white writer and filmmaker to use this word without evoking the history of white oppression and abuse that it carries with it. The term "nigger" has of course been used widely by black artists such as Richard Pryor and contemporary hip-hop culture as a "signifyin'" strategy against white oppressive uses of the term, but such use, according to Lee's position, is not possible by a writer and director who is white.[2] The underlying focus of Lee's comments is that Tarantino's dialogue is a kind of "blackvoice" which, like "blackface," is a white symbolic construction based on the "power to make African-Americans stand for something besides themselves."[3] Without the experience of being black, Tarantino's use of this term, and his appropriative references to African-American culture as a whole, are a cynical and exploitative attempt to cash in on the politicized shock, cultural authenticity, and "coolness" which contemporary African-American culture signifies in the white American cultural imagination. In other words there is a fetishizing of black culture as a desirable "other" which in the end reaffirms white power relations of racism. Tarantino's response to these criticisms is firmly embedded within liberal ideology arguing that "no one word should be allowed to stay in prison." At the same time Tarantino defends the use of the word by claiming a kind of novelistic verisimilitude, expressing the belief that the word only appears in his dialogue "because it is a word that the characters would use," and that it is used to mean different things, depending on the character using it.[4]

This argument briefly raged through newspapers and popular journals in 1997 and 1998 and subsequently disappeared almost as soon as it appeared. But I want to argue here that the issues touched upon by Lee's criticism and Tarantino's defense point toward a much more complex and fundamental series of mimetic relations between contemporary white Hollywood film and African-American culture—and African-American film in particular. In broad terms I want to explore the relations between the cinematic body and urban space in two films, *Menace II Society* (Hughes Bros, 1993) and *Pulp Fiction* (Tarantino, 1994), to argue that Tarantino's films seek to provide a new form of immediacy—a new way of making audiences sense and experience the cinematic image through the body first. This drive toward a new kind of cinematic "affect" is based on the immediate fear and paranoia provoked in white American viewers when confronted by images of black bodies and black culture—and in particular the urban black male body. These sensations emanate from what Judith Butler, after Frantz Fanon, has called "a racial disposition of the visible" in which images of black masculinity are seen and felt in American popular culture as sites of anarchy, primitivism, and meaningless, random violence.[5]

But this chapter also contends that *Pulp Fiction* is not simply reproducing a racist othering of black culture. The film reveals what Toni Morrison calls (in a different context) a contemporary "American Africanism" at work. Morrison detects a tendency to associate blackness with immediacy, authenticity, primitivism, the hip, and the affective within canonical texts of American literature.[6] She goes on to argue that the white cultural association of African-Americans with both a savage, meaningless violence and hipness and modernity, acts as a kind of feeding ground for the construction of white American cultural identity itself. This chapter argues that these kinds of associations are present within the images of whiteness and blackness within *Pulp Fiction*, and that the film's American

Africanism is most clearly manifested in the way that the cinematic body is placed in relation to images of the milieux of contemporary LA.

More specifically *Pulp Fiction* mimics the structure of the spatial and temporal relations between the body and urban space which form a major aspect of the aesthetics of the genre of the "hood film" or New Black Realism.[7] The relationship between images of African-American masculinity and images of the hood are key to the way that films like *Menace II Society* have been received by critics and commentators as a cinema which assaults the senses, and as being somehow more "real" than what is often referred to as formulaic Hollywood action film. The reasons for this can be explored by analyzing the structural relations between the cinematic black male body and the urban milieu. *Menace II Society* both reproduces and disturbs these relations through its manipulation of different styles of image—all of which have been conceptualized as signs of the real in the history of film and image criticism.

Pulp Fiction's mimesis of the urban spatial structures of the hood film is symptomatic of an aesthetic and political crisis in the Hollywood action film, and reveals a desire in *Pulp Fiction* to produce a white cinema beyond the nostalgic intertextuality of postmodern narrative film. The very fact that the film reveals this political and aesthetic crisis means the significance of this mimesis is more complex than the criticisms voiced by Spike Lee. It is the imagined blankness of white culture, and its need to feed off what it constructs as an affective and substantive blackness, that is placed under the spotlight. It is for this reason that I want to discuss these films in terms of what will be called the "white cultural imagination" of the United States—a deliberately loose term, designed to identify a viewing position, but a term that is fluid enough not to be fixed or essentialist. The white cultural imagination also signals a move in this chapter away from psychoanalytic discourses which tend to construct the relationship between white viewers and images of blackness in terms of fetishism and disavowal.[8] Tarantino's films are at times guilty of these practices, but the mimesis of black culture in *Pulp Fiction* is less a matter of repressing the anxieties aroused by the "other" than it is part of what Michael Taussig identifies as mimetic processes of contagion and tactility, in this case where the differences between the white cultural self and the "other" are always "polluted" by that "other."[9] Whiteness in the US is always affected and altered by the agency of black culture to the point where the racial boundaries between white and black have become blurred and difficult to determine.

THE GANGSTA FILM AND THE DANGEROUS BLACK BODY

Critical reception of New Black Realism and "gangsta" films, like *Menace II Society* and *Boyz N the Hood* (Singleton, 1991), has often tended to stress their ability to assault the senses of the viewer, and be more culturally authentic than roughly contemporaneous white action films such as the *Die Hard* and *Lethal Weapon* series. For instance, *Sight and Sound* called *Boyz N the Hood* "a tough raw film," while the *Hollywood Reporter* called the film a "knock-down assault on the senses" and "no mere studio genre piece."[10] The performances of African-American actors in the films have also provoked responses from critics which also stress the affective immediacy of the genre. Tom Doherty argues that "Ice Cube is Singleton's ace in the hood, the authentic human presence without whom the melodrama would play as travelogue."[11] He goes on to assert that "Ice Cube has the pent-up intensity of a caged panther . . . playing a role so close to home, he has the stance, the style, the slang, and the gaze that means business, and the girth to back it up."[12] This extraordinary construction of the animalistic qualities of Ice Cube's heavily stylized performance in *Boyz* is symptomatic of the way the hood film has been perceived as carrying an immediate viscerality within its images.

Boyz N the Hood in particular tended to arouse sensations of immediacy before it was even released, and one of the predominant instant responses to the film centered around its marketing strategies, and specifically its trailer. Many commentators condemned the film on the basis of the trailer alone because they felt that it would provoke black audiences into acts of "copycat" violence. Ed Guerrero notes this paranoia, arguing that "critics were quick to assert that *Boyz* raised the expectation of violence among its volatile youth audience" because of the inclusion in the trailer of "every instance of gunplay in the film." Guerrero goes on to argue that this emphasis was at odds with the reception of the film's narrative content with its "anti-violence message [and] father–son relationship at the film's moral center."[13]

Gene Siskel's reaction was typical of this response. Within the space of one paragraph this influential mainstream critic attacked the trailer on the basis of its images of violence and praised the film for its anti-violence message:

> If you look at the trailer you would think that the movie was strictly about gang action. I had heard a lot about the film in Cannes and then saw the trailer, and thought "this looks like trash." But then I saw the movie and thought it superb and very clearly anti-violence and very pro- taking responsibility for one's children and brothers and sisters.[14]

Responding to the criticism of the trailer, John Singleton, the film's director (and the editor of the trailer), defended the promotional campaign on the grounds that *Boyz* was a Hollywood product, arguing that "[the trailer] got the motherfuckers into the theater and that's the bottom line. If the trailer for *Terminator II* showed the part where he agreed not to kill anyone, nobody would have gone to see it."[15] In the event, the *Hollywood Reporter* did report several cases of violence at the film's first screenings in the US, although the fact that several cinemas had taken extra security measures (close circuit cameras and extra security staff) was not cited as a provocative factor contributing to the violence.[16]

Todd Boyd has argued that white American fears of black audiences being provoked into copycat violence by images of black violence date back to the 1911 motion picture footage of the African-American boxer Jack Johnson fighting white champion Jim Jeffries.[17] The interracial fight, and Johnson's victory in particular, was perceived by white audiences as a spark that would induce similar interracial fight scenes on the streets of American cities—for Jane Gaines, a fundamentally racist anxiety:

> In this racialized image phobia we recognize a familiar old assumption about the public as dupes, unable to make a distinction between fiction and "reality," which takes on a special racial tinge here with the implication that blacks cannot see the difference between motion picture images and events that "happen" in real historical space and time.[18]

A similar assumption about potential black audiences of *Boyz N the Hood* underpinned the condemnation of the trailer by critics, suggestions that black audiences would be unable to distance themselves from the fictional events that the film portrayed, and the extra security measures taken at cinemas where it was first screened. But, judging from Siskel's comments, the people who were unable to distance themselves from the immediacy of the trailer were the white critics who condemned it. They were unable to perceive the trailer in terms of the accepted knowledge shared by audiences and the marketeers of action films—namely, that trailers are designed to assault the senses by bombarding the viewer with as many peaks of the action as possible in a very limited time span. One of the reasons for this is suggested by Jane Gaines when she argues that "white middle class talk about violence is smug and self righteous . . . this talk always fails to make a distinction between actual acts of brutality and representations of them."[19] This misrecognition is exactly what the white critics of the trailer of *Boyz N the Hood* were accusing its potential black audience of being guilty of. But, paradoxically, it was the failure of the critics to make a distinction between the represented violence of the trailer and the imagined violence of the potential audience of the film that was most noticeable in early reviews. This inability to distinguish between two types of black violence—images and real—is connected to the way that the white cultural imagination fabricates images of black bodies as immanently violent.

Frantz Fanon's work on the way that black male bodies connote an immediate sense of danger for the white Western subject is important here. In a well-known passage describing an encounter with a white French child on a train, he suggests that the perception of the black male as an entity to be scared of is produced by a historical racial schema where the black body is sketched out by "the other, the white man, who had woven me out of a thousand details, anecdotes, stories."[20] In other words, the history of the West has produced what Judith Butler calls a "racial disposition of the visible."[21] The significant point, in terms of the affective power of the hood film, is that this historical, schematic racial organization of perception is experienced as something immediate and real by the white cultural imagination. Fanon primarily engages with the ways in which othering of the black body by white culture affects the psyche of the colonial black male subject. But the association of the black male body in terms of anarchic violence and authenticity is also interesting in terms of what it reveals about white American identity—or what it is to be American in the late-twentieth century. As I noted earlier, Toni Morrison argues that there is an American Africanism present in white cultural identity, where not only are African-American people othered in terms of random violence and as a sign of urban modernity, but these attributes both constitute and are desired by the white cultural imagination. This desire is paradoxically expressed in terms of an immediate fear and powerlessness. As Judith Butler notes:

> In Fanon's recitation of racist interpellation, the black body is circumscribed as dangerous, prior to any gesture, any raising of the hand, and the infantilised white reader is positioned in the scene as one who is helpless in relation to that black body.[22]

When it comes to the relationship between American Africanism and American cinema of the 1990s, this anxiety, and the denial it reveals, is manifested in very particular ways.

In American popular culture it is black bodies in urban milieux which tend to evoke immediate sensations of fear and paranoia that such bodies are immanently dangerous and violent. One has only to think of the Rodney King episode and the two very different readings of the videotape by, first, the people who interpreted it as the police assaulting Rodney King, and, second, those people—including the Simi Valley Jury—who saw the tape as evidence of Rodney King's threat to the thin blue (white) line of the LAPD. What strikes Judith Butler as particularly significant about this second reading of the video is that it was not framed as a reading at all. The video as read by the jury of Simi Valley was still conceived as seen rather than interpreted—as evidence of the innate threat of African-American males rather than as a racially constructed meaning.[23]

The tendency to see the hood film as more real and immediate than white Hollywood action film is visible in the way that commentators have categorized and evaluated hood films by the accuracy of their representation of black life in South Central Los Angeles. Manthia Diawara describes hood films in a manner "that links them . . . to existent reality in Black communities," and indeed the filmmakers themselves have sometimes appeared to encourage this approach.[24] The Hughes brothers have made direct comparisons between their film and John Singleton's *Boyz N the Hood*, and are quoted as saying that in comparison to the latter, *Menace II Society* is based on "true, day to day life in Watts."[25] Both of these films focus on the story of a teenage African-American male facing the everyday, random violence and crime of the hood, and the racism of institutions, such as the police and schools, which exist outside of this milieu. The protagonists of both films face the inevitability of being caught up in these social crises, and are presented with the choice of escape. But in order to uncover the affective impact of these films (and *Menace II Society* in particular) we have to go beyond narrative representation. If we look at the films purely in terms of representation and narrative structure, it could be argued that both *Boyz N the Hood* and *Menace II Society* display very familiar patterns. Both are Oedipal linear narratives which have been seen dozens of times before in countless Hollywood films, and which familiarity and postmodernism have taught us bear no concrete relation to social reality.

MENACE II SOCIETY, AFFECT AND THE DISRUPTION OF WHITENESS

In spite of the comments made by the Hughes brothers, *Menace II Society* itself actively discourages the direct links between the images of the film and social reality of life in Watts by self-consciously drawing attention to the aesthetics and stylistics of the image itself. Even in the opening scenes of the film the images of Los Angeles reference several cinematic and non-cinematic styles of image, from the *noir*-like voice-over, to the sweeping movements and sudden close-ups of Scorsese's films, to black and white footage of 1960s newsreels, to the pixellated images of the videotape used on "true crime" TV shows such as *Cops*. This intertextual referencing continues throughout the movie and tends to negate the idea that what we are watching is intended to be viewed purely on the level of social realism. Indeed the social realism of the film calls to mind the classical gangster film, where violence and crimes—in films such as *Angels With Dirty Faces* (Curtiz, 1936)—were also "explained" in terms of the hard social conditions inhabited by the gangsters.

In this sense *Menace II Society* and other hood films are self-reflexive in the way they reference both the history of the gangster genre and non-cinematic images of urban crime. In the light of this postmodern sensibility we need to ask why questions of authenticity and realism seem to be at the forefront of their critical reception. We also need to ask why these films are described and perceived as assaulting the body and senses first.

In white postmodern film, intertextuality is, as Fredric Jameson notes, one of the key aesthetic constituents. He argues that intertextuality is largely a matter of surface play, of referencing and pastiche between texts and discourses, and that as such its aesthetic dominance in postmodern culture has contributed toward the waning of affect.[26] Part of the pleasure of watching a postmodern film is the game of "spot the reference"—an activity born out of an initiated, authoritative knowledge and, in Jameson's view, part of a contemporary situation in which feelings, emotion, and subjectivity have been displaced by "the emergence of a new kind of flatness or depthlessness, a new kind of superficiality."[27] To a large extent, and as Brian Massumi implies, Jameson makes this argument because he tends to equate affect with emotion to suggest that modernism was able to produce a distinctive depth of feeling.[28]

Massumi argues that, rather than affect and emotion being synonymous, "emotion and affect . . . follow different logics and pertain to different orders."[29] Emotion is derived from the narratives which are made from images, where affect is inserted into "semantically and semiotically formed progressions, into narrativizable action–reaction circuits, into function and meaning."[30] In other words, emotion is caused when the viewer either produces or is given narrative by which to make sense of and recognize images. In contrast, Massumi equates affect with intensity, suggesting that "intensity is embodied in purely automatic reactions most directly manifested in the skin—at the surface of the body, at its interface with things," with vision being one of the most tactile of these surfaces.[31] Intensity or affect is disconnected from the signifying order or meaning, in the sense that it is a moment which is outside of the spatial coordinates of a narrative, and outside of the meaning we make of films through narrative, as Brian Massumi has explained:

> It is a state of suspense, potentially of disruption. It is like a temporal sink, a hole in time as we conceive of it and narrativize it. It is not exactly passivity, because it is filled with motion, vibratory motion, resonation. And yet it is not exactly activity, because the motion is not of a kind that can be directed (if only symbolically) toward practical ends in a world of constituted objects and aims (if only on screen).[32]

At the affective moment when the image first assaults us, we are temporarily outside meaning. At the same time this moment of disruption also has an impact on the way in which we make meaning. Massumi is describing a body-first way of knowing in the sense that in the reception of images, we are subject to affect in the first instance and this material bodily response subsequently becomes meaning. If affect is manifested at the surface of the body, postmodernism, argues Massumi, is characterized by a surfeit of affect rather than a waning because of the proliferation of images which characterizes postmodernity.

The distinction between affect produced by and feelings or emotions derived from the narrative organization of images is important in thinking through the ways in which *Menace II Society* seeks to provoke a visceral response in the white cultural imagination. It is also a distinction which is difficult to absolutely maintain when considering the question of the dangerous black male body in contemporary American popular culture. On the one hand, the dangerous black body can be thought of in narrative or discursive terms as a stereotype and representation constructed through years of American history. On the other hand, Judith Butler's discussion of the Rodney King case and the initial critical reaction to the hood film suggests that images of black male bodies are experienced as powerfully affective before meaning (conscious or unconscious) is made.

With Massumi's definition of affect in mind, it is no surprise that the abundance of intertextuality in films like *Menace II Society* should produce an immediate bodily response rather than a cognitive one. Keeping up with the range and speed of the intertextual allusions in the opening sequences of the film alone makes it difficult to produce a coherent narrative by which one might explain or "own" the images. But the intertextuality in the film is also combined with the affective power of the dangerous black male body on the white cultural imagination both to reveal a crisis in the aesthetics and politics of white Hollywood action genres, and to disturb the authority of white discourses around Hollywood film, in both its classical and contemporary forms.

This is most marked in the figure of O-Dog who is seen murdering Korean shopkeepers in the opening scenes of the film. O-Dog is an exaggerated embodiment of all the white cultural imagination's affective responses to images of black masculinity. He is shown as unpredictably and randomly violent, liable to kill at the slightest provocation, and with no regret. He is described in the film by Caine's voiceover as the "craziest nigger alive, young, black and doesn't give a fuck, America's nightmare" (**16**). The film seems to be trying to gain as much

16 "America's nightmare," O-Dog (Larenz Tate) in the Hughes Brothers' *Menace II Society* (1993) (Copyright New Line Cinema, 1993)

affect as possible by inflating the fears and paranoia of the white cultural imagination. But at the same time, the film draws attention to the fact that O-Dog is also connected to a cultural and cinematic history—a history that has been conceived in white terms. The figure of O-Dog is drawn from a tradition of white gangster films, ranging from Jimmy Cagney's unpredictable, grapefruit-squashing, refinery-burning outlaw in classic gangster films like *The Public Enemy* (Wellman, 1931) and *White Heat* (Walsh, 1949) to the Scorsesean figure who does not recognize the limits of his gangster milieu—figures such as Johnny Boy in *Mean Streets* (1973) and Tommy in *Goodfellas* (1990). *Menace II Society* creates a connection between the affective responses provoked by the images of violent black masculinity and the constant evocation of the history of the genre—the film makes this link quite clear at several points when we see Caine watching old gangster movies. This resonation between affect and cultural knowledge forces the white imagination to realize that the immediacy with which the figure of O-Dog is randomly violent is drawn from predominantly white figures in predominantly white cinema. There is a kind of feedback from the affective and bodily response produced by O-Dog, which, perhaps, forces the viewer to reflect on the apparently non-racial construction of the white gangster.

The film does more than just reaffirm white fears of unpredictable black violence by highlighting a white American racist organization and disposition of the visible. The film *also* reveals the crisis of belief in the structures of what Gilles Deleuze calls the cinema of the action-image. The cinema of the action-image portrays characters in an organic relationship to the milieux in which they find themselves, such that the milieu and the actions they undertake reciprocally condition and are logically connected to each other through narrative; this cinema is in crisis once this relationship appears to be broken. The structures of action-image cinema are most firmly embedded within classical Hollywood. Deleuze argues that one of the fundamental constituents of the realism of the action-image in classical Hollywood cinema is the belief that there are concrete sensory-motor relations between the individual protagonist and the milieu of the film, and moreover that the individual protagonist can have a definable effect on his milieu—that protagonists have the ability to change their cinematic milieu through individual actions.[33] The realism of, or belief in, the action-image is, in other words, dependent on the ideology of the American Dream, where individuals are strongly rooted in a community, and at the same time have the power to recognize, be recognized and, on an individual level, change that community. Perhaps the ultimate example of this structure is George Bailey and the community of Bedford Falls in *It's a Wonderful Life* (Capra, 1946)—a film which is directly referenced by *Menace II Society* as being anachronistic and beyond belief. Deleuze argues that this belief in the concrete sensory-motor relations between the individual protagonist and cinematic milieu is no longer possible—largely because such belief no longer has any grounding in the extra-cinematic world, and is no longer a dominant ideology.[34]

The striking aspect of *Menace II Society* (and other New Black Realism films) is that there is an overwhelmingly concrete connection between the main protagonist, Caine, and the community of the hood. Like the milieux of the cinema of the action-image, the space of the hood is presented as a social totality in which the bonds between the protagonists and their particular milieu are concrete and immutable. The film constantly draws attention to this with its focus on LA as a partitioned city full of no-go areas for its main protagonists and more marginal characters. Like George Bailey in *It's a Wonderful Life*, the central protagonist, Caine, is never able to leave his cinematic world.

Part of the reason for this is that *Menace II Society* is, to some extent, aiming at a representation of the social reality of the limited mobility of young African-American audiences in Watts. But the film also works in another, more cinematic way on the white cultural imagination. The strictly enforced confines of the cinematic milieu of the hood evoke the violent affective structures of the cinematic experience itself. As Noël Burch notes, there are structures of aggression in the cinematic experience which have their "source in that very special, almost hypnotic relationship," a relationship

> that is established between screen and viewer as soon as the lights go down in the theatre . . . Whatever his level of critical awareness, a viewer face to face with the screen is completely at the mercy of the filmmaker, who may do violence to him at any moment and by any means.[35]

The physical and psychic constraints of the images of the hood which New Black Realism conveys echo the restraints the film viewer experiences in terms of physicality and consciousness—assaulted by the rays of light flickering on the screen in the darkened auditorium of the cinema. There is, in other words, a particularly strong mimetic connection between the affective black body and urban milieu, on the one hand, and the white cinema viewer, on the other.

Menace II Society strategically uses the affective urban black body to do violence to the white cultural imagination. The constant referencing to predominantly white genres of urban cinema and the way that urban space is configured and structured in *Menace II Society* highlights the fact that it is no longer possible for white cinema to produce an affective response with these familiar spatial structures. The white cultural and cinematic imagination is constructed as a kind of blank space which needs to, and has always needed to, feed off an American Africanism to provide affective substance. This crisis is not one defined in terms of box office performance—there are of course still very commercially successful films made which display strong sensory-motor connections between the protagonist and the milieu, but the response provoked by these films is one of nostalgia through intertextual knowledge rather than that of affect.

PULP FICTION AND MIMING THE HOOD

Pulp Fiction displays both a knowledge of the crisis of the action-image and a desire to resolve that crisis by miming the aesthetic spatial structures of the "gangsta" film.

   This self-reflexive awareness of the crisis of the action-image is nowhere more apparent than in the relations between the milieu of Los Angeles and the protagonists. The LA of *Pulp Fiction* is predominantly a space of rootlessness, with no visibly present central milieu or individual protagonist. LA is shown as what Deleuze would call an "any-space-whatever" in both temporal and spatial terms.[36] Characters appear to drift in and out of neutral, non-definable spaces, such as coffee shops, motel rooms, bars, and apartments. The protagonists appear to have no concrete relations with these spaces, and seem to stroll, like Deleuze's nomad, from one to another. The sense of instability is compounded by the non-definable era of these spaces. We travel from the contemporary space of the apartment block, to *The Big Combo's* boxing ring backstage, to the Godardian motel room where Butch and Fabienne play out their interminable love scene. Characters wander in and out with what on first viewing seems to be no definable purpose or reason. Unlike the well-defined and tightly structured space of the hood, this LA seems to be a space of surface and postmodern intertextuality with no concrete sensory-motor relations between protagonists and milieu.

   But beneath this surface flow and "never-never land" texture, there is an often unseen center to this LA present in the omnipotent figure of the black gangsta, Marcellus (**17**). Marcellus hovers over all the narratives and functions as the one concrete link between the protagonists and the milieu of the LA underworld. He

17 "The omnipotent figure of the black gangsta," Marcellus (Ving Rhames) in Quentin Tarantino's *Pulp Fiction* (1994) (Copyright Buena Vista International, 1994)

is the authoritative and controlling center of the movie's narrative in the sense that it is he who can get things done, and it is he who functions as the limit of what the other characters can and cannot do.

The construction of the African-American as a sign of cultural authority within the flux of modernity and postmodernity is of course one aspect of Toni Morrison's American Africanism, but Marcellus also functions as a fantasy site of non-symbolizable affect within the nomadic and dream-like milieu of *Pulp Fiction*. By intertextual association, *Pulp Fiction* also constructs the gangsta film as a cinematic genre in which affect is still possible. This construction is carried out as a mimesis of what, for the white cultural imagination, is the unpredictable, random violence and unsymbolizable depth of black bodies.

It is the film's torture and rape scene that above all equates the unknowable depth of blackness with the affective potential and "depth" of the cinematic experience. It is also this scene which most clearly illuminates *Pulp Fiction*'s construction of the gangsta film as a cinematic genre in which affect is still possible. The build-up to this scene self-reflexively plays out the racialized construction of the random meaningless violence of the black gangsta. The shots fired by

Marcellus at Butch which hit an innocent bystander echo white paranoid fears around the urban black body as a site of random, unpredictable violence—even though the viewer knows that Marcellus has very good narratological reasons for shooting Butch. After the randomness of this violence and the banal, nomadic, "any-space-whatever" setting of the chase, the film places Butch, Marcellus, and the viewer within the confines of a torture basement. The spatial coordinates of the torture room, like the warehouse in *Reservoir Dogs*, evoke the space of the hood in its limitations and constraints, from which there is no escape. The two protagonists are literally tied into the milieu as they sit bound to their chairs by their hillbilly captors, Zed and Maynard. The space and situation of the protagonists echoes that of the cinematic apparatus in which the cinematic affect comes from the assault of the images as the viewer sits in a darkened auditorium. But, as well as being a place of affective visual assault, the torture chamber, through intertextual association, suggests that the space of the urban hood and the black body are spaces of the Real and of unsymbolizable bodily depth. Through its use of depth-of-field and slow-motion as Marcellus is carried away to be raped, the scene presents the viewer with a series of spaces which, like Butch, we want to see, but cannot. Eventually most of these spaces are opened up to our voyeuristic view—with the exception of one. The camera cannot move into the body of Marcellus. The interior of the body of Marcellus presents a barrier to representation, and therefore a space of unsymbolizable affect, beyond white cultural knowledge.

The way that blackness and the black body become a barrier to the viewer's curious gaze in this scene is also reminiscent of the titillating but obstructive language of rap, as it is used in the hood film. The difficulty that white audiences have in understanding rap occurs at the time when the desire to find meaning in the dialogue in the hood film is at its most intense. Mark Winokur notes that our "own ignorance of black codes is being signified—our desire to be titillated is turned against us."[37] The rape of Marcellus works in a similar fashion. Once Butch opens the door to the torture room, our desire to see behind it is replaced by the shock of the rape. Our voyeuristic gaze is turned back onto us as in the "reactive gaze" that Carol Clover notes assaults the viewer in many horror films.[38] Not only is Marcellus' body a space where the desire to see depth in the image is thwarted, but it is also the source of an affective shock.

The fact of Marcellus' body being penetrated by hillbillies—straight out of movies such as *Deliverance* (Boorman 1973) and *The Hills Have Eyes* (Craven 1977)—is also significant here, in terms of identifying *Pulp Fiction*'s politics of race. Carol Clover suggests that the figure of the hillbilly has become a kind of repository of all the racist features reserved in classical Hollywood for the African-American—unpredictable violence, sexual deviancy, lack of intelligence, sophistication, or moral code.

Clover argues that films like *Deliverance* appeal to both white and black audiences because of the hillbilly's association with the unsophisticated racism of the Ku Klux Klan. Hillbillies are easy targets because they are other to the sophisticated urban white or black viewer.[39] But the hillbillies in *Pulp Fiction* also point toward the more complex issue of the construction of white culture as surface, discursive blankness, and blackness as a substantive bodily source of affective depth. The self-conscious citationality of the film's portrayal of Zed and Maynard reveals the American Africanism which saturates *Pulp Fiction*. White culture as embodied by these cinematic figures is a surface space of random and meaningless intertextuality which constructs blackness as a condition of desirable authenticity.

CONCLUSION

As we have seen, the dynamics of mimesis in the aesthetic structures of urban space and urban bodies in both *Pulp Fiction* and *Menace II Society* raises some deeply complex political questions. Spike Lee's criticisms of Tarantino depend on a notion of the fetish which is too rigid a concept to describe the cultural flow between white and black culture. The fetish ultimately depends on the phallus in the sense that underlying the imitation of black culture is a knowing authority and a clear and substantive definition of what white culture is. This knowledge is not always present in *Pulp Fiction*. In fact, the authority of white culture is a question which the film is always provoking, through the ways that the milieu of LA and its protagonists are displayed in terms of rootlessness, and its intertextuality has an almost arbitrary quality. At the same time, despite the affect of randomness provoked by the film on first viewing, there is quite clearly a precise spatial and temporal structure governing it, and this is largely based around the figure of Marcellus. But the torture scene demonstrates a self-reflexive awareness that the film (and, by extension, the white cultural and cinematic imagination) depends on an American Africanism which constitutes black culture as being more real, affective, and hip.

In the end, to try and explain the political meaning of these films in terms of what they are "trying to say" is a futile gesture. They do not work as directly discursive political commentaries on the mimetic flow between white and black culture. But at the same time they do shed light on the way in which US cultural and cinematic identity has been constructed in racial terms and through the use of bodies and urban spaces as sites of affect.

NOTES

1. Lee accuses Tarantino of wanting to be an "honorary black man," placing the word "nigger" in his screenplay because of the word's "cool and trendy" connotations. See *Daily Variety*, December 17 1997, p. 1. For the history of, and discussion provoked by, this criticism see Carter, *The Independent*, December 3 1998, p. 32.
2. Perhaps one of the most famous examples of this is the former West Coast hip-hop band NWA ("Niggers with Attitude").
3. Michael Rogin, "Blackface, White Noise: The Jewish Jazz Singer Finds His Voice," *Critical Inquiry*, 18, 1992, pp. 417–53.
4. Quentin Tarantino, quoted in *"Jackie Brown," Sight and Sound*, 4, 5, 1998, pp. 10–11.
5. Judith Butler, "Endangered/Endangering: Schematic Racism and White Paranoia," in Robert Gooding-Williams, ed., *Reading Rodney King, Reading Urban Uprising*, London: Routledge, 1993, pp. 15–23. Butler argues that the Rodney King episode is symptomatic of this organization of the visible.
6. Toni Morrison, *Playing in the Dark: Whiteness and the Literary Imagination*, London: Picador, 1993.
7. New Black Realism is a term derived from Manthia Diawara's article "Black American Cinema: The New Realism," in Manthia Diawara, ed., *Black American Cinema*, London: American Film Institute/Routledge, 1993, pp. 3–25. Diawara categorizes a number of films (all of them directed by African-Americans in the early 1990s) which set their actions within the urban 'hoods of both East and West Coast US cities. Diawara includes films such as *Boyz N the Hood* (John Singleton, 1991), *Juice*

(Ernest Dickerson, 1991) and *Straight Outta Brooklyn* (Matty Rich, 1991). See also Manthia Diawara, "*Noir* by *Noirs*: Toward a New Realism in Black Cinema," in Joan Copjec, ed., *Shades of Noir*, London: Verso, 1993, pp. 261–79.

8. See, for instance, the discussions around fetishism, disavowal, and race in Stuart Hall, ed., *Representation: Cultural Representation and Signifying Practices*, London: Sage, 1997, pp. 264–9.

9. Michael Taussig, *Mimesis and Alterity: A Particular History of the Senses*, London: Routledge, 1993, p. 25.

10. Peter Brunette, "Singleton's Street Noises," *Sight and Sound*, 1, 4, 1991, p. 4; and the *Hollywood Reporter*, 318, July 12 1991, p. 16.

11. Jaquie Jones and Tom Doherty, "Two Takes on *Boyz N the Hood*," *Cineaste*, 18, 4, 1991, p. 16.

12. Ibid., p. 16.

13. Ed Guerrero, *Framing Blackness*, Philadelphia: Temple University Press, 1993, p. 183.

14. Gene Siskel, quoted in Andrea King, *Hollywood Reporter*, July 15 1991, p. 122.

15. Quoted in Brunette, p. 2.

16. Andrea King, *Hollywood Reporter*, 318, July 16 1991, pp. 1, 6; and *Hollywood Reporter*, 318, July 12 1991, pp. 9, 16.

17. Todd Boyd in Jane Gaines, "Films That Make You Want to Fight Back (And Why White People Fear Them)," unpublished manuscript.

18. Ibid.

19. Ibid.

20. Frantz Fanon, *Black Skins, White Masks*, New York: Grove Press, 1967, pp. 110–13. The passage I am referring to reads as follows:
"In the white world the man of color encounters difficulties in the development of his bodily schema. Consciousness of the body is solely a negating activity. It is a third-consciousness. The body is surrounded by an atmosphere of certain uncertainty.
'Look a Negro!' It was an external stimulus that flicked over me as I passed by. I made a tight smile.
'Look a Negro!' It was true. It amused me.
I made no secret of my amusement.
'Mama, see the Negro! I'm frightened!' Frightened!
Frightened! Now they were beginning to be afraid of me. I made up my mind to laugh myself to tears, but laughter had become impossible."

21. Judith Butler, "Endangered/Endangering: Schematic Racism and White Paranoia," in Robert Gooding-Williams, ed., *Reading Rodney King, Reading Urban Uprising*, London: Routledge, 1993, p. 18.

22. Butler, p. 18.

23. Butler, pp. 18–23.
24. Manthia Diawara, ed., *Black American Cinema*, London: American Film Institute/ Routledge, 1993, p. 24.
25. Amy Taubin, "Girl N the Hood," *Sight and Sound*, 3, 8, 1993, p. 14.
26. Fredric Jameson, *Postmodernism, or the Cultural Logic of Late Capitalism*, London: Verso, 1991, p. 10. Jameson's larger analysis of the place of affect and intertextuality within postmodernism is pertinent to my argument and can be found in *Postmodernism or The Cultural Logic of Late Capitalism*, pp. 1–54. Brian Massumi has also pointed toward the importance of Jameson's thesis that postmodernism is characterized by the "waning of affect." See Massumi, "The Autonomy of Affect," in Paul Patton, ed., *Deleuze: A Critical Reader*, Oxford: Blackwell, 1996, p. 221.
27. Jameson, pp. 9–10.
28. Massumi in Patton, ed. *Deleuze: A Critical Reader*, pp. 217–40.
29. Massumi, p. 221.
30. Massumi, p. 221.
31. Massumi, p. 219.
32. Massumi, p. 219.
33. Gilles Deleuze, *Cinema 1: The Movement-Image*, trans. Hugh Tomlinson and Barbara Habberjan, London: Athlone Press, 1986, pp. 115–215.
34. Deleuze, *Cinema I*, p. 206.
35. Noël Burch, *Theory of Film Practice*, Princeton, NJ: Princeton University Press, 1981, p. 124.
36. Deleuze defines the any-space-whatever as the "marshalling yard, disused warehouse—the undifferentiated fabric of the city." Deleuze, *Cinema I*, p. 208.
37. Mark Winokur, "Marginal Marginalia: The African-American Voice in the Nouvelle Gangster Film," *Velvet Light Trap*, vol. 35, Spring 1995, p. 26.
38. Clover, pp. 191–202.
39. Clover writes, "If 'redneck' once denoted a real and particular group, it has achieved the status of a kind of universal blame figure, the 'someone else' held responsible for all manner of American social ills. The great success of the redneck in that capacity suggests that anxieties no longer expressible in ethnic or racial terms have become projected onto a safe target—safe not only because it is (nominally) white, but because it is infinitely displaceable onto someone from the deeper South or the higher mountains or the further desert." Clover, p. 135.

10

CITY SPACES AND CITY TIMES: BAKHTIN'S CHRONOTOPE AND RECENT AFRICAN-AMERICAN FILM

PAULA J. MASSOOD

In the early 1990s, African-American filmmaking experienced what has been called a "renaissance" because an unprecedented number of films directed by Black filmmakers were released.[1] Referred to as "New Jack Cinema," "New Black Realism," "Black Urban Cinema," or "hood films," films such as *New Jack City* (Mario Van Peebles, 1991), *Straight Out of Brooklyn* (Matty Rich, 1991), *Boyz N the Hood* (John Singleton, 1991), *Juice* (Ernest Dickerson, 1992), and *Menace II Society* (Allen and Albert Hughes, 1993) signified a change in style and thematic focus in American cinema.[2] All of the films were written, directed, and produced by young African-American men and focused specifically on Black subject matter. Most included narratives set in time frames that were contemporaneous with the year of their release. And the majority of hood films located their drama (and sometimes melodrama) in what would soon become the recognizable Black neighborhoods of Los Angeles and New York—two cities (or parts of cities) with long histories of African-American occupancy and cultural (though not always material) ownership.

More specifically, these films focused on young male protagonists, included an inner city *mise en scène*, and incorporated a stylization referencing the fashion, the dialect, and the music associated with urban African-American youth culture at the time of their release. In narrative, setting, costume, and sound, the city played a central role in the focus and concerns of all of the films. These characteristics of hood films became so familiar that by mid-decade they were standardized and packaged both domestically and globally as a means of connoting an African-American social sphere that foregrounded the importance of specific urban spaces, the related issues of poverty and crime, and a focus on defining Black masculinity. In the United States, hood film conventions subsequently appeared in genres as disparate as the Western (*Posse*, Mario Van Peebles, 1993), the action film (*Lethal Weapon 3*, Richard Donner, 1992, and *Die Hard With a Vengeance*, John McTiernan, 1995), the political satire (*Bulworth*, Warren Beatty, 1998), and the horror film (*Leprechaun 5: In the Hood*, Rob Spera, 2000). Furthermore, the conventions had international significance as they crossed over into films such as Matthieu Kassovitz's *La Haine* (1995), Lee Tamahori's *Once Were Warriors* (1995), and Jean-Pierre Beckolo's *Quartier Mozart* (1992). In these latter examples, African-American cultural referents were particularly adaptable to post-colonial political situations and were used to signify the social, economic, and cultural repression and struggle experienced by "minority populations" living in large cities—Paris, Auckland, and Yaoundé, respectively.

Many of the critical discussions of hood films have focused on the industrial, aesthetic, and political questions raised by the films to the exclusion of an in-depth analysis of the role of the city in African-American life and culture in the twentieth century in general, and its relationship to the hood genre in particular. The city is a given. It is true that city spaces such as Los Angeles and New York enable hood films by providing an environment which instantiates certain elements of the narrative. It is equally true, however, that hood films did not begin cultural representations of African-Americans in cities. City spaces, especially Harlem and Chicago's South Side, have a long history in African-American film and literature before that—a history that precedes Spike Lee's cinematic inscriptions of Brooklyn and John Singleton's or Allen and Albert Hughes' constructions of the South Central urbanscape. This history is both industrial and sociological in nature, extending through race film production of the early twentieth century and blaxploitation film from the 1970s and referencing the often fraught policy positions taken by the US government toward the urban African-American poor.

The city's often contradictory, though paramount, role in Black American life first made an extended appearance in African-American film in the "race films" produced by Black, white, and mixed production companies from the 1920s through the mid-1940s.[3] Films such as The Colored Players' *Scar of Shame* (1921), Oscar Micheaux's *Within Our Gates* (1920) and *Murder in Harlem* (1935), and Spencer Williams' *Dirty Gertie from Harlem* (1946), were both relevant to and popular with an African-American audience that was increasingly urbanized because of successive waves of migration that brought Black migrants from the rural South to the industrialized North (often referred to as "The Great Migration") during and after World War One. During World War Two, many migrants moved to the cities of Los Angeles, Oakland, and San Francisco in order to work in the defense industries located on the West Coast. In these films, as in the Harlem Renaissance novels, short stories, plays, and poems published at roughly the same time, the image of the city promised freedom and mobility on a personal, political, and economic level. Yet the actual cities were also perilous (especially to the Black bourgeoisie alarmed at the large influx of uneducated, unmannered migrants to the city), and many films and novels from the 1920s and the 1930s were concerned with exposing the lure and threat of crime (what would simply be called "the life" by the 1970s) presented by urban spaces. Race film producers were actually developing these focuses and urban tropes from earlier writers and thinkers. For example, in 1899, W. E. B. DuBois voiced his concerns about the city in *The Philadelphia Negro*. According to DuBois, the "peculiarly pressing social problems of poverty, ignorance, crime, and labor" presented the greatest threat to Philadelphia's Black residents.[4] This literary and cinematic tradition also can be read with reference to the context of its literary and cinematic equivalents in modernism. In particular, modernism's use of the nineteenth-century topos of the "Dark City" created urban spaces that had "many contradictory meanings," most clearly exemplified in modernist poetry by writers such as T. S. Eliot and in films such as *Metropolis* (Fritz Lang, 1926), *Sunrise* (F. W. Murnau, 1927), and, later, in the *films noir* produced by Hollywood in the 1940s and early 1950s.[5]

Ironically, while the city was a main focal point in literature and film produced by both African-Americans and whites at this time, its explorations were almost exclusively segregated from one another, at least in their narratives and viewing situations. While the city promised freedom, it often, even in the northern United States, did not extend to the public spheres of most theaters. When Blacks and whites mixed, especially in the diegesis of films, they did so in places and times far removed from the city as if the narratives themselves were trying nervously to quell the fear of racial mixing. During the same years as companies produced early sound-era race films (1930s–1940s), for example, Hollywood released a series of musicals featuring all-Black casts. These films, such as *Hallelujah!* (King Vidor, 1929), *The Green Pastures* (Marc Connelly and William Keighley, 1936), and *Cabin in the Sky* (Vincente Minnelli, 1943), featured narratives focusing exclusively on Black subject matter and were set in a timeless, Southern space rather than in a contemporary urban setting that would have been more familiar to the films' African-American audiences. If the city entered the narratives, it was often in the form of a threat to the idyllic stability of the family and of the home. This would remain the case until the release of *Stormy Weather*, directed by Andrew L. Stone, in 1943, when Hollywood acknowledged the city—or the cities of New York, Memphis, Chicago, and Los Angeles—and its African-American communities.[6] These films ultimately exhibit a similar fear about the evils of the city as race films, but unlike the uplifting narratives of the latter, Black-cast musicals repressed and literally contained the fear of a rising African-American urban population within an idyllic rural past.

After disappearing from screen narratives from the late 1940s through the late 1960s, African-American city spaces reappeared in African-American film in the 1970s, playing a crucial role in both blaxploitation films and the films made by the LA School throughout the decade. While differing in conditions of production, projected audience, and political intent, films such as Melvin Van Peebles' *Sweet Sweetback's Baadasssss Song* (1971), Gordon Parks, Jr's *Superfly* (1972), and Haile Gerima's *Bush Mama* (1976) indicate the complex and contradictory roles the city played in African-American life in the 1970s, a time influenced by waves of urban rebellions in the 1960s and the demonization of the Black family by Daniel P. Moynihan's *The Negro Family* (1964), which projected an urban world of absent Black fathers and single welfare mothers into the nation's imagination. Additional stresses included increasing poverty, the warehousing of many poor urban residents in housing projects, and the abandonment of the inner city as a whole by the United States government in the 1970s as more affluent middle class whites and Blacks left the cities for the suburbs.

What this brief overview suggests is the ways in which the history of African-American movement and migration, and the rising importance of urban spaces in Black life contributed to contemporary Black popular culture, especially (though not limited to) the cinematic representation of African-American urban experiences. African-American culture is not only linked but specifically identified with the city, as made evident by Charles Scruggs' observation that "In the twentieth century it became Blacks . . . whose orientation was distinctly urban."[7] The relationship between twentieth-century African-American culture and the city, especially the tropes of migration and modernity that such a framework foregrounds, introduces history and the concomitant questions of mobility, progress, and stasis into a discussion of contemporary African-American city spaces in film because it was migration that brought many Blacks to the cities and it was the city that would place economic and social limits on a multitude of Black residents. It is precisely these tropes that still fuel many of the present-day films as well, even playing a central role in Singleton's *Shaft* (2000), which includes a sub-plot involving a character's desire to maneuver through the white world of Manhattan's more affluent downtown neighborhoods, an area that he feels is both off-limits and far removed from his impoverished South Bronx home. What we have to take into account then is the ways in which contemporary African-American film registers and responds to this history (or time) in its representations of certain cities (or spaces).

Mikhail Bakhtin's concept of the "chronotope" offers a productive framework toward understanding the complex intertwining of a text's spatial and temporal coordinates, whether it be the contemporary city presented in hood films or, as we see in films such as *A Rage in Harlem* (Bill Duke, 1992), *Devil in a Blue Dress* (Carl Franklin, 1995), and more metaphorically in *Clockers* (Spike Lee, 1995) and *Down in the Delta* (Maya Angelou, 1998), the acknowledgment of the city's rural past.[8] As defined by Bakhtin a "chronotope" is "a unit of analysis for studying texts according to the ratio and nature of the temporal and spatial categories represented."[9] It is, as the term suggests, a *topos* (a place, person, figure) which embodies (or is embodied by) *chronos*, time. The chronotope—Bakhtin offers the road, the castle of Gothic fiction, Balzac's salon, and the threshold, as examples—functions as "materialized history," where temporal relationships are made literal by the objects, spaces, or persons that embody them.[10]

In hood films the chronotope of "the hood" is the recognizable African-American city spaces of South Central Los Angeles and Brooklyn, and a time frame whose immediacy is connoted by references to contemporary popular culture and historical events and figures (for example, to rappers like Ice Cube and politicians such as Ronald Reagan in John Singleton's *Boyz N the Hood*). Additionally, the films' narratives and sign systems stress the trope of constraints on mobility, especially on movement within and the ability to move out of the clearly defined (and often strictly maintained) borders of the Black city. Identifying the hood chronotope in such a manner indicates how space and time come to bear on cinematic inscriptions of the Black city because it illustrates the interconnections between the present moment and these spaces. It also provides a means for re-historicizing the contemporary city so that the hood can be understood in relation to its historical precedents, for instance, in references to a neighborhood's, an individual's, or a community's past.

Although for Bakhtin the chronotope was a novelistic device, it is relevant to cinematic narratives as well. Robert Stam states that the chronotope is

> even more appropriate to film than literature, for whereas literature plays itself out within a virtual, lexical space, the cinematic chronotope is quite literal, splayed out concretely across a screen with specific dimensions and unfolding in literal time . . . quite apart from the fictive time/space specific films might construct.[11]

Besides the "time/space" implied by its narratives and its actual material qualities (film and select digital-video speed, 24 fps, is defined in spatio-temporal terms), film offers an expanded way of understanding Bakhtin's concept of dialogism because it encompasses the specificity of cinematic discourses such as casting, performance, costume, setting, and sound, that are not as readily available to the literary text. In the cinema such discourses help to illuminate a text, a fact that is apparent in the aesthetic strategies of hood films, especially in many directors' decisions to cast hip-hop personalities such as Ice-T and Ice Cube, and to use their music on the soundtrack.[12] Ice Cube's presence in *Boyz N the Hood*, for example, initiates a chain of meanings related to his involvement in the rap group NWA (Niggas With Attitude) and his identification with the Los Angeles neighborhood of Compton. These references contribute authenticity to his role in *Boyz N the Hood* as a tough, drug-dealing thug from South Central.

Rather than existing as some arbitrary, unlocatable trope, the chronotope is directly linked to narrative, or, of particular concern to Bakhtin, narrative as it

relates to genre. As Katerina Clark and Michael Holquist observe, "The chronotope both defines genre and generic distinction and establishes the boundaries
between the various intrageneric subcategories of the major literary types."[13]
Specific chronotopes are linked to specific genres, often defining, or enabling, a
genre or subgenre. For example, in Bakhtin's construct, the road is almost
always associated with the quest tale. In cinematic terms, theorists such as
Vivian Sobchack have argued that night clubs and cocktail lounges are essential
elements in the *film noir* because they substitute for the home and contribute to
noir's ambivalence toward normative domesticity.[14]

The chronotope's links to genre make it a central theoretical construct for the
analysis of contemporary African-American film and toward an understanding
of the hood film as a genre. If we are to understand the chronotope as determining genre, then it makes sense that particular African-American genres might
be enabled by elements of space and time, especially those genres that privilege
certain spatio-temporal tropes, such as the contemporary city. This is especially
the case with the hood film because it is indisputable that it is defined by the
places and times in which its films are set, so much so that the genre is explicitly
named by the space mapped out by its films. In addition, references to the city—
place names, both specific and less determined, for example—were used in many
of the titles (*Boyz N the Hood*, *Straight Out of Brooklyn*, *South Central*). Without
such an acknowledgment of the city space, made even more contemporary
through the use of colloquialisms and slang, the hood film would have little
meaning for its audience.

This is particularly relevant when we analyze the hood chronotope in contemporary African-American film, especially in the hood films' rendering of what
appears to be reality. When we take into account the discourses of realism and
authenticity generated by contemporary African-American cinema and certain
strains of African-American film aesthetics, theory, and criticism, we can see the
burden of the assumption that the images under consideration somehow mirror
their historical context in a one-to-one correspondence. But the filmmakers'
conscious construction of a hood chronotope helps us to unpack these claims by
reminding us that what appears onscreen is a mediated construction of reality.
Clark and Holquist argue that "The chronotope is a bridge, not a wall [between]
the actual world and the world represented."[15] As this observation suggests, the

chronotope offers a more complex understanding of the relationship between the spatio-temporal discourses that generate genres and the world outside the text.

While Bakhtin discusses the direct link between the actual world and the text, he cautions against confusing one with the other:

> there is a sharp and categorical boundary line between the actual world as a source of representation and the world represented in the work. We must never forget this, we must never confuse . . . the *represented* world with the world outside the text (naive realism); nor must we confuse the author-creator of a world with the author as a human being (naive biographism).[16]

Bakhtin's comments bear directly on the consideration of urban cinematic chronotopes in his acknowledgment of the role that exterior reality may play in a text. This is also relevant to the whole of film theory, which for much of its existence has been occupied by interrogations of the relationship of either the film text or the cinematic apparatus to reality, from Rudolf Arnheim's identification of film's aesthetic distortions of reality to Baudrillardian evocations of hyper-reality. Such considerations are even more relevant when we take into account African-American filmmakers' overarching concern for representational and cultural verisimilitude as related to Hollywood's history of negative stereotypes and caricature. It is this concern that has been translated into the discourses of authenticity and "realness" that have circulated around African-American film since its very first inception in the Foster Photoplay Company's *The Railroad Porter* (1912). It seems particularly relevant to the hood film of the 1990s because of the style and techniques, many of which have been drawn from documentary filmmaking practices such as *cinéma vérité*.

However, many of the texts themselves caution against the "naive realism" feared by Bakhtin, thus complicating such notions as Clyde Taylor's description of African-American cinema's "realness dimension," defined as the establishment of "only the slightest departure from . . . contiguous offscreen reality."[17] This use of caution has been especially the case with many of the films of the 1990s. That filmmakers like Spike Lee, Allen and Albert Hughes, Mario Van Peebles, and (to a lesser extent) John Singleton consciously announce the constructed nature of their own films reminds us that what we are witnessing is not actuality, but rather a "refraction of a refraction" of reality.[18] For example, the

18, 19, 20, 21 "The link between politics and inner-city violence," John Singleton's *Boyz N the Hood* (1991) (Copyright Columbia Pictures Industries, 1991)

opening minutes of Singleton's *Boyz N the Hood* directly link Ronald Reagan's domestic policies as both governor of California and president of the United States to the economic and social conditions of South Central Los Angeles. The Hughes Brothers' *Menace II Society* follows a similar structure, but the causes of the living conditions in present-day Watts are traced further back in time, first to the Watts Rebellion of 1965 and then to the subsequent increase in drugs in the neighborhood in the 1970s. In both examples, the filmmakers foreground diegetic and extradiegetic references through technique. In *Boyz N the Hood*, shots of bullet-ridden posters from Reagan's 1984 presidential re-election campaign are synthesized in an Eisensteinian visual/aural montage sequence in which Reagan's visage (in cowboy hat and bandanna) collides with the sounds of gunshots. The audio-visual technique ruptures the diegesis, standing out in a film with a highly conventional narrative structure and continuity editing patterns, and it continues the link between politics and inner-city violence first introduced at the beginning of the film in title cards that provide sociological information about Black-on-Black crime (**18, 19, 20, 21**).

The Hughes Brothers, wanting to make a film that challenged Singleton's version of events, foreground technique much more explicitly and systematically

in *Menace II Society*.[19] Not only do they use the main protagonist's (Caine's) voiceover to narrate events, but he is unreliable at best and unlikeable for most of the film, thus preventing an unproblematic identification with the character as well as undermining the melodramatic potential of the narrative. While it may be a tragedy when one of the characters in *Boyz N the Hood* is murdered, it is less so in *Menace II Society* if we are to believe that tragedy depends at least in part on the attractiveness of a character.[20] Moreover, in *Menace II Society*, not only grainy black and white film stock demarcates the Watts Rebellion from what precedes and follows it, but the footage is also pixellated, making it nearly impossible to decipher the images. The scenes that follow, from a party during Caine's childhood in the 1970s, immediately appear in saturated reds and blues, not only mimicking color schemes associated with blaxploitation films from the same period but acting, in combination with both diegetic and nondiegetic music, to seduce the viewer into the almost celebratory and nostalgic pleasure of the party scenes, a pleasure which a brutal murder ruptures, effectively ending the scene.

As these examples indicate, many films, rather than reflecting reality (perhaps an impossibility from the beginning) instead dialogue with extradiegetic political discourses (many of which are visual), acknowledging context while concurrently using history for the film's own political and aesthetic ends, whether those are the increased visibility of African-American subject matter (a disarmingly simple and yet for white audiences a potentially threatening intent) or the attempt to examine race relations in Hollywood or in the United States as a whole. This point is vital for understanding the impact of the histories of African-American migration, the growth of urban areas, the Civil Rights movement, and American social policy in the films' narratives. Singleton's references to the speculative acquisition of South Central neighborhoods by outside investors in Furious' speech to Tre, Ricky, and some residents of Compton and the Hughes Brothers' rendering of nihilism in the character of O-Dog as "America's nightmare—young, Black, and don't give a fuck," are further examples of this dialogue. This double reflexivity with history and technique indicates that the construction of particular cinematic chronotopes, such as the hood chronotope, should be seen in relation to a larger historical framework yet should not be mistaken for that history because they are, as Ella Shohat and Robert Stam explain, "historically situated 'utterance[s]' . . . addressed by one socially constituted subject or subjects [the filmmaker, the cinematic apparatus, the conditions of production] to other socially constituted subjects, all of whom are deeply immersed in historical circumstance and social contingency."[21] Ultimately, hood films, and especially the chronotope that defines and enables them, help us understand the pressures and the constraints that context brings to representation and its analysis.

Furthermore, the relationship between the hood chronotope and context enables us to theorize difference (race, ethnicity, gender, sexuality) and its relationship to the construction of urban space in film texts. Shohat and Stam observe that chronotopes

> mediat[e] between the historical and the discursive [and] provid[e] fictional environments where historically specific constellations of power are made visible . . . There is nothing inherently sinister in this process, except to the extent that it is deployed asymmetrically, to the advantage of some national and racial imaginaries and to the detriment of others.[22]

When we analyze the hood chronotope we can identify the ways in which hood films self-consciously point to the "asymmetrical" relations of power that have often (over)determined representations of Black urban space. Not only have hood films placed historically invisible spaces on the screen, but their dialogue with their historical situation also links the politics of the film industry and the cinematic apparatus to a larger social context.

One of the best ways to chart the relationships between text and context, and between space and history, is through the identification of chronotopic motifs. Often texts and genres may be characterized by a primary chronotope, for instance the hood chronotope in *Boyz N the Hood*, a film set in a contemporary time and a recognizable city space by means of locators such as street signs, opening intertitles, and verbal referents. Yet other chronotopes may exist as either motifs or traces in texts that originate in other genres. In a sense, these motifs transcend particular genres or create new ones. Gary Morson and Caryl Emerson define a chronotopic motif as "a sign of a generic chronotope that is present in another genre. [It] serves as an 'aura' of another genre—a reminder of another space and time."[23] But this is not a passive relationship: chronotopes can co-exist and dialogue with one another as separate and yet related utterances. As Bakhtin explains, a fundamental characteristic of chronotopes is that they are "mutually inclusive, they co-exist, they may be interwoven with, replace, or oppose one another, contradict one another or find themselves in ever more complex relationships."[24]

Spike Lee's *Clockers* provides a complex example of this interrelationship of chronotopic motifs. In a film that combines the conventions of two city-based genres, the hood film and the *film noir*, Lee inexplicably inserts references to trains both by means of the main character's fascination with model trains and in his escape from the city via Amtrak at the film's conclusion, both of which are changes from the Richard Price novel upon which the film was based.[25] It is possible to read these references as chronotopic motifs of another time (the early twentieth century) and another place (the rural South), and their inclusion in the film helps solidify the relationship between African-American social and economic mobility and the train. Through the motif of the train, Lee expands the film's contemporary urban narrative with an explicit acknowledgment of Brooklyn's history as an African-American community formed soon after the Great Migration. In doing so, he links the urban present to its rural past.[26]

Mario Van Peebles' *Posse* offers another interesting use of chronotopic motifs, reversing those found in *Clockers*. *Posse* is a Western, set in the late nineteenth century and featuring a mostly African-American cast. In an attempt to situate the film in a larger generic tradition, Van Peebles includes many references to both classical and revisionist Westerns, often quoting from John Ford, Arthur Penn, and Sam Peckinpah. Additionally, he posits that the film continues the long history of the African-American Western because of his casting of performers such as Woody Strode, who made his career in white Westerns, and through the inclusion of footage from a number of films, such as *Harlem Rides the Range*, produced by race film companies in the late 1930s. This intertextuality was a novelty at the time because it referenced little known films from African-American history. More recently, Spike Lee has taken a similar approach to quoting from African-American film history in *Bamboozled* (2000).

Posse also references many of the conventions of the hood film. This is evident from the use of contemporary musical forms (especially rap and R & B) on the soundtrack, to the casting of rap personalities such as Big Daddy Kane and Tone Loc, to specific references to the 1992 riots in Los Angeles (with the inclusion of Rodney King's famous phrase "Can't we all just get along?").[27] Besides being a strategy to increase box office appeal, Van Peebles' references to more contemporary generic motifs connect the situation in present-day urban areas to the history of American settlement. He thus makes the suggestion that the problems of American inner cities are not so much the result of contemporary pressures such as drugs and crime as they are a result of a long history of economic materialism which led to the displacement of many mostly non-white peoples.

Since the mid-1990s the production of hood films has decreased and the renaissance seems to be over. Films directed by African-American filmmakers and featuring Black subject matter continue to be made but not nearly at the rate in which they were made in the early 1990s. Additionally, stories with an inner city focus have been replaced by films set in the more middle class milieu of American suburbs. Still, the hood continues as a motif in many films, most notably in Maya Angelou's *Down in the Delta* (1998), where it functions as the foil for a tale of southern, rural regeneration. Lee's *Bamboozled* (2000) also contains chronotopic motifs of the hood. Again, the specific conventions of the hood film, especially its links to urban youth culture, are used as the foil, this time, ironically, to suggest the absence of a knowledge of African-American, American, and film history.

African-American city spaces did not just appear with the release of *Boyz N the Hood*, *New Jack City*, *Straight Out of Brooklyn*, *Menace II Society*, or even Spike Lee's *Do The Right Thing* in 1989. They have a longer, more complex history in African-American culture which can be traced in African-American literature and film from the earliest decades of the twentieth century. Bakhtin's concept of the novelistic chronotope can be adapted for an African-American cinematic context, allowing us to see how the representation of Black city spaces brings together space and time. While enabling us to theorize the roles of history and the influence of context on the texts, the chronotope can also provide us with a means to a more complex understanding of the roles of exterior reality and the aesthetics of realism in the films by foregrounding a text's constructed nature. The chronotope reminds us that African-American city spaces have long and complex histories in American and African-American cinema.

NOTES

1. This is a reference to a cover story appearing in *Time Magazine* on October 10 1994 which proclaimed a "renaissance" in a cross-section of African-American arts, from dance and painting to literature and film. The number of films released supports the view that African-American film obtained increased visibility in the early 1990s; for example, in 1991, Hollywood studios and major independent distributors released a record twelve such feature films.

2. The phrase "New Jack" comes from Barry Michael Cooper's "New Jack City." The term was used by Cooper in 1987 as a reference to the city of Detroit. For more on this, see Nelson George, *Buppies, B-Boys, Baps and Bohos*, New York: HarperCollins, 1992, p. 31. "New Black Realism" comes from Manthia Diawara's "Black American Cinema: The New Realism," in Manthia Diawara, ed., *Black American Cinema*, New York: Routledge, 1993; and "Black Urban Cinema" comes from Elizabeth Mermin's "'Searing Portraits': The Persistence of Realism in Black Urban Cinema," *Third Text: Third World Perspectives on Contemporary Art and Culture*, 34, Spring 1996. I prefer the term "hood film" because I feel that it more accurately describes what young African-American filmmakers and musicians were trying to communicate about the world around them. More importantly, the term is adapted from their own words.

3. "Race films" were a group of films that were produced and exhibited for African-American audiences and which featured Black performers and subject matter. While many of the production companies featured African-American personnel,

the majority had some form of white technical or financial involvement as well. The best-known African-American producers were Oscar Micheaux, George and Noble Johnson, and Spencer Williams. The production of race films extended from shortly after 1910 through the 1940s, with the bulk of films produced in the 1920s and 1930s. Most companies were under-financed and operated on shoe-string budgets, often folding before a film was released. For more on race films, see Thomas Cripps, *Slow Fade to Black: The Negro in American Film, 1900–1942*, New York: Oxford University Press, 1977.

4. W. E. B. DuBois, "The Negro Problems of Philadelphia," in Richard T. LeGates and Frederic Stout, eds, *The City Reader*, New York: Routledge, 1996, p. 57.

5. James Naremore, *More Than Night: Film Noir in its Contexts*, Berkeley, CA: University of California Press, 1998, p. 44.

6. *Stormy Weather* is virtually an allegory for African-American migration. Its main character travels from Harlem, down the Mississippi to Memphis, back up to Chicago and finally west to Los Angeles through the course of the narrative. These migrations coincide with African-American migration between World Wars One and Two, which is also the timeframe of the narrative.

7. Charles Scruggs, *Sweet Home: Invisible Cities in the Afro-American Novel*, Baltimore: Johns Hopkins University Press, 1993, p. 15.

8. Of these films, *A Rage in Harlem* and *Devil in a Blue Dress* are revisionist adaptations of detective novels—the first from Chester Himes' *A Rage in Harlem* (original title *For the Love of Imabelle*) and the second from Walter Mosley's *Devil in a Blue Dress*, itself a revisionist *noir* novel. *Clockers* is also an adaptation of a novel by Richard Price. Like the other films, *Clockers* also utilizes *noir* conventions, though the film is more of a hybrid.

9. M. M. Bakhtin, in Michael Holquist, ed., *The Dialogic Imagination*, trans. Caryl Emerson and Michael Holquist, Austin: University of Texas Press, 1981, p. 425.

10. Bakhtin, p. 247.

11. Robert Stam, *Subversive Pleasures: Bakhtin, Cultural Criticism, and Film*, Baltimore: Johns Hopkins University Press, 1989, p. 11.

12. Films that employ such casting include: *New Jack City* and Ice-T; *Boyz N the Hood* and Ice Cube; *Juice* and *Above the Rim*, featuring Tupac Shakur; *Menace II Society* and Pooh Man, MC Eiht, and Yo Yo; *Posse* and Big Daddy Kane and Tone Loc; *Clockers* and Mekhi Phifer; *Set It Off* and Queen Latifah; and *Shaft* (2000) and Busta Rhymes. Hood films also went through a stage in which many of the films' links with rap music were parodied. The most notable example of this is *CB4*, a mockumentary of a gangsta rapper who moves into acting in film.

13. Katerina Clark and Michael Holquist, *Mikhail Bakhtin*, Cambridge, MA: The Belknap Press, 1984, p. 280.

14. See Vivian Sobchack, "Lounge Time: Postwar Crises and the Chronotope of *Film*

Noir," in Nick Browne, ed., *Refiguring American Film Genres: Theory and History*, Berkeley, CA: University of California Press, 1998, pp. 129–70.

15. Clark and Holquist, p. 279.

16. Bakhtin, p. 253.

17. Clyde Taylor, "Decolonizing the Image: New US Black Cinema," in Peter Steven, ed., *Jump Cut: Hollywood, Politics, and Counter Cinema*, New York: Praeger, 1985, p. 168. Taylor focuses specifically on the LA School from the 1970s, but his approach to film and authenticity has been reiterated in the 1980s and 1990s, most often by Spike Lee. For a response to Lee's appropriation of the language of authenticity, see Wahneema Lubiano's "But Compared to What?: Reading Realism, Representation, and Essentialism in *School Daze, Do The Right Thing*, and the Spike Lee Discourse," in Valerie Smith, ed., *Representing Blackness: Issues in Film and Video*, New Brunswick, NJ: Rutgers University Press, 1997, pp. 97–122.

18. Ella Shohat and Robert Stam, *Unthinking Eurocentrism: Multiculturalism and the Media*, New York: Routledge, 1994, p. 180.

19. See Henry Louis Gates, Jr., "Blood Brothers: Albert and Allen Hughes in the Belly of the Hollywood Beast," *Transition*, 63, 1994, pp. 164–77.

20. In their treatment of Caine, the Hughes Brothers are also referencing Spike Lee's *Do The Right Thing*, in which Lee presented the death of a "difficult" character, Radio Raheem, in order to problematize audience response. Lee asks his audience to feel as much sympathy for a sometimes rude homeboy with a loud radio as it would for a stellar athlete and student.

21. Shohat and Stam, p. 80.

22. Ibid., p. 102.

23. Gary Saul Morson and Caryl Emerson, *Mikhail Bakhtin: Creation of a Prosaics*, Stanford: Stanford University Press, 1990, p. 375.

24. Bakhtin, p. 252.

25. *Clockers* presents an interesting case study in this regard because it combines chronotopic motifs from three different spaces and times: the *noir* city, the contemporary African-American city, and the rural past. For more on chronotopes in *noir* see Julian Murphet's "*Film Noir* and the Racial Unconscious," *Screen*, vol. 39, no. 1, Spring 1998, pp. 22–35, and Vivian Sobchack's "Lounge Time: Postwar Crises and the Chronotope of *Film Noir*."

26. For more on the use of chronotopic motifs in *Clockers*, see Paula J. Massood, *Cities in Black: Visualizing African-American Urban Experiences in Film* (forthcoming, Temple University Press, 2002).

27. For more on *Posse*'s references both to Western conventions and to the hood film, see Alexandra Keller's *Re-Imagining the Frontier: American Westerns Since the Reagan Administration* (forthcoming, Westview Press).

11

AGAINST THE LOS ANGELES SYMBOLIC: UNPACKING THE RACIALIZED DISCOURSE OF THE AUTOMOBILE IN 1980s AND 1990s CINEMA[1]

JUDE DAVIES

"Gangs are mainly based on colors and race," raps M. C. Shan on the soundtrack to Dennis Hopper's 1988 movie *Colors*, "it's not everywhere, just in particular places."[2] Shan's words conjure up several ironies, not least because the track contests the violence of LA gang culture and its representation in the then-dominant forms of rap itself. Echoing down from NWA's 1988 album *Straight Outta Compton*, and seen clearly in John Singleton's *Boyz N the Hood* (1991), an insistence on the specificity of the local has been a principal focus for Black cultural producers in Los Angeles, for whom specific neighborhoods are locations of authenticity. Yet the commodification of locatedness through hip-hop culture has been heavily conditioned by the desires of a.majority white male youth for the vicarious consumption of violence and other forms of sexist and homophobic aggression. More particularly, the rap soundtrack was related in complex ways to the production and dissemination of *Colors*. In general, along with the LA gang culture portrayed in the film, the soundtrack provided an "authentic" local color backdrop to what was essentially a white-centered police buddy thriller. But the appearance of the soundtrack album itself, presented as a rap compilation and lacking any pictorial reference to the film, suggested the acknowledgment by Warner Bros records of a dynamic Black cultural presence largely independent of the film itself. Shan's rap, an attempt to resist the symbolic appropriation of South Central LA neighborhoods, yet partially circumscribed within their commodification as "gangland," emblematizes how the decade from the late 1980s on was a particularly intense period of struggle over Los Angeles and its representations.

While these ironies have wider resonances, they are also specific examples of a widely recognized attribute of Los Angeles—what might be called the symbolic overdetermination of the city. Cinema has made a powerful, perhaps preeminent contribution to this LA symbolic. From 1940s *noir* to *Chinatown*, from *Blade Runner* to *Strange Days*, Los Angeles has been made into a series of "locations" in a process whereby historical and spatial specificity are dissolved by being subjected to generic conventions such as the testing of masculinity in *noir*, or abstracted to provide generalizations about the human condition, and increasingly from the 1970s on, the state of the nation, or "the future." The resulting symbolic overdetermination has become a commonplace for geographers and cultural historians of Los Angeles such as Edward W. Soja, Mike Davis, and Norman M. Klein, summed up by Soja's reference in the seminal *Postmodern Geographies* to what were, by 1989, already familiar notions; that "Los Angeles is everywhere" and "Everywhere seems also to be in Los Angeles."[3]

In *City of Quartz*, Davis suggests several reasons for the intensification of the LA symbolic during the late 1980s and early 1990s: in the arts, the development of a commercialized, tokenistic, and largely international official policy of multiculturalism, combined with social and cultural neglect of the inner city; the ambivalent growth of rap as a forceful and prominent cultural medium, yet one in hock to dominant ideologies of possessive individualism; and the explicit promulgation of Los Angeles as emblematic of a national and international future under the sign of postmodernity.[4] This promulgation has been exemplified most notoriously by Jean Baudrillard, but also, albeit inadvertently, by critics such as Soja and Fredric Jameson.[5] Hence the particular importance, for leftist critics such as Davis and Klein, of combating the erasure or "forgetting," to use Klein's term, of ethnic and classed spaces and histories.[6] Significantly, the work of both Davis and Klein includes the direct recovery of histories previously forgotten or unwritten, and critical interventions on filmic and other representations of

Los Angeles. The latter takes on particular force in the early 1990s, when the dominant notion of Los Angeles as an exemplary totality is made all the more powerful through its configuration, via the most vulgar of multiculturalisms, as inclusive diversity.[7]

In this chapter, I want to trace how race and ethnicity are configured in three Los Angeles movies from these years: firstly, *Colors*; secondly, a film that might be seen almost as its sequel, Joel Schumacher's *Falling Down* (1993); and a third film that is in some ways its antithesis, *Devil in a Blue Dress*, directed by Carl Franklin and released in 1995. I hope to show how the ways that these films represent race are inseparable from discourses of postmodernity, gender, and space. Out of these overlapping themes, Hollywood depictions of the automobile as a symbolic object emerge as a key means of sustaining discourses of Los Angeles as exemplary, and as a significant focus of racialized meaning and contestation over the erasures and exaggerations of the cinematic LA.

Before looking at these films in more detail, I want to suggest an overview of the discursive production of the exemplarity of Los Angeles by reference to one of its most extreme, but nonetheless symptomatic and influential elaborations, in Jean Baudrillard's 1986 travelogue, *America*. In particular, it is worth focusing on the ways in which Baudrillard's use of the automobile as a symbol strategically engages with and disengages from explicit notions of race.

Baudrillard cites the automobile in a seemingly neutral or universalist discourse through most of the book. From its very first paragraph, car-based perception, film, LA, the USA, and the hyperreal are continually associated with one another.[8] "Drive ten thousand miles across America," according to Baudrillard, "and you will know more about the country than all the institutes of sociology and political science put together." Focusing on Los Angeles itself, he continues

> The city was here before the freeway system, no doubt, but it now looks as though the metropolis has actually been built around this arterial network. It is the same with American reality. It was there before the screen was invented, but everything about the way it is today suggests it was invented with the screen in mind, that it is the refraction of a giant screen.[9]

Through its primary status in relation to the freeway and the cinema screen, communications systems seen as taking precedence over "reality," Los Angeles here is taken to exemplify America as hyperreal. In passages such as this it is the car as a symbolic object that connects and grounds the theorization of the hyperreal and its concretization in America, and especially Los Angeles. Later in the book, Baudrillard reiterates the importance of car transport for the hyperreality of LA:

> No elevator or subway in Los Angeles . . . the hyperreal scenario of deserts, freeways, ocean, and sun.[10]

For Baudrillard, Los Angeles is not only a specific space—it also typifies America and, in particular, the interpenetration of American actuality and ideal self-image. This exemplary status of the city is generated in a section of *America* entitled "Los Angeles Freeways," partly through Baudrillard's sense of the American city as being (especially to the European) inherently cinematic:

> Where is the cinema? It is all around you outside, all over the city, that marvellous, continuous performance of films and scenarios . . . It is not the least of America's charms that even outside the movie theatres the whole country is cinematic.[11]

While Baudrillard's discourse here is strikingly generalized, referring to "[t]he desert you pass through" and "[t]he American city," the surrounding paragraphs are firmly located in California and especially in Los Angeles.[12] Hence LA stands metonymically for America as a whole. This sense of the exemplarity of LA is further grounded by Baudrillard's juxtaposition of cinematic and car-based perception, so as to suggest homologies between the two.

This trajectory in *America* has proved highly suggestive for recent attempts to theorize the relations between the cinema and the city.[13] The cinematic emerges from this frame as a cultural form embedded in everyday life through the similarities between the activity of watching a film and the experience of postmodern urbanity as being structured by or analogous to driving. Critics such as David Harvey and Arie Graafland have reiterated the homologies between driving, the cinematic, and the "time/space compression" considered to be indicative of the postmodern.[14] As Graafland has put it, "The speed of driving creates a cinematographic effect that many underestimate. The result is a loss of sensible referents and a decay of architectonic markers."[15]

But the textual practices of Baudrillard's *America* have rightly been challenged. Elisabeth Mahoney notes the "persistence of metanarratives, objectification and marginalization" within "playful, postmodern text(s)," including *America*.[16] Elsewhere John Rundell has argued that Baudrillard's notion of hyperreality, heavily dependent as it is on notions of the car and the freeway as paradigmatic social forms, is itself a "totalizing meta-narrative" in which a certain modernism "goes unnoticed."[17] Moreover, in certain parts of *America*, the apotheosis of car culture can be seen to collude with, if not actually to require, the presence of objectified racialized and gendered others. Consider, for example, Baudrillard's description of a group of people he calls the "Black and Puerto Rican women of New York." Remarking upon their "beauty," he adds

> it must be said that black, the pigmentation of the dark races, is like a natural make-up that is set off by the artificial kind to produce a beauty which is not sexual, but sublime and animal—a beauty which the pale faces so desperately lack. Whiteness seems an extenuation of physical adornment, a neutrality which, perhaps by that very token, claims all the exoteric powers of the Word, but ultimately will never possess the esoteric and ritual potency of artifice.[18]

The overt sexism and racism of these remarks derives directly from the skewed racial history of modernism. This is compounded by Baudrillard's reiteration of whiteness as neutrality and blankness, the self-image historically associated with the occupation by white men of the subject positions of viewers and possessors of knowledge and desire. Both the voyeuristic pleasure and the stable, secure sense of white selfhood evident in this passage are made possible by the positioning of the white viewing subject within the safe, interior space of the automobile. As such, the typology of car-based perception establishes white masculinity as the dominant subjectivity of the hyperreal, while simultaneously disavowing any sense of whiteness as a racial category.

If car-based perception is in this example implicitly racialized, Baudrillard does acknowledge the racialization of car culture in LA with the infamous comment that "Only immigrants from the Third World are allowed to walk. It is, in a sense, their privilege."[19] The sophisticated irony of this position is only possible from a position of power, being in the driving seat as it were. These are some of the most powerful but extreme fantasies of car culture; not only a vision of the freeways as unhindered flows, without congestion or gridlock, but also a paradise for the (white, male) voyeur. The freeway is never jammed, the gaze is never returned. Women, African-Americans, and immigrants are offered up as specular and abstracted models of absolute difference. Read against the grain like this, what turns out to be remarkable about Baudrillard's *America* is the frankness with which it acknowledges the interweaving of gendered and racial power with visions of hyperreality—"the America of the empty, absolute freedom of the freeways."[20] It is only when the freeways are conceived of as empty, expunged of racial difference, that they can function to reiterate the hyperreal symbolic of America.

Here and in reference to the "privilege" of walking, *America* betrays a nostalgia that is recognizably modernist. Truly Baudrillard's ideal driver replicates the characteristics of the *flâneur* "in an intensified form."[21] In terms of its interiority this ideal driver may be considered to be subject to an intensified version of the modernist double-bind, as defined for example by Adorno and Horkheimer in terms of enlightenment and reification, or perhaps more directly in terms of empowerment and alienation.[22] However, if it is not to remain within the unreflectively white, male, and heterosexual subjectivities of dominant modernisms, this (post)modernist sense of the dialectical nature of the interiority of the ideal driver must be supplemented by a concern with the structural and contingent exclusions generated by cars as both material and symbolic objects.

Among others, Marshall Berman, Mike Davis, and Norman Klein have drawn attention to such material exclusions in the respective contexts of New York and Los Angeles. For such critics, the costs of the apparent freedoms conferred by automobile travel are to be seen not only in terms of the individual alienation of the driver, but also in the destruction of city neighborhoods for highway construction, the decay of public transportation systems, the geographical concentration of wealth and poverty associated with suburbanization and disinvestment in downtown areas, and a host of further environmental problems.[23] What is suggested by this work is a very different modernist sense of the car as a symbolic object. Via Marx, the car appears as a dialectical combination of civilization and barbarism, and against this totalizing, fantastical, and implicitly white and masculinized discourse of automobile freedom, historians such as Berman, Davis, and Klein assert the specificity of those ethnicized communities erased to make way for the freeway.

Pursuing a different but complementary trajectory, in the remainder of this chapter I want, therefore, to examine in more detail the ways in which automobiles function in film to produce certain kinds of white and Black masculinity.[24] This examination will entail a process of unmasking the manipulation of racial and gender difference (found more explicitly in Baudrillard), whereby Hollywood's presentation of the automobile as an apparently universal symbolic object is part of a reiteration of the centrality of white middle class masculinity. Yet I want to call attention also to the ways in which the spatial representation of cars and car relations on film can be seen as showing up the fissures, uneven developments, and inequalities of power relations mediated by the automobile, and highlighting the contestation of this dominant discourse of the car.

Throughout the 1980s and 1990s, in Hollywood representations of Los Angeles the car was a potent emblem of the positive pole of modernity, a "mobile intimate realm" epitomizing an ideology of masculinized self-sufficiency.[25] In general, recent Hollywood films have reiterated the traditionally dominant associations of the car with mobility both geographical and social, with personal security and self-fulfillment. Like "America" itself, the car in Hollywood movies embodies a fantasy of democratic freedom, self-presence, and control, characterized, as John Orr has observed, by "possessive individualism, the open road and the triumph of the heroic machine."[26]

In movies set in Los Angeles from *Pretty Woman* (Garry Marshall, 1990) to *Get Shorty* (Barry Sonnenfeld, 1996), from the *Beverly Hills Cop* series (Martin Brest, 1984; Tony Scott, 1987; John Landis, 1994) to *Grand Canyon* (Lawrence Kasdan, 1991), automobiles are framed by dominant and long-standing US discourses of cross-country travel strongly linked with notions of social mobility, escape, and leisure. Such representations of the automobile connect it self-evidently to security, glamor, freedom, and power, in ways that are so naturalized as to be taken for granted by most audiences. These semiotic links have become so conventional in Hollywood representations of private autos, police cars, and limousines that they are used as the basis for the production of further meanings.

For example, in the opening minutes of *Pretty Woman*, the power and status of the Richard Gere character Edward are confirmed by his use of his lawyer's expensive sports car. Yet his inability to control the car's manual transmission signals a lack in his classed and gendered identity, which in the film is elaborated in two contexts: Edward's personal relationships, such that previous romances have failed due to his lack of commitment; and his professional life as a corporate capitalist. He is, the audience learns later, a corporate raider who profits from closing down companies rather than producing commodities. The ease with which prostitute Vivian (Julia Roberts) operates the stick-shift is a token of her good sense, which the film asks audiences to read both in terms of practicality and of morality. By the end of the film this good sense has enabled the regeneration not only of Edward, but also, symbolically, of American business in general. Vivian, meanwhile is rewarded by being able to marry both for love and for money, a happy ending achieved in the film's closing scenes which again invoke the automobile as symbolic object. Edward depends upon his chauffeur to find Vivian's flat, but leaves his limousine waiting as he climbs the fire escape to propose. Thereby *Pretty Woman* signals Edward's willingness to forgo the enervating, confined security of economic privilege, and to take the driving seat, as it were, in his personal life.

Vivian's trajectory, which as Hilary Radner has pointed out takes the form of negotiating her way from prostitute to wife, is anticipated in the early scene on Sunset Boulevard, when Vivian talks her way from streetwalker to driver.[27] As a streetwalker, Vivian/Roberts had been the object of the looks both of the camera and of Edward as he drove up Sunset Boulevard. However, it is far from clear that the film goes on to grant to her the privileges of the look associated with the driver's position. The sense of Vivian's empowerment, as D. Soyini Madison has suggested, derives instead from the covert workings of codes of racial identity.[28] Vivian's whiteness links her to the female stars of screwball comedy, and distinguishes her from the largely Black and Latina prostitutes of the real Sunset Boulevard. A key figure here, as I have argued elsewhere, is "Skinny Marie," a streetgirl who at the beginning of the film is said to have been murdered and left in a dumpster.[29] While the film does not assign racial or ethnic identity to this character, she occupies the position of the racialized and ethnicized underclass in contrast to which Vivian is defined. Vivian's whiteness is thus highly symbolic while remaining unspecified and in a sense "invisible."

Elsewhere in Hollywood, and far less frequently, car culture is associated with modernity in its negative sense. Probably the best example is *American Gigolo* (Paul Schrader, 1980), in which Richard Gere also starred, where automobile transport, along with designer clothes and interiors, signifies Los Angeles in terms of a moral and ethical vacuum. In *American Gigolo*, the black Mercedes which Gere drives around a bleak LA is an instrument of self-alienation. As John Orr has suggested, that Gere is driving a foreign car helps to preserve the dominant fantasy of car ownership in American cinema.[30] It is in such moments of disavowal that the car becomes most visible in terms of the interior dialectic of modernist selfhood, signaling both empowerment and alienation.

As I suggested earlier, this dialectic of modernity in car culture is itself ideological, and can serve to displace a sense of the exclusionary practices predicated on the automobile both historically and symbolically. It was significant then that in the late 1980s and 1990s questions of power and exclusion were made visible in a series of films and television spectacles. Dysfunctional or limit-cases of driving-as-autonomy were broadcast nationwide via the video footage taken by George Holliday of the beating of Rodney King (widely shown in 1991–92), the LA uprising (April/May 1992), and the pursuit and arrest of O. J. Simpson in June 1994. Each of these raised questions of the racial and economic limits of the dominant ideology of car freedoms, or what I have termed the "ideal driver." For many viewers of these spectacles, the protection offered by the automobile was revealed actually and symbolically as being subjected to power relations based on race and class. Rodney King was, of course, allegedly stopped for motoring offenses, while often-replayed footage from the LA uprising of the attack on white truck driver Reginald Denny provided a graphic illustration of the breakdown of law and order where not even the high cab of the truck could protect its occupant.

Although less important in terms of historical actuality, the much-replayed live television coverage of O. J. Simpson's flight in his friend Al Cowling's white Ford Bronco, and its low-speed pursuit by numerous police cars is perhaps the most complex of these representations. It also garnered the highest viewing figures—some 100 million.[31] On one level, the coverage demonstrated the limits of the protection that can be afforded by the automobile. Here, on national television, was played out the tension between juridical and police power and the freedom of the individual as emblematized by auto-mobility. And for many miles and many minutes of screen time this tension was in fine balance. The forces of law and order, emblematized by at least twelve police cruisers, pursued Simpson, but for whatever reason were unable or unwilling to penetrate the interior of the Bronco. At the same time, as part of the Simpson episode more generally, the incident raised the questions of race and wealth in connection with access to privilege and protection from the racially skewed power of the LAPD. In this sense, the television coverage served as a precursor to popular and racially inflected readings of the subsequent murder trial. As such, the Ford Bronco occupied the metaphorical position of Simpson's legal defense team. At yet another level, for purely technical reasons the incident enacted some elements of the hyperreal. The slow speed of the pursuit made it appear an inferior copy of car chases familiar from film representations. On its action alone, the footage would not be dynamic enough for one of the "true life" shows such as *Cops* or *The World's Most Dangerous Car Chases* that it helped to spawn, and which are now more popular than their fictive counterparts.

But there was something more going on here than simply a demonstration of the ideological limits of car culture. These examples were not just limit cases of a dominant ideology, but could also be read in terms of an alternative or counter-discourse whereby cars are represented as emblems of power and tools for patrolling limits of exclusion and inclusion. This counter-discourse is articulated in much African-American film of the 1980s and 1990s, most obviously in the representations of police cars in the films of Spike Lee, Matty Rich, and Mario Van Peebles, and in Lee's use of the video footage of the Rodney King beating in the opening titles of *Malcolm X* (1992), presumably to signal the historical continuities of African-American experience. Both dominant and counter-discourses were articulated with racial inflections in gangsta films such as *Menace II Society* (Allen Hughes and Albert Hughes, 1993), where private cars were presented as embodying economic success and social status, and police cars as the mobile panopticons of the state.

It is important to bear in mind these multiple and overlapping, though still power-inflected, ideological discourses of the car when considering *Colors*, *Falling Down*, and *Devil in a Blue Dress*. In each of these films a dominant point-of-view, offered cinematographically, strongly resembles, and is frequently identified as, that from a car window. However, due in no small part to the film grammar of shot and reverse shot, these movies cannot help but also offer at least a doubled point of view, whereby the driver is presented in the positions of the viewer and the viewed. Each of these films offers a direct representation of the historical Los

Angeles (of the 1980s, 1990s, and 1940s respectively), and each represents the experiential and cultural spaces of LA in connection with both automobile culture and power relations articulated on racial lines.[32]

Against the background of gang conflict in downtown Los Angeles, *Colors* focuses on the relationship of two white cops, macho authoritarian rookie McGavin (played by Sean Penn), and the more avuncular Hodges (Robert Duvall) who is one year from retirement when the two are partnered at the opening of the film. This scenario re-enacts the abstraction of the local associated with classic *noir*. Put simply, gangland tension between Crips and Bloods, and the alleys of Watts, become backgrounds to a narrative about the relationship between and testing of different models of blue-collar white masculinity. Hence *Colors* is subject to the criticism Norman Klein makes of classic *noir* as "essentially a mythos about white male panic—the white knight in a cesspool of urban decay."[33]

Yet two related aspects of the film suggest a more complex representation of race and space. In parallel to the Penn/Duvall narrative, *Colors* was marketed on the back of a notion of authenticity derived from research in Watts and the featuring of actual gang-members, together with several scenes dramatizing gang life. Such scenes convinced reviewer Roger Ebert of the film's representational value, and even Pauline Kael, who rejected what she regarded as Hopper's aestheticization of LA gang life, nevertheless classed the film as "muck-raking melodrama."[34] However, this aspect of the film in general, and in particular its misleading depiction of an attack by a Black gang on Chicanos, is excoriated by Davis.[35] More complex than its deployment of gangs for local color were the ways that, as briefly mentioned above, *Colors* also signified itself as authentic by reference to the localized Black cultural forms of rap and hip-hop. The soundtrack featured not only specially written tracks by artists such as Ice-T and Roxanne Shante, but also a version of Eric B. and Rakim's seminal "Paid in Full"—probably the archetypal assertion of rap as a politicized take on the history of Black cultural production. However compromised by commodification, this overlap of gang with gangsta introduces into the racial symbolic economy of *Colors* a Blackness which derives from *cultural production* rather than simply location. At the same time, the exclusion from the album of material featured in the film but not performed by African-Americans, emphasizes the interpenetration of commercial imperatives with the racial identification of rap as a cultural form.

In some respects, cars function in *Colors* as a means of negotiating these racial and gender relations. The film directly invokes associations of the car with power and the privileged position of the subject of the gaze. For much of its length, Hodges and McGavin patrol Watts in a succession of unmarked police cars, getting out to make contact with gang members and to take part in a series of raids, during one of which Hodges is eventually killed. Moreover, the opening title sequence normalizes both the association of the car with the gaze of power and white racial identity, and the driver's perspective on Los Angeles.

The title sequence takes viewers on a car journey radiating outwards from central LA, to the sound of Latino band Los Lobos (a song not included on the exclusively rap soundtrack CD). The film cuts from the interior of the LAPD Headquarters, (the scene of a pre-credit sequence I will discuss shortly), to an exterior shot of City Hall from a car, which fleetingly suggests the intimidating height of the Citadel. Cinematic point-of-view maintains the perspective of driver and/or front-seat passenger as the car exits the Central Business District and traverses the run-down areas of downtown, where African-Americans and Latino/as are visible as individuals and in groups on the sidewalk. These images are interspersed very occasionally with views of McGavin and Hodges through the car windscreen. Significantly, this is not a reverse shot but stands in for one. Viewers are positioned with the (white) policemen as they gaze at the (non-white) pedestrians on the sidewalk, but instead of returning this look cinematic point-of-view switches to the front rather than the side of the car. The titles sequence is concluded by a cut to a wide focus view of the skyscrapers downtown at night, which must be either from a tall building or a helicopter. Although seamless for viewers (and this seamlessness illustrates the mutually sustaining normative power of car-based perception and Hollywood conventions of point-of-view), this shift of perspective can also be regarded as the first of a series of ways in which the film shows up the limits of the power attributed to car-based subjectivity.

Throughout the film, their car is a haven of security for McGavin and Hodges, yet they must frequently leave it and become vulnerable. The space they traverse is always difficult—primarily it is the bumpy, dusty alleys of Watts. The pair are never shown driving the freeways, but only on these alleys and city streets. Like their contrastive styles of masculinity, linked in the film to notions of community policing (Hodges) and overt aggression (McGavin), the power of the car is presented in terms of performativity. And it is exactly the testing of these masculinities and the power conferred by the car that forms the narrative interest of the film, displacing to a large extent the dynamics of gang conflict and overt racial difference which, though privileged in terms of the film's title and soundtrack, function largely as a backdrop.

The opening pre-title sequence of *Colors* begins with a washroom discussion of masculinity, in which Hodges compares contemporary gangbangers invidiously with John Wayne, before McGavin introduces himself jokingly as "Rocky Six." When the older Hodges sarcastically asks what his job is, McGavin responds, "I'm a guardian of masculinity, man." This statement is quickly ironized when the effectiveness of Hodges' brand of masculinity becomes apparent, while McGavin's aggression only alienates the public. McGavin's aggressive driving occupies a pivotal point in the narrative, linking his own rite of passage into mature and caring masculinity with the gang strife that provides the film's background. His determined pursuit of gang members in a car driven by a Latina results not only in the death of the occupants but also in the destruction of the unmarked police car. The replacement car, a shabby yellow sedan, draws ridicule from their colleagues and results in a temporary loss of prestige.

By the end of *Colors*, car use is repositioned in terms of stasis rather than mobility, in contradistinction to the helicopter. After a raid on a drug-dealer in the middle section of the film, a police chopper is shown occupying exactly the position of the powerful subject of the gaze that in the opening titles sequence had been identified with a car-based point-of-view. Later, as Hodges lies fatally shot, the sound of a helicopter vies to drown out his last words. Most strikingly of all, at the instant Hodges dies, McGavin raises his face to the sky and cries out in anger, sorrow, and frustration, and the cinematic point-of-view moves back sharply to give an aerial view of the death scene, as from a helicopter.

Hodges' death is followed by a brief coda, in which McGavin is shown imparting the wisdom of his dead colleague to his new partner, a rookie African-American. The film proper then closes with a wordless twenty-five-second shot of McGavin at the wheel. The effect is a somewhat contradictory mixture of glamor and dull professionalism, of submission to the disciplines of police work while invoking also the Western motif of the cowboy's fundamental marginality and exteriority to "civilization." Having looked down on McGavin and the dead Hodges from the position of the helicopter, viewers are encouraged by these cinematic conventions to read driving from outside, differentiating themselves from it as driving is fixed as a blue-collar activity which places the cops in proximity to the gangs on which they seek to impose their authority.[36]

A second coda of sorts follows during the end titles.[37] These are interspersed with stills and very brief shots of downtown street scenes as seen from a car, as in the opening titles, but this time alternating with images of an arrest of several African-American and Latino gang members. These are closely cropped, focusing in on handcuffs and groups of the arrested until, in the final shot, a wider perspective reveals the arresting officer, who is Black. As with the final scene of the film proper, the effect is ambiguous. Following from that scene, in one sense this sequence suggests a trajectory whereby African-Americans are now inhabiting the position of the ideal driver, a position whose whiteness was taken for granted in the opening title sequence. Yet this is tokenistic: there has been no countershot to establish the presence of the African-American driver, and audiences are enabled to read the driving position in terms of Blackness only retrospectively, and with a little effort.

1993's *Falling Down* in part employs a similar grammar of car and helicopter to *Colors*. The opening and initializing scene is set in a traffic jam. The gridlocked highway is just the first of a series of emblematic images and discourses in the film representing Los Angeles in terms of a highly territorialized and socially fragmented space (territory is policed by Latino gang members, a golf club, helicopters, and white police officers, among others) (**22**). These territories are traversed by the film's central protagonist D-Fens (named for his car license plate), a sacked defense worker played by Michael Douglas, whose decision to abandon his car in the gridlock not only initiates the action but also symbolizes the failure of the automobile as modernist ideal.

The opening scene presents automobile dysfunction in both general and specific ways. D-Fens' lost status is exemplified by his perspiration, the lack of air conditioning in his car, and his broken window winder, while the gridlock suggests a more general malaise. This conjunction opens up the car interior to the

22 Joel Schumacher's *Falling Down* (1993) (Copyright Warner Bros, An AOL-Time Warner Entertainment Company, 1993)

penetrating stare of gendered, ethnicized, and generational others, most obviously in the form of children on a school bus. Here then the car window no longer functions as both wind*screen* and wind*shield*, and can therefore be read as demonstrating the racial, gendered, and economic limits of automobile fantasies, at least for this particular unemployed white male. *Falling Down* has been widely seen as relating specifically to the development of a new cultural visibility of white masculinity in the 1990s.[38] In this context, the abandonment of the car by D-Fens emblematizes what the film portrays as his exclusion from the economic and social status traditionally associated with whiteness. Its significance is underlined by the helicopter sounds that recur throughout the film, especially noticeable at the close of the scene when he abandons his car, and at later moments of crisis, signaling unease and surveillance, as do similar sounds in *Boyz N the Hood*.

Like *Colors* (with which it shares some locations), *Falling Down* makes a symbolic accommodation between white and African-American males. Unlike *Colors* which hardly admits the possibility of police racism, *Falling Down*, which was made in the wake of the dissemination of the Rodney King video, and whose production was interrupted by the LA uprising, presents the association of African-American and disenfranchised white males as being generated against police power. In a scene superfluous to the main narrative, D-Fens is associated with an African-American protesting against the alleged racism of a bank. Played by Vondie Curtis Hall, the protester is identified in the film's closing credits as the "not economically viable man," after the words on a placard he holds. As he is arrested and driven away in an LAPD squad car, he exchanges glances with D-Fens. His words, "Don't forget me" are heard. At the conclusion of the film, when D-Fens is involved in a face-off with cop Prendergast (Robert Duvall), he repeats the words on the protester's placard, "I'm not economically viable."

The territorialized city of *Falling Down*, and its symbolic representation of car and helicopter, is heavily overdetermined by debates over race and gender issues integrated into its action and extra-textually framing its consumption as a "state of the nation" film. D-Fens' encounter with the Black protester has been read, for example by Liam Kennedy, as appropriating Black history imperialistically, using the protester figure to give extra credibility to white suffering. However, its representation of the LAPD car links it to the counter-discourses described above.[39] The complexity of *Falling Down* in this respect is thrown into relief by comparison with *Grand Canyon* (Lawrence Kasdan, 1991), which is initiated with a similar representation of the potential dysfunctionality of the car as modernist symbol. Kasdan's film begins when the Lexus of Mack (Kevin Kline) breaks down in Inglewood and he is threatened by Black gang members. Mack is "saved" by an African-American tow-truck driver played by Danny Glover. Both *Grand Canyon* and *Falling Down* explicitly display a concern with whiteness as a racialized identity, in addition to the focus on styles of masculinity in *Colors*. This can be seen most clearly by comparing the characters played by Robert Duvall in *Colors* and in *Falling Down*. Duvall reprises his role as an avuncular, caring cop due for retirement, only this time the film's action takes place on what is intended to be his last day in the job. But in contrast to *Colors*, the later film goes out of its way to portray Duvall's character, Prendergast, as a white officer in a multi-ethnic force, negotiating racial and ethnic distinctions, as well as gender status, with his colleagues. While *Grand Canyon* and *Falling Down* alike call attention to the importance of reconciling racial difference, *Grand Canyon* keeps faith with modernity, the automobile, and American exceptionalism, all of which are employed to realize a heavily symbolic racial accommodation via a family road trip to the Grand Canyon at its climax. Yet for all their comparable gestures of racial negotiation and their different constructions of whiteness itself, all three remain white-centered films.

More generally, *Falling Down*'s bid to be taken as a "state of the nation" film also relies on two versions of the exemplarity of Los Angeles. Kennedy persuasively reads the film through the lens of what Mike Davis calls "paranoid spatiality," the territorialization of space associated with "fortress LA."[40] At the same time, the narrative sequencing of the film, as a series of discontinuous scenes of conflict, reiterates the decentered, post-urban landscape widely associated with Los Angeles and car culture—a city of voids and open, empty spaces.[41] Reliant in any case, as Elisabeth Mahoney has shown, on a gendered distinction between public and private space, *Falling Down* sometimes erases, sometimes rewrites the racial and ethnic specificity of Los Angeles.[42]

In comparison with both *Colors* and *Falling Down*, *Devil in a Blue Dress* makes no claims for topicality (it is set with meticulous detail in the Los Angeles of 1948), but its evocation of the racialized and class-based power of automobile ownership amounts to a revisionist take on Hollywood traditions of car ownership. Carl Franklin's film does feature a scene in which a police car functions to maintain white power, as two policemen cruise by abusing the African-American protagonist Easy Rawlins (Denzel Washington) (**23**). But as an aspirational blue-collar African-American, who has left the South to pursue industrial work in California, Easy Rawlins' own car is very important to him. The film opens with Rawlins driving home through his suburban neighborhood and the car remains visible in much of the film, largely as a safe haven. These representations place Rawlins firmly in the driving seat, occupying the normative space of the driver as exemplified in *Colors*. In a scene that deliberately echoes *Chinatown* and reiterates the logic of *Colors*, the mobility conferred by the car is potentially dangerous as soon as one steps outside it. Rawlins is attacked by two white police officers just as he gets out of the car in his drive. This danger is also articulated in specifically racialized terms when the car allows Rawlins to travel to parts of town where his presence attracts the attention of white racists. During the course of the film, as Rawlins is drawn somewhat unwillingly into the role of private eye, the conventions of classical Hollywood are reworked around racial difference. At one point, while driving a white woman across town, he wonders to himself at the danger of being found by the police with her in his car. (In an ironic twist it is eventually

23 Carl Franklin's *Devil in a Blue Dress* (1995) (Copyright Columbia Pictures Industries, 1995)

revealed that the woman, Daphne Monet, played by Jennifer Beales, is actually passing for white.)

Hence, *Devil in a Blue Dress* engages a dual Black history—the struggle for access to postwar suburbia, and the continued threat of legalized white-on-black violence outside the South—while at the same time self-consciously rewriting the *noir* genre. Another scene calls attention to the ways in which the ideology of the car is imbricated within power relations structured by economic power and racial and ethnic identity. Here, while walking home at night from a police station, Rawlins is persuaded to get into an expensive car. The passenger compartment is dark, gloomy, and threatening. A middle-aged and rather overweight white man kisses a Latino boy, whom he introduces as "Jésus, my adopted son," and begins to address Rawlins. Here Franklin effectively reverses the logic set up in the opening scenes. The interior space of the automobile is white-dominated and threatening, part of an over-arching field of power which

Rawlins has already experienced at the hands of the LA cops. At the same time, the identification of the young boy as Latino implies that to be outside the dominant ideology of car culture is to be positioned not as "Black" but as "non-white." In this scene, with both the boy and Rawlins incarcerated against their own interests, the automobile is for them more akin to a mobile jail than a liberatory mode of transport.

In conclusion, I hope I have suggested some of the ways in which contemporary philosophical and cinematic representations of Los Angeles configure race, gender, and class through the automobile as a symbolic object. I have tried to unmask the persistence of modernist subjectivities centered on white masculinity in the LA symbolic epitomized by Baudrillard's *America*, visible in the strategic deployment of racialized and non-racialized descriptions of relations between drivers and pedestrians. This combined symbolism of LA and the automobile has its analogues in conventions shared by many classical and contemporary Hollywood films. However, I have also pointed to the complexity of cinematic renderings of cars and Los Angeles in the late 1980s and 1990s. In *Colors*, *Falling Down*, and *Devil in a Blue Dress* instances of the dysfunctionality of the automobile as symbolic object, and/or of the limitations of car culture, serve to carry a range of significances, especially in configuring relations between different racial, gendered, and classed positions.

In both *Colors* and *Falling Down* the automobile is presented as a fragile protection for the status of white males, threatened by their dangerous work or the loss of status engendered by unemployment and divorce. While Hopper's film operates within white-centered genre conventions and uses a simplistic vision of Black gang violence as a context for the testing of white masculinities, this racial hierarchy is inverted by the forcefulness of rap/hip-hop as the cultural form of urban authenticity. *Falling Down* again deploys the magical discourse that presents white masculinity as both specific and universal, but makes explicit, if highly problematic, attempts to identify the condition of its white male in crisis with that of African-Americans. "Guardians of masculinity" as Hodges and McGavin are, they lack the everyman status that Schumacher claims for D-Fens both through his whiteness and through the victimhood that he supposedly shares with the Black protester.

If *Falling Down* pivots uncertainly between explicit and implicit discourses of race, *Devil in a Blue Dress* is doubled in a different way. Franklin's film plays out positive and negative versions of the symbolic automobile, exemplified by Rawlins' own car, on the one hand, and those of the police and white officials, on the other. More obviously than the other films discussed here, *Devil* thus shows up the ambivalence of automobiles as cinematic symbols, as much indices of power as they are instruments of self-fulfillment.

NOTES

1. Many of the ideas that inform this chapter were initially developed in connection with the collaborative work of the Ghent Urban Studies Team (GUST), in whose edited collection, *The Urban Condition*, some of them were first worked out. My thanks are due to GUST, and in particular to Bart Eeckhout, for comments and suggestions on that early draft. Thanks are also due to Mark Shiel and Tony Fitzmaurice for their helpful and suggestive comments, and to the delegates and hosts at the Dublin *Cinema and the City* Conference (1999), especially James Hay. Finally, I am grateful to Russell White for first drawing my attention to the continued production of "authenticity" under the sign of the local in rap culture, and for sustaining a long and fruitful dialogue.
2. M. C. Shan, "A Mind is a Terrible Thing to Waste" (S. Moltke, M. Williams), Cold Chillin' Music Publishing/Merley Marl International, ASCAP, from *Colors, Original Motion Picture Soundtrack*, Warner Bros Records, #25713, 1988.
3. Edward W. Soja, *Postmodern Geographies: The Reassertion of Space in Critical Social Theory*, London: Verso, 1989, pp. 222–3. Soja uses these phrases to set up a double problematic for the study of LA. On the one hand, LA is multiply over-exposed. The city is "everywhere" through "its almost ubiquitous screening of itself as a rectangular dream machine for the world," composed to its "countless seers" as "perhaps the epitomizing world city." On the other hand, the sheer diversity of goods, peoples, and cultures flowing through and stopping in LA constitutes an "extraordinary heterogeneity." Between them, these twin excesses, of what might be called representation and reproduction, pre-empt any definitive totalization of Los Angeles. Setting himself the task nevertheless of displacing them with a "critical human geography" of Los Angeles, Soja launches a tactical combination of local analysis and general reflection, "to appreciate the specificity and uniqueness of a particularly restless geographical landscape while simultaneously seeking to extract insights at higher levels of abstraction." Soja, *Postmodern Geographies*, p. 223. My emphasis here is different and complementary, focusing on the production of LA's exemplarity itself in order, often, to unmask it, rather than seeking to displace it by reference to a material social geography.

4. Mike Davis, *City of Quartz: Excavating the Future in Los Angeles*, London: Verso, 1990, pp. 76–88.

5. For an example of Jameson's writing on Los Angeles, see his discussion of the Bonaventure Hotel in the Bunker Hill area of downtown LA in *Postmodernism, or The Cultural Logic of Late Capitalism*, London and New York: Verso, 1993.

6. Norman M. Klein, *The History of Forgetting: Los Angeles and the Erasure of Memory*, London: Verso, 1997.

7. The structure of Davis' first chapter provides an index of the particular problematic of the late 1980s and early 1990s. It is organized around a rough antithesis between "sunshine" (the fantasy LA of boosterism) and *noir* (in general, realist exposé on the part of those marginalized in terms of race and class), an antithesis which, Davis shows, breaks down when faced with the prominence of NWA and what he calls "the entire burgeoning *Colors* genre." Davis, *City of Quartz*, p. 87.

8. Jean Baudrillard, *America*, trans. Chris Turner, London: Verso, 1988, pp. 1, 52–5, 124–6.

9. Baudrillard, *America*, pp. 54–5.

10. Ibid., pp. 125–6.

11. Ibid., p. 56.

12. Ibid., p. 56.

13. See David E. Clarke, ed., *The Cinematic City*, London: Routledge, 1997.

14. David Harvey, *The Condition of Postmodernity: An Enquiry into the Origins of Cultural Change*, Oxford: Basil Blackwell, 1989.

15. Arie Graafland, *Architectural Bodies*, Rotterdam: 010 Publishers, 1996, p. 41.

16. Elisabeth Mahoney, "'The People in Parentheses': Space Under Pressure in the Post-modern City," in Clarke, ed., *The Cinematic City*, p. 184. The same volume includes an exemplary tracing of the historical and spatial specificities of cinema and the urban in James Hay's "Piecing Together What Remains of the Cinematic City," pp. 209–29.

17. John Rundell, "Beyond Crisis, Beyond Novelty: The Tensions of Modernity," in *New Formations*, 31, Spring/Summer 1997, pp. 158–74, 165.

18. Baudrillard, *America*, pp. 15–16.

19. Ibid., *America*, p. 58.

20. Ibid., *America*, p. 5.

21. For a highly lucid and concise discussion of the indebtedness of theorizations of the postmodern and hyperreal to overtly modernist notions of identity, via the *flâneur*/driver, see Ghent Urban Studies Team, "Consumer Aesthetics and the neo-*flâneur*," in GUST, *The Urban Condition: Space, Community, and Self in the Contemporary Metropolis*, Rotterdam: 010 Publishers, 1999, pp. 131–5.

22. T. W. Adorno and M. Horkheimer, *The Dialectic of Enlightenment*, London: Verso, 1986, pp. xiv–xv.

23. Marshall Berman, *All That Is Solid Melts Into Air: The Experience of Modernity*, London: Verso, 1982; Davis, *City of Quartz*; Klein, *The History of Forgetting*.

24. This trajectory can be identified with the critical turn to identity representation associated not only with the fall-out from identity politics, but with a growing sense of the instability of dominant and emergent cinematic forms exemplified by the complex manipulation of some discourses from feminism and civil rights within mainstream Hollywood. I am thinking of the work of a large number of critics, such as Manthia Diawara, James Doty, Richard Dyer, Henry Giroux, Ed Guerrero, bell hooks, Amy Kaplan, Liam Kennedy, Susan Jeffords, Wahneema Lubiano, D. Soyini Madison, Tania Modleski, Elizabeth G. Traube, Cornel West, and Sharon Willis, which demonstrates a concern with the cultural meaning of identity representations arising out of, but not confined to, politicized debates over positive and negative images of identity. This is brought alongside a sense of the mutually constitutive function of codes of race, ethnicity, gender, sexuality, and others in forming identity constructions through binary oppositions such as those between black/white, male/female, heterosexual/homosexual. In radically destabilizing these binaries and the identity constructions predicated upon them, such work seeks to spatialize, and to historicize what might otherwise be abstracted in terms of a post-structuralist deferral of signification, or individuated by a Lacanian sense of the exclusions and repressions necessary to produce full subjectivity. Instead, it simultaneously highlights the traditions of those filmmakers previously marginalized by a monolithic notion of Hollywood as American film, and the reading strategies evolved by consumers not directly interpolated by the default audience position of straight white masculinity. For a fuller development of this position, see Jude Davies and Carol R. Smith, *Gender, Ethnicity and Sexuality in Contemporary American Film*, Edinburgh: Keele University Press, 1998, pp. 1–8.

25. On the connections between the car as "mobile intimate realm" and politically powerful fantasies of identity, see René Boomkens, "The 'Middle Landscape' and the Myth of Mobility: Coming Home in Commuter Country," trans. Bart Eeckhout, in GUST, *The Urban Condition*, pp. 214–27.

26. John Orr, *Cinema and Modernity*, Cambridge, MA: Polity Press, 1993, p. 129. Orr's chapter, "Commodified Demons II: The Automobile" is a highly suggestive critical account of car symbolism. While reiterating Orr's discussion of the automobile as exemplary of dominant American ideology, in this chapter I want to draw attention to differences within US cinema that complicate the symbolic status of the car.

27. Hilary Radner, "'Pretty is as Pretty Does': Free Enterprise and the Marriage Plot," in Jim Collins, Hilary Radner, and Ava Preacher Collins, eds, *Film Theory Goes to the Movies*, New York and London: Routledge, 1993, pp. 56–76.

28. D. Soyini Madison, "*Pretty Woman* Through the Triple Lens of Black Female Spectatorship," in Elizabeth Bell, Lynda Haas, and Laura Sells, eds, *From Mouse to Mermaid:*

The Politics of Film, Gender, and Culture, Bloomington and Indianapolis, IN: Indiana University Press, 1995, pp. 224–35.

29. Davies and Smith, *Gender, Ethnicity and Sexuality*, pp. 10–13.
30. Orr, *Cinema and Modernity*, p. 130.
31. John Fiske, *Media Matters: Everyday Culture and Political Change*, Minneapolis and London: Minnesota University Press, 2nd edition, 1996, p. 255.
32. A longer study would be necessary in order to fully understand the inflection of filmic discourses of the automobile by the various important codes of identity such as race, gender, sexuality, and class. The concentration here on masculinity and race reflects the focus of the majority of Los Angeles movies, but remains theoretically exemplary rather than exhaustive.
33. Klein, *History of Forgetting*, p. 79.
34. Roger Ebert, review of *Colors*, *Chicago Sun Times*, April 15 1988; Pauline Kael quoted in *Microsoft Cinemania* CD-Rom.
35. Davis, *City of Quartz*, p. 322, fn. 118.
36. As such, *Colors* anticipates many elements of the loss of prestige experienced by the LAPD in the early 1990s, as detailed by Klein, *History of Forgetting*, pp. 263–91.
37. I am working here, as throughout, from the UK video release; video copies of the film contain some material cut from the first cinema release.
38. See Jude Davies, "Gender, Ethnicity and Cultural Crisis in *Falling Down* and *Groundhog Day*," *Screen*, vol. 36, no. 3, 1995, pp. 214–32; Jude Davies, "'I'm the bad guy?' *Falling Down* and White Masculinity in 1990s Hollywood," *Journal of Gender Studies*, 4, 2, 1995, pp. 145–52; Fred Pfeil, *White Guys: Studies in Post-modern Domination and Difference*, London: Verso, 1995; Liam Kennedy, "Alien Nation: White Male Paranoia and Imperial Culture in the United States," *Journal of American Studies*, 30, 1, 1996, pp. 87–100; Davies and Smith, *Gender, Ethnicity*, pp. 31–8; John Gabriel, "What Do You Do When the Minority Means You? *Falling Down* and the Construction of 'Whiteness'," *Screen*, vol. 37, no. 2, 1996, pp. 129–51; Richard Dyer, *White*, London and New York: Routledge, 1997, pp. 217–22.
39. See Kennedy, "Alien Nation"; for further discussion of the complex negotiations going on here and in the film in general, see especially Davies and Smith, *Gender, Ethnicity and Sexuality in Contemporary American Film*.
40. Liam Kennedy, *Race and Urban Space in Contemporary American Culture*, London: Pluto Press, 2000, pp. 36–7.
41. See Ghent Urban Studies Team, "Urban Discontinuities and Urban Voids," in GUST, *The Urban Condition*, pp. 38–43.
42. Mahoney, "The People in Parentheses," pp. 174–7. See also Klein, pp. 107–9, for a detailed account of the ethnic specificities of LA neighborhoods and their rewriting in *Falling Down*.

12

ALLERGY AND ALLEGORY IN TODD HAYNES' [SAFE]¹

MATTHEW GANDY

We are one with the world who created us, we are *safe*, and
all is well in our world.
Peter Dunning, fictional environmental guru in Todd Haynes' [Safe]

We should feel we're in a world where nature has been completely over-
come by man and there's no trace of it. It should feel like space but it's really
LA. It should feel like an airport where you never touch real ground.
Todd Haynes describes his depiction of Los Angeles in [Safe]²

A figure in protective clothing stumbles across a desolate landscape (**24**). The scene is reminiscent of an astronaut making tentative steps across the surface of the moon yet this is no visual paean to human achievement. The harsh sunlight and complete isolation of the slowly moving figure are not suggestive of scientific progress but are indicative of a kind of pastoral inversion within which the relationship between modern society and nature has become utterly dislocated. In Todd Haynes' critically acclaimed movie [Safe] (1995) we are presented with a dystopian diorama of environmental estrangement. The film depicts a contemporary America in which fears of chemical contamination pervade even the most affluent sections of society, provoking a mix of anger, disbelief, and despair. Sufferers are caught between the Scylla of a skeptical medical establishment and the

24 A figure in protective clothing outside the Wrenwood Center retreat for the chemically sensitive in Todd Haynes' *[Safe]* (1995) (Copyright Sony Pictures Entertainment Inc., 1995)

Charybdis of New Age hokum promulgated by self-styled healers and charismatic eco-philosophers.

In *[Safe]*, Todd Haynes presents one of the first cinematic depictions of severe chemical allergy, a newly emerging source of ill health which has been variously referred to as "multiple chemical sensitivity," "chemical AIDS," "environmental illness" or "twentieth century sickness."[3] Yet this film is far more than an accurate reconstruction of this medical phenomenon; it is also an exploration of declining faith in the capacity of modern societies to satisfactorily handle newly emerging threats to public health. The cinema of Todd Haynes can be compared to the work of other North American directors such as David Cronenberg, Atom Egoyan, and Abel Ferrara, who have produced highly innovative and often controversial works which tackle complex and contentious issues such as disease, sexuality, and death.[4] In many ways, *[Safe]* marks an elaboration of earlier themes developed by Haynes in *Superstar* (1987) and *Poison* (1991) and his continuing exploration of the genre of "dystopian urbanism" and the cinematic uncanny.[5] Critical commentaries on *[Safe]* have alluded to the wider significance of his work but have not satisfactorily explored the social and political implications stemming from the resurgence of disease-based metaphors in the post-AIDS era.[6] Haynes himself has suggested that the film is best conceived as an allegory for the decline of the American Left within which existing connections between modernity, science, and collective ideals of social progress have become unraveled:

> I think what *[Safe]* is really about is the infiltration of New Age language into institutions. And about the failure of the Left; how it imploded into these notions of self and self-esteem . . . And it's such a loss because what was once a critical perspective looking out, hoping to change the culture, is turning inward and losing all of its gumption and power.[7]

The structure of this chapter mirrors that of the film. We begin by witnessing the deteriorating health of the principal character, Carol White (Julianne Moore). A series of interrelated themes are introduced: her disaffection with conventional sources of male authority; the increasing severity and complexity of her symptoms; and the gradual emergence of her environmental consciousness. Following the complete breakdown of her health, we then follow Carol's progress at a retreat for chemically sensitive people located in the New Mexico desert. We find that her earlier environmental awareness becomes subverted into a highly individualized form of personal healing and New Age spirituality. The depiction of the desert retreat develops into a powerful satirical indictment of alternative health care regimes which fail to challenge the underlying causes of ill health in affluent Western societies.

SAN FERNANDO VALLEY, 1987

In the opening sequence of *[Safe]* we observe a suburban neighborhood through the windscreen of a slowly moving car. No people are visible in the evening light—only the lights of other cars. A large electronically controlled gate draws back and we enter the garage of Carol White's home. She and her husband step from the car and a film caption informs us that this is "San Fernando Valley, 1987," an affluent Los Angeles suburb near the end of the Reagan era. In the 1950s the San Fernando Valley had been the focus of major planning conflict between existing residents seeking to preserve some semblance of the "urban pastoral" ideal of semi-rural settlement patterns and intense demographic and economic pressures to unleash further development activities at the urban fringe. With the opening of the 101 Freeway in the 1960s a new cycle of change instituted an increasingly polarized social and economic structure. On the one hand, the Valley was dotted with prosperous white enclaves and the growth of hi-technology industrial clusters, but, on the other hand, there were new waves of Latino migration and the emergence of a burgeoning sweatshop production sector. During the 1970s the wealthy communities of the San Fernando Valley became part of the vanguard for the Reaganite anti-liberal backlash in public policy-making. The residents' associations of the Valley "functioned as political lightning rods for tax revolt and opposition to school busing," thereby initiating a prolonged and unresolved fiscal crisis for the provision of adequately funded public services.[8] This, then, is a fragmentary, fearful, and myopic urban land-scape in which spatial and social boundaries remain tightly defended.

In Haynes' representation of the San Fernando Valley he builds a minutely detailed parody of a hermetically sealed urban enclave where forms of social interaction are limited and sharply demarcated by class, gender, and race. A series of early sequences in the film emphasize the isolation of Carol White within a succession of austere and claustrophobic interiors. Once inside their home, for example, we witness Carol's joyless submission to her husband's sexual demands. The next day we see Carol tending roses in their garden as her husband reminds her to call the landscape architect. Like the roses, Carol's pres-ence in the garden is purely ornamental: all "real work" is left to an array of service employees. Through cinematography, Haynes conveys Carol's sense of disorientation through the extensive deployment of wide-angle lenses to empha-size the empty wan interiors of her home (25).

Later in the day we see Carol at an aerobics class where she briefly engages in conversation with some of the other women who enthuse over a self-help book by

25 A succession of wide-angle frames is used to emphasize Carol White's increasing isolation from her upper-middle-class lifestyle in *[Safe]* (Copyright Sony Pictures Entertainment Inc., 1995)

a popular health writer. She then visits a friend who is grieving the loss of her brother. In the first of Haynes' oblique references to AIDS, the cause of death is only ever alluded to indirectly and the conversation moves briskly on to interior design. When Carol returns home she finds herself in the midst of diverse home-making activities. In a scene of opulent chaos reminiscent of a Hogarth engraving we find her surrounded by furniture delivery men, carpenters, and a new female servant being trained to polish silverware. She seems preoccupied and detached from what is going on around her; her day is marked by the constant murmur of FM radio, distant traffic, and the whirring of helicopters and light aircraft (we are never sure whether this aerial din is due to police surveillance or medfly containment). We are confronted with a spectacle of contemporary America as a "Niagara of visual gabble."[9] The motif of traffic-clogged roads is also repeatedly invoked in the film to denote a dystopian urban diorama. The earlier promise of "autopia," to use Reyner Banham's memorable classification of the Los Angeles landscape, has gradually dissipated into a kind of threatening repository of existential meaninglessness.[10]

The sense of foreboding intensifies as Carol drives along the freeway listening to apocalyptic religious callers on FM talk-radio. A van in front of her spews out thick smoke from its exhaust and Carol has a prolonged coughing fit. Desperate to leave the freeway, she enters a multi-story car park where she drives around and around in a state of mounting panic and disorientation. Back in the safety of her own home we find her lying listlessly on a sofa. It is here that we encounter the first trace of contact with radical ecological thinking. Presented in a documentary style (though we cannot be sure that this is not a sophisticated piece of extended advertising), a television program presents images of the earth from space juxtaposed with scenes of ecological devastation. "A movement to save the trees," intones a soothing male narrator, "some say it goes deeper than that":

> Today environmentalists from all over the globe are adopting a new, more holistic approach to their studies which they call "deep ecology." Deep ecology goes beyond the traditional scientific framework to create a greater spiritual awareness of the planet, or as eco-philosopher Carlo Grass puts it, "an understanding of the one-ness of all life."

As the voice gradually fades out we focus on Carol's face. Haynes' choice of ecological sentiment carefully reflects the kind of "deep ecological" literature which developed in the 1980s through the writing of Bill Devall, George Sessions, Michael Tobias, and others. The fictional eco-philosopher "Carlo Grass" is invoked to provide a veneer of scientific authority. The holistic perspective advanced combines romantic idealism with a highly reductionist conception of human agency. It is precisely the kind of ecological awareness which mirrors the intensified individualism of the Reagan era. A central political tension to be explored in the film begins to crystallize around the search for individual self-fulfillment rather than any recognition of the scope for collective social action to solve environmental problems.

Carol's health continues to deteriorate and she seeks medical advice for the first time. It is in these encounters with medical and scientific authority that Haynes begins to develop a gendered dimension to his depiction of environmental illness. Carol's doctor is clearly baffled by her illness and admits that he cannot find anything wrong with her "outside of a slight rash and congestion." After arriving home that evening Carol's sense of anxiety is intensified as she listens to her ten-year-old stepson read out his homework essay on the theme of crime:

> In the '80s, there are more and more gangs in the Los Angeles basin. Plus many more stabbings and shootings . . . LA is now the gang capital of America. Rapes, riots, shooting innocent people, slashing throats, arms and legs being dissected, are all common sights in the black ghettos of LA. Today black and Chicano gangs are coming into the valleys and mostly white areas more and more. That's why gangs in LA are a big American issue.

In this scene Haynes develops the broader theme of middle class anxieties over personal safety and the "containment" of urban violence. Haynes' representation of middle class paranoia echoes the kind of arguments made by Mike Davis in *City of Quartz* concerning the fortified spaces of southern California where "middle class imagination, absent from any first-hand knowledge of inner city conditions, magnifies the perceived threat through a demonological lens."[11] In the affluent and gated communities of Los Angeles, physical security is placed on a par with financial security as an indicator of social status. Differential degrees of personal and environmental safety emerge as a metaphor for social structure. With multiple chemical sensitivity, however, even the most intimate and secure spaces of the home become alien and threatening through the dissipation of pre-existing boundaries.

Over the next few days we see Carol developing her interest in alternative health regimes through a fruit-only diet and the elimination of dairy products. Her behavior becomes more erratic: she sits impassively through a restaurant meal ignoring the conversation around her; she wanders aimlessly around the garden at night; and a coffee morning with friends induces a panic attack. Her continuing lack of interest in sex provokes anger in her husband: in one scene, for example, she hugs her husband only to be violently sick. This intense sense of claustrophobia and domestic malady underlies a connection between the social and environmental determinants of her ill health. On a second visit to her doctor (this time accompanied by her husband) she is referred to a psychiatrist. The implication is clear: if the illness has no readily identifiable physiological cause then it must be psychological in origin.[12] In a later scene, a psychiatrist stares at Carol from behind a vast desk, his office adorned with expensive-looking Oriental wall hangings. "Do you work?," he asks. "No," replies Carol, "I'm a house . . . um . . . homemaker. I'm working on some designs for our house, though, in my spare time." There is an awkward silence broken by another question from the psychiatrist: "We really need to be hearing from you. What's going on in you?" There are clear parallels here between the long-standing attitudes of the medical establishment toward mental illness in women and the contemporary skepticism of many (often male) doctors toward the existence of environmental illness in its predominantly women sufferers.[13] This is a significant point because it emphasizes the complexity of the phenomenon in question as it cuts across a series of pre-existing gendered constructions of scientific knowledge and medical authority.

Carol's attempt to educate herself about her health progresses further at a public meeting on the theme of "environmental illness." In this scene Haynes is careful to present us with a mixed audience, no longer simply a depiction of affluent white America but a broad array of people by age, class, and ethnicity. Some of the audience are also clearly ill and wear masks during the meeting (the ontological status of chemically induced illness is never in doubt). We see the audience listening attentively to an educational video. "Who are you?" asks a reassuringly calm male voice, "You are of all ages and from all walks of life":

> But you find you all have one thing in common: strange never-ending ailments. Suddenly you can't cook dinner anymore because the smell of the gas from the stove makes you ill. Or if you take the freeway you feel as if you might choke on the fumes. Your family and friends tell you that you're over-reacting; it's all in your head. But your symptoms worsen. Fatigue and depression turn into migraines, blackouts, even seizures. Now if this sounds familiar, you're not alone. What you most likely are is one of a vastly growing number of people suffering from environmental illness. That means that for reasons not yet known to us certain people's natural tolerance to everyday substances is breaking down, usually as a result of some kind of chemical

exposure. Today there are 60,000 chemicals in everyday use yet only ten per cent are tested for human toxicity. This is a disease that you catch from your environment.

The next encounter with medicine is through the services of a clinical ecologist who tests Carol's allergic responses to a variety of everyday foods, molds, and other potential allergens. She suddenly reacts very strongly to one of the tests, thereby confirming that a severe allergy forms part of her deteriorating health. The doctor acknowledges that "we can turn it on and off like a switch," but adds ominously that "we just don't know how to make it go away." In this one scene, then, there is some scientific recognition of the legitimacy of her illness but it is clear that the extent of knowledge and understanding remains incomplete. Indeed, there is no sense in which the allergies might be alleviated through any form of collective action: the implication of her encounter with clinical ecology is that people affected should alter their own lifestyles in order to protect their damaged immune systems. She attends yet another public meeting (this time accompanied by her husband) and we hear testimony from individual sufferers. One woman blames her condition on a fumigation company which is being sued for the flouting of environmental laws. Another woman in the audience claims that her condition has greatly improved since attending a desert retreat for chemically sensitive people (it is through this probable plant in the audience that we are first made aware of the Wrenwood Center's existence). Meanwhile, Carol's condition deteriorates: she tells her friend how she has been poisoned by oranges which had been wrapped in newsprint, how their new couch proved to be "totally toxic," and that she can no longer wear make-up. Her friend is clearly impressed by Carol's growing knowledge about the toxicity of different foods and everyday materials. Carol has developed a more confident identity for herself now as a "chemically sensitive person," devoted to clearing her body of its chemical load and to proselytizing her new found health awareness.

The first half of the film concludes with Carol's ill-timed arrival at the local dry cleaners during a bug-spraying operation. She collapses to the floor with a life-threatening seizure and is rushed to hospital. Her doctor visits her in hospital but continues to doubt that her illness could be environmental in origin. Carol is now openly scornful of her doctor's disbelief and blames her condition on "the chemicals." During her hospitalization she sees a television program about the Wrenwood Center for chemically sensitive people. "Nestled in the foothills of Albuquerque," we are told, "the Wrenwood Center describes itself as a non-profit communal settlement dedicated to self healing, offering the services of a combined health retreat and community center." The stage is now set for the second part of the film and Carol's encounter with New Age philosophies of personal healing and environmental well-being. We follow Carol's taxi journey through a jumble of industrial and suburban zones on the urban fringe as she heads for the New Mexico desert. She peers out from the taxi window onto a confused assortment of unregulated real estate speculation, unsightly billboards, and scattered remnants of former industrial activity. The presence of nature intensifies from sidewalk weeds and straggling palm trees to a gradual opening out of the arid landscape. A growing sense of light and space now pervades a vista which has been emptied of any obvious signs of human artifice apart from the interstate highway twisting away into the hazy distance.

THE WRENWOOD CENTER, NEW MEXICO

A roadside sign informs us that the Wrenwood Center was founded in 1978, a critical year during which liberal political coalitions began to experience serious setbacks across the United States and a new kind of right-wing populist agenda gathered pace. In California, for example, 1978 saw the passing of the infamous Proposition 13 resolution which instituted a decisive shift away from adequately financed local services such as health and education.[14] The late 1970s also marked a significant turning-point in the development of American environmentalism, marked by a weakening of earlier alliances between the labor and environmental movements which succeeded in driving through a progressive legislative agenda in the early 1970s.[15] These earlier priorities became gradually displaced through the economic marginalization of environmental quality issues and the diffusion of "deep ecological" ideas which ran counter to any productive engagement between social and environmental concerns.[16]

The founder and director of the fictitious Wrenwood Center is the charismatic Peter Dunning (Peter Friedman) who gazes out of the center's publicity literature like a suave matinée idol. Dunning is introduced to us as an influential

26 The director of the Wrenwood Center, Peter Dunning (Peter Friedman), addresses the center's staff and residents, in *[Safe]* (Copyright Sony Pictures Entertainment Inc., 1995)

environmentalist, well known from his TV appearances, who describes the retreat as a "safe haven for troubled times." After Carol's arrival we encounter Dunning for the first time at a gathering of the center's staff and residents (**26**). A friendly African-American woman informs Carol that Peter is a "chemically sensitive person with AIDS," thereby emphasizing an ostensible social inclusivity at the center which could be easily mistaken for a continuation of the diverse gatherings of people depicted at the public meetings held in Los Angeles. Dunning deploys remarkable rhetorical aplomb in his effortless drift from humorous introductory preamble to a powerful reiteration of the Wrenwood philosophy:

> So we're feeling good, huh? We're feeling warmth, we can look into each other's eyes and actually see rejuvenation and personal transformation happening. Why? Because

we've left the judgmental behind. Phew! [*Dunning wipes his brow in an ironic gesture of release*] . . . Because when you look out on the world from a place of love and a place of forgiveness what you are seeing outside is a reflection of what you feel. Does that make sense? [*nods and murmurs from the audience*] So [*rubbing his hands together*] what do I see outside me? I see the growth of environmentalism and holistic study. I see a decline in drugs and promiscuity [*applause from the audience*]. I see [*raising his voice*] sensitivity training in the workplace. Yeah! [*louder applause from the audience accompanied by cheers*] and the men's movement and multiculturalism [*prolonged applause and yells from the audience*]. I see all these positive things outside in the world because what I am seeing is a global transformation identical to the transformation [*he pauses*] I revel at within. And with that: [*the audience and Dunning speak together in prayer-like fashion*] We are one with the power that created us, we are safe, and all is well in our world.

The implication of this scene is clear. The Wrenwood Center is not a health center but a kind of sophisticated retreat in which the residents are persuaded to adopt a highly moralistic philosophical agenda. There is repeated reference to some kind of inevitable transition toward a new kind of society through the gathering pace of individual revelation and self-healing. This kind of quasi-spiritual New Age philosophy has been prominent within the development of environmental thinking in the West since the late 1960s and can be traced through the writings of Fritjof Capra, Charlene Spretnak, and a number of other influential contributors.[17] The role of nature as a powerful source of symbolic legitimation to these strands of thinking is repeatedly emphasized in the film. In one particularly poignant moment, for example, Dunning sits on the verandah of Carol's room and describes how "words are just the way to get to what's true," and then, as if by a sleight of magical timing, he points to a coyote on the desert hillside. The coyote is especially significant in this context as a classical beast of North American mythology. Dunning's metaphysical hubris is sustained in this instance by a flash of ecological serendipity and the appropriation of non-Western belief systems. The desert landscape also provides a poignant contrast with the urban sprawl of the San Fernando Valley. The dichotomy between culture and nature recreated within the film's narrative structure skillfully presents a tension between two non-dialectical conceptions of nature. We find that a rationalist bio-medical ethos is counterpointed with a nature-based philosophical system of personal salvation advanced through the repudiation of modernity.

Meanwhile, Carol's health continues to deteriorate. She is now permanently accompanied by her breathing apparatus which she must wheel around with her wherever she goes. Haynes is careful to show us that not only is the Wrenwood Center ineffectual in a political sense but it is also of little practical value in a medical sense. That evening there is another lecture from Dunning, who sits in avuncular fashion at the edge of the lecture hall podium in order to invoke a sense of informality and trust:

> Ladies and gentlemen I have a confession to make. I've stopped reading the papers! I've stopped watching the news on TV! I've heard the media doom and gloom and I have seen their fatalistic negative attitude and I've finally realized once and for all: I don't need it! And so I transform that negative stimulus into something that will not do harm to me. Because if I really believe that life is [*pauses for effect*] that devastating, that destructive, I'm afraid that my immune system will believe it too, and [*making an oblique reference to his HIV status*] I can't afford to take that risk. Neither can you.

The rage against "chemicals" which marked Carol's earlier environmental consciousness at public meetings in Los Angeles is now turned inward at Wrenwood where patients are told that they have made themselves sick. This connection between morality and health through the advocacy of personal responsibility and self-growth marks a distinctive feature of many New Age health philosophies.[18] This view of human well-being returns us to a kind of pre-Pasteurian and pre-Chadwickian conception of disease and public health in which human suffering was routinely ascribed to feckless or immoral behavior. As the residents become indoctrinated with the Center's philosophical mantra of self-blame they become convinced that it is anger and disappointment about their own lives which has led to a breakdown in their immune systems. In group therapy sessions the Center's residents are encouraged to reveal their sense of self-hatred and low self-esteem. Dunning nods approvingly: "nobody out there made us sick," he tells them, "The only person who can make you get sick, is you . . . If our immune system is damaged, it's because we have allowed it to be." Yet this transposing of physical illness into moral metaphor condemns the ill through "punitive or sentimental fantasies" which not only worsen the experience of ill health but also undermine the possibilities for effective treatment.[19] Even after the passage of the 1906 Pure Food and Drugs Acts the anti-rationalist impulse which combines pseudo-medicine with fear of illness has continued to provide fertile ground for the unscrupulous exploitation of sickness. The historian James Young, for instance, in his classic study of medical quackery entitled *The Toadstool Millionaires*, shows how "alternative medicine" has been an enduring theme in American social and intellectual history. Dunning's "self-cure" philosophy is simply a late-twentieth-century variant on the Harry Hoxseys of the past.[20]

The Wrenwood Center is not only a retreat for chemical detoxification but also a site of political cleansing, a place of joyful collective amnesia.[21] The multicultural and multi-ethnic nature of the people at the retreat provides a glib veneer of socially inclusive harmony, yet this cult-like business venture successfully exploits the inadequacies of social policy by diverting creative energies toward individual rather than society-wide advancement. We can argue that the Wrenwood Center is best interpreted as a distant outpost of the suburban enclaves of southern California. Rather than representing polar opposites, these kinds of places are intimately related. Their apparent contrast is sustained through the long-standing ideological antinomy between city and country. As Raymond Williams observed, this historic juxtaposition has served "to promote superficial comparisons and to prevent real ones."[22] In this case, much of the rhetorical power of New Age environmental thought rests on a profoundly anti-modern and anti-urban sentiment which not only obscures the cause of environmental illness but also subverts the possibilities for any kind of rational analysis or collective response to ecological problems.

Haynes portrays Dunning as self-delusional, or, at worst, cynically manipulative of vulnerable and gullible people in order to finance his lavish lifestyle: when Carol's husband visits Wrenwood he asks her who lives in the huge house on a hill overlooking the Center. "Oh, that's where Peter lives," replies Carol, seemingly unconcerned about the foundation's claim to be non profit-making. In the final scene, we find Carol alone in her isolation "igloo," her face now swollen and covered with reddish lesions. She sits in front of a mirror and repeats to herself in a plaintive voice, "I love you." The credits roll and we are left in little doubt that she will soon be dead. There is no concession made to the narrative expectation of a "happy ending" characteristic of commercial cinema in this powerful and disturbing portrayal of illness in late-twentieth-century America.

CONCLUSIONS

The tessellated landscapes of Los Angeles and its vast semi-arid hinterland have long held a peculiar fascination for writers, scholars, and filmmakers. The juxtaposition of the raw energies of nature and culture has produced an ideological fault line between the self-conscious products of human imagination and a primordial arena of "first nature" untrammeled by the forces of modernity. Los Angeles has emerged as a pivotal city within this renegotiation of the boundary between nature and culture. Fragments of nature and landscape have been woven into the urban fabric in order to create the semblance of a Jeffersonian small town idyll. The San Fernando Valley, which provides the setting for the first half of [Safe], is in many respects an axiomatic example of this transformation of the American landscape. The orchards and farms which made up the original backdrop for the development of suburban garden cities were rapidly displaced by new development pressures as the feeble greenbelt zoning of the 1940s and other legislative safeguards were swept aside.[23] From the sunny modernity of Reyner Banham to the Marxist *noir* of Mike Davis, a range of literature has delved into Los Angeles in order to explicate the role of nature within the process of capitalist urbanization. The ideological power of the fictional Wrenwood Center, tucked away in the New Mexico desert, is rooted in a fetishization of the "urban" as a discrete entity which can be cordoned off from a "natural" realm of wild nature. The powerful juxtaposition of alternative utopian landscapes in [Safe] is periodically unsettled by highways and other "contaminated" spaces that demarcate the boundaries between Carol's search for a safe haven and the "chemicals" which threaten her well-being. Her journey from the San Fernando Valley to New Mexico, which passes through an "undesigned" urban fringe landscape of unspecified industrial activities, low income housing and ecological blight, is her only prolonged encounter with the spatial complexity of Los Angeles and the kind of places which underpin her affluent lifestyle as the unseen habitat of low-paid workers. These are the people who really live in close proximity to chemical refineries, noxious waste processing plants, and other significant sources of urban pollution, yet their story is largely absent from epidemiological disputes over Multiple Chemical Sensitivity. Though we encounter some sense of this wider debate over environmental justice at the public meeting Carol attends in Los Angeles, the narrative structure of the film excludes any engagement with the radical anti-pollution campaigns of groups such as the Mothers of East Los Angeles.[24] In *[Safe]* we witness a disengagement of middle class environmental politics from any kind of broader agenda for social change as the progressive legislative agendas of the past have been displaced by an inward looking anti-rationalism.

In *[Safe]* we are presented with a satirical condemnation of the existential emptiness of wealthy suburban enclaves along with a withering assault on the solipsistic alternatives promulgated by New Age gurus of "non-Western" thinking. The fictional Wrenwood Center is simply an exaggerated extension of the spatial separation and political myopia of the gated communities of the San Fernando Valley. The phenomenon of multiple chemical sensitivity among affluent middle class Americans is used to illuminate the political weaknesses of New Age responses to issues of public health and environmental justice. In *[Safe]*, Haynes sets out to critique both conventional medicine and the alternative health communities which have emerged to treat AIDS, cancer, chemical sensitivity, and other illnesses which lie at the edge of scientific knowledge and understanding. The medical establishment is portrayed as a masculinist science, irresponsive to patient testimony, and hidebound by outmoded diagnostic dogma. New Age alternatives are presented in an even less favorable light, as little more than half-baked quackery which plays on the existential fears of the ill. As Haynes has noted of his fictional environmental guru Peter Dunning:

> Peter's cure is to adhere completely to these very basic ideas about self that affirm the society as it is. His kind of New Age philosophy comes out of a '60s ideology, using Eastern traditions to re-examine the West. It claims to change the world through self-esteem or a softening of basic structures of resistance, but I see it as a reiteration of basic conservative arguments about the self, which are closely aligned with masculinity and patriarchy.[25]

The film's narrative structure traces Carol's progression from disorientation to recognition of her environmentally induced chemical allergies. Yet this second phase in her awareness is never allowed to develop. The implication is clear: the possibilities for collective action become subverted by her search for self-development. Her quest for inward self-fulfillment buries any recognition of the underlying causes of environmental illness. Carol also eschews any kind of engagement with feminist ideas and fails to recognize the degree to which her sense of powerlessness has contributed to her declining mental health.[26] Her creative energies are devoted to pursuits such as interior decorating and the exploration of alternative health therapies rather than any direct confrontation with the structures of power and authority which are destroying her life. This is significant because not all chemical sensitivity sufferers have followed this route. Since the late 1980s, there has been growing political awareness of the causes of chemical sensitivity marked by a spate of law suits under the US Rehabilitation Act, the Americans with Disabilities Act, the Fair Housing Amendment Act, and also under negligence or product liability actions.[27] Yet this regulatory progress is by no means easy given the lack of consensus among health care workers, lawyers, scientists, and public health advocates. The contemporary debate over chemical sensitivity is characterized by mutually reinforcing spheres of uncertainty which cloud the possibilities for any kind of collective response to the immunological disruption of American health.

Recently, calls have emerged for rational science to prevail in discussions and policy recommendations surrounding multiple chemical sensitivity. Gio Batta Gori has argued that "the quest for rationality and objectivity slowly fought its way through history," and that multiple chemical sensitivity presents a new challenge for science in the face of competing "mystical, magic, or emotional interpretations of reality."[28] The distinction between what Gori terms "rational" and "mystical" modes of explanation mirrors the impasse between conventional and alternative health care responses to chemical sensitivity which are portrayed in [Safe]. This tension is also suggestive of a broader philosophical chasm which has opened since the early 1990s between reductionist and social constructivist conceptions of physical reality.[29] This dichotomous representation of competing analytical frameworks has led conventional scientific responses to newly emerging sources of ill health (and environmental change) to ignore dialectical or historically based modes of analysis as a viable alternative to postmodern philosophies of science.[30]

Haynes' depiction of chemical sensitivity develops a richly layered iconography of fear and anxiety. Los Angeles provides a powerful setting for an exploration of these themes through its contradictory intersection of utopian fragments amid an ever-present malaise of existential meaninglessness. It is the political vacuity of the Reagan era which lends such poignancy to this striking representation of social and spatial dislocations. The inability to clearly distinguish between the physical and psychological origins of illness reflects a wider uncertainty over the structural origins of ill health in an era of "self actualization" and hyper-modernity. The experience of disease in Los Angeles is thus a metaphor for social and spatial contamination as well as a concrete manifestation of physiological harm. Uncontrolled urban space is depicted in [Safe] as synonymous with the threat of disease and crime to the well-being of bourgeois society.[31] With the advent of chemical sensitivity we find that the distinction between self and nonself is greatly magnified to the extent that virtually any element within the everyday environment can become alien and threatening.[32] In psychoanalytic terms, the "return of the repressed" can take many forms: fears of the urban underclass; anxieties over risk and health; or more diffuse and abstract concerns with global disequilibria and chaos. The sociologist Avery Gordon has elaborated on contemporary metaphors of unease through her investigation of "haunting" as a shared "structure of feeling" in contemporary society. This intervention begins to sketch possible linkages between our understanding of the "uncanny" as a specific kind of aesthetic and philosophical phenomenon and the kind of cultural materialism developed in the writings of Raymond Williams.[33] Though [Safe] is primarily concerned with environmental illness, the "haunting" of upper middle class Los Angeles is clearly a more diffuse and complex set of existential fears surrounding aging, morbidity, and personal security. In particular, [Safe] can be read as an allegory for the handling of AIDS in the Reagan era, where a mix of moral and quasi-spiritual responses developed in place of a coordinated public health response.[34] [Safe] is a film about what happens to societies under some kind of collective threat where there is no clearly defined collective response. It is a film which charts our retreat into private worlds of political disengagement and social isolation. It is, above all, the congruence between New Age philosophies and conservative individualism which constitutes the most disturbing element in this complex allegorical depiction of affluent Western societies.

NOTES

1. I would like to thank Mark Shiel and Emer Williams for their helpful comments on an earlier draft of this chapter.

2. Todd Haynes, "Nowhere to Hide: Interview with Amy Taubin" in *Sight and Sound*, May 1996, p. 34.

3. The film, whose production was delayed for some time, was eventually funded from various sources including American Playhouse, the Public Broadcasting Service, the Corporation for Public Broadcasting, the National Endowment for the Arts and the UK-based Channel Four Television. A range of environmental organizations are thanked in the closing credits including the Response Team for the Chemically Injured, the Allergy Research Group, the Chemical Connection, and Greenpeace. In making the film Haynes researched the phenomenon of chemical sensitivity extremely carefully and Julianne Moore, who plays the central character Carol White, studied the testimony of chemically sensitive patients in detail. The existing scientific literature suggests that symptoms of chemical sensitivity are typically chronic and recurrent and often occur after an initial exposure, with subsequent reactions triggered by progressively smaller degrees of exposure to the same substance. The symptoms of chemically sensitive people vary widely and are often linked to the central nervous system with sufferers affected by a combination of fatigue, depression, headaches, asthma, and panic attacks. Triggers to chemical sensitivity include many different foods, pesticides, detergents, solvents, certain metals (such as nickel and lead), and less clearly defined triggers such as air conditioning, central heating systems, newly installed materials, and the operation of office machinery. Non-chemical triggers include stress, trauma, and personal injury (including surgical operations). We also find that sufferers are typically affected by multiple and chemically unrelated substances: the removal of these various triggers usually leads to some improvement in the reported symptoms. For recent medical and scientific debates on multiple chemical sensitivity see I. R. Bell, G. E. Schwartz, C. M. Baldwin, and E. E. Hardin, "Neural sensitization and physiological markers in multiple chemical sensitivity," *Regulatory Toxicology and Pharmacology*, 24, 1996, S39–47; D. I. Bernstein, "Multiple chemical sensitivity: state of the art symposium—the role of chemical allergens," *Regulatory Toxicology and Pharmacology*, 24, 1996, S28–31; K. I. Bolla, "Neuropsychological evaluation for detecting alterations in the central nervous system after chemical exposure," *Regulatory Toxicology and Pharmacology*, 24, 1996, S48–51; E. J. Calabrese, "Biochemical individuality: the next generation," *Regulatory Toxicology and Pharmacology*, 24, 1996, S58–67; M. Castleman, "This place makes me sick," *Sierra*, September–October 1993, pp. 105–16; R. E. Gots, "Multiple chemical sensitivities: distinguishing between psychogenic and toxicodynamic," *Regulatory Toxicology and Pharmacology*, 24, 1996, S8–15; B. J. Kunz, J. Ring, and O. Braun-

Falco, "Are allergies really increasing?," *Fortschritte der Medizin*, 109, 1991, pp. 353–6; E. Nelson, "The MCS debate: a medical streetfight," *Washington Free Press*, February–March 1994; J. R. Nethercott, L. L. Davidoff, B. Curbow, and H. Abbey, "Multiple chemical sensitivities syndrome: toward a working case definition," *Archives of Environmental Health*, 48, 1993, pp. 19–26; J. E. Salvaggio, "Understanding clinical immunological testing in alleged chemically induced environmental illness," *Regulatory Toxicology and Pharmacology*, 24, 1996, S16–27; R. S. Schwartz and S. K. Datta, "Autoimmunity and autoimmune diseases," in W. E. Paul, ed., *Fundamental Immunology*, New York: Raven Press, 1989, pp. 819–66.

 4. See G. Brown, "Out of This World," *Village Voice*, June 27 1995; B. Reynaud, "Les indépendents et les fleurs du mal," in *Cahiers du cinéma*, 489, 1995, pp. 14–15; C. Stephens, "Gentlemen Prefer Haynes: Of Dolls, Dioramas, and Disease—Todd Haynes' Safe passage," *Film Comment*, 31, 1995, pp. 76–9.

 5. The 1990s has seen a number of films which could be loosely grouped within the genre of "dystopian urbanism," such as Robert Altman's *Short Cuts* (1993), Kathryn Bigelow's *Strange Days* (1995), and Lawrence Kasdan's *Grand Canyon* (1991). Needless to say, Los Angeles is the standard setting for many of these types of films. See M. Davis, *Ecology of Fear: Los Angeles and the Imagination of Disaster*, New York: Metropolitan Books, 1998.

 6. See, for example, R. Reid, "Unsafe at Any Distance: Todd Haynes' Visual Culture of Health and Risk," *Film Quarterly*, 51, 1998, pp. 32–44; R. Grundmann, "How Clean Was My Valley: Todd Haynes' *Safe*," *Cineaste*, 21, 1995, pp. 22–5.

 7. Todd Haynes, "Nowhere to Hide. Interview with Amy Taubin" in *Sight and Sound*, May 1996, p. 33.

 8. Allen J. Scott, "High-technology Industrial Development in the San Fernando Valley and Ventura County: Observations on Economic Growth and the Evolution of Urban Form," in Allen J. Scott and Edward J. Soja, eds, *The City: Los Angeles and Urban Theory at the End of the Twentieth Century*, Berkeley, CA: University of California Press, 1996, p. 288.

 9. Robert Hughes cited in Perry Anderson, *The Origins of Postmodernity*, London and New York: Verso, 1998, p. 89.

10. Reyner Banham, *Los Angeles: The Architecture of the Four Ecologies*, London: Penguin, 1971.

11. Mike Davis, cited in G. Naismith, "Tales From the Crypt: Contamination and Quarantine in Todd Haynes' *[Safe]*," in P. A. Trichler, L. Cartwright, and C. Penley, eds, *The Visible Woman: Imaging Technologies, Gender, and Science*, New York: New York University Press, 1998, p. 361.

12. See S. Kroll-Smith and A. E. Ladd, "Environmental illness and biomedicine: anomalies, exemplars, and the politics of the body," *Sociological Spectrum* 13, 1993, pp. 7–33.

13. H. M. Kipen, W. Hallman, and K. Kelly-McNeil, "Measuring chemical sensitivity prevalence: a questionnaire for population studies," *American Journal of Public Health*, 85, 1995, pp. 574–7; J. Rea, *Chemical Sensitivity: volume 1*, Boca Raton, FL: Lewis Publishers, 1992; Schwartz and Datta, "Autoimmunity and autoimmune diseases," pp. 819–66. See also G. Naismith, "Tales From the Crypt: Contamination and Quarantine in Todd Haynes' [Safe]," in Trichler et al., *The Visible Woman*.

14. Mike Davis, *Prisoners of the American Dream: Politics and Economy in the History of the US Working Class*, London and New York: Verso, 1986; M. Kettle, "End of the Californian Dream," *The Guardian* (London), May 25 1998, p. 11.

15. S. Dewey, "Working for the Environment: Organized Labor and the Origins of Environmentalism in the United States, 1948–1970," *Environmental History*, 3, 1998, pp. 45–63; D. Faber and J. O'Connor, "Capitalism and the Crisis of Environmentalism," in R. Hofrichter, ed., *Toxic Struggles: The Theory and Practice of Environmental Justice*, Philadelphia, PA: New Society, 1993, pp. 12–25.

16. The emergence of the environmental justice movement in the 1990s signals an important exception to this trend. See, for example, R. D. Bullard, *Dumping in Dixie: Race, Class and Environmental Quality*, Boulder, CO: Westview Press, 2nd edition, 1994; C. Levenstein and J. Wooding, eds, *Work, Health, and Environment: Old Problems, New Solutions*, London and New York: Guilford Press, 1997; D. Pena, "The 'Brown' and the 'Green': Chicanos and Environmental Politics in the Upper Rio Grande," *Capitalism, Nature, Socialism*, 3, 1992, pp. 79–103; R. Rosen, "Who Gets Polluted? The movement for Environmental Justice," *Dissent*, Spring 1994, pp. 223–30; A. Szasz, *Ecopopulism: Toxic Waste and the Movement for Environmental Justice*, London and Minneapolis: University of Minnesota Press, 1994.

17. Other examples of influential deep ecological literature which make explicit connections with New Age health philosophies include M. J. Cohen, *Well Mind, Well Earth*, Roche Harbor, WA: World Peace University Press, 1994; B. Devall and G. Sessions, *Deep Ecology*, Layton, UT: Peregrine Smith Books, 1985; P. Devereux, J. Steele, and D. Kubrin, *Earthmind*, New York: Harper and Row, 1989; D. LaChapelle, *Earth Wisdom*, Silverton, CO: Finn Hill Arts, 1984; D. LaChapelle, *Sacred Land, Sacred Sex, Rapture of the Deep: Concerning Deep Ecology and Celebrating Life*, Berkeley, CA: Parallax Press, 1988; J. Macy, *World as Lover, World as Self*, Berkeley, CA: Parallax Press, 1991; J. Seed, J. Macy, P. Fleming, and A. Naess, *Thinking Like a Mountain: Toward a Council of All Beings*, Philadelphia, PA, and Santa Cruz, CA: New Society Publishers, 1988.

18. See R. Coward, *The Whole Truth: The Myth of Alternative Health*, London: Faber and Faber, 1989; G. Naismith, "Tales from the Crypt: Contamination and Quarantine in Todd Haynes' [Safe]," in Trichler et al., *The Visible Woman*, p. 361.

19. Susan Sontag, *Illness as Metaphor*, New York: Vintage Books, 1977, p. 3.

20. See James Harvey Young, *The Toadstool Millionaires: A Social History of Patent*

Medicines in America before Federal Regulation, Princeton, NJ: Princeton University Press, 1961, pp. 260–1. Harry Hoxsey was a profitable Dallas based medical charlatan who from the 1930s until the 1950s claimed to be able to cure cancer.

21. Reiner Grundmann, "How Clean Was My Valley: Todd Hayne's *Safe*," *Cineaste*, 21, 1995, pp. 22–5.

22. Raymond Williams, *The Country and the City*, Oxford: Oxford University Press, 1973, p. 54. On the ideological dimensions to city–country relations, see also Leo Marx, "The American Ideology of Space," in S. Wrede and W. H. Adams, eds, *Denatured Visions:Landscape and Culture in the Twentieth Century*, New York: Museum of Modern Art, 1991, pp. 62–78; A. Wilson, *The Culture of Nature*, Oxford: Blackwell, 1992.

23. See Mike Davis, "How Eden Lost its Garden: A Political History of the Los Angeles Landscape" in Scott and Soja, *The City*, pp. 160–85.

24. See, for example, Laura Pulido, *Environmentalism and Economic Justice: Two Chicano Struggles in the Southwest*, Tucson: University of Arizona Press, 1996.

25. Todd Haynes, "Nowhere to Hide: Interview with Amy Taubin," in *Sight and Sound*, May 1996, p. 32.

26. See Naismith, "Tales from the Crypt."

27. M. S. Lieberman, B. J. Dimuro, and J. B. Boyd, "Multiple chemical sensitivity: an emerging area of law," *Trial*, 31, 1995, pp. 22–6.

28. G. B. Gori, "The role of objective science in policy development: evidence versus conjecture," *Regulatory Toxicology and Pharmacology*, 24, 1996, S3.

29. For recent examples of this sharply polarized epistemological divide, see the misrepresentations of radical science contained in P. Gross and N. Levitt, *Higher Superstition: The Academic Left and its Quarrels with Science*, Baltimore, MD: Johns Hopkins University Press, 1994; M. Soulé and G. Lease, eds, *Reinventing Nature: Responses to Postmodern Deconstruction*, San Francisco: Island Press, 1995.

30. See, for example, the combination of biology and cultural anthropology in the work of Emily Martin and especially the path-breaking dialectical approaches to biological science developed by Richard Levins and Richard Lewontin.

31. C. Grunenberg, *Gothic: Transmutations of Horror in Late Twentieth Century Art*, Boston: Institute of Contemporary Art and Cambridge, MA: MIT Press, 1997; Anthony Vidler, *The Architectural Uncanny: Essays in the Modern Unhomely*, Cambridge, MA: MIT Press, 1992.

32. Donna Haraway, "The Biopolitics of Postmodern Bodies: Constitutions of Self in Immune System Discourse," in *Simians, Cyborgs and Women: The Reinvention of Nature*, London: Free Association Books, 1991, pp. 203–30; E. Martin, *Flexible Bodies: Tracking Immunity in American Culture—From the Days of Polio to the Age of AIDS*, Boston: Beacon Press, 1994.

33. A. F. Gordon, *Ghostly Matters: Haunting and the Sociological Imagination*, Minneapolis: University of Minnesota Press, 1997.
34. O. Moverman, "And All is Well in our World—making *[Safe]*," in J Boorman and W Donohue, eds, *Projections 5*, London: Faber and Faber, 1996; Naismith, "Tales from the Crypt"; S. Sontag, *AIDS and its Metaphors*, New York: Farrar, Strauss, and Giroux, 1988.

13

THE DELEUZEAN EXPERIENCE OF CRONENBERG'S *CRASH* AND WENDERS' *THE END OF VIOLENCE*

DARRELL VARGA

The conflicting desires for proximity and escape, like the technologies of mechanical reproduction and internal combustion, come together in the road movie, but the twentieth century, the century of the car and the cinema, ends with David Cronenberg's *Crash* (1996). Here, the road is neither path to escape nor mediation zone between locations in the city—these are inconsequential. It is the road itself as site of transformation that is engaged. This chapter begins with this process of transformation in *Crash*, and then considers the *end* of the city, in Wim Wenders' *The End of Violence* (1996). Our experience of cinema and mass culture cannot be thought separately from the particular instrumentalization of space and time which is the modern city, but the twentieth-century automobile myth of flight as freedom offers a fantasy of escape from that urban mass. As J. G. Ballard described it in a 1970 interview:

> One spends a substantial part of one's life in the motorcar and the experience of driving condenses many of the experiences of being a human being [today] . . . the marriage of physical aspects of ourselves with the imaginative and technological aspects of our lives. I think the twentieth century reaches just about its highest expression on the highway. Everything is there, the speed and violence of our age, its love of stylization, fashion, the organizational side of things—what I call the elaborately signaled landscape.[1]

Vivian Sobchack has incisively pointed out that Ballard's novel (and I would add Cronenberg's film) is by no means a Baudrillardian neo-conservative celebration of the disavowal of the body but instead explores desire in bodily transformation while at the same time articulating the limits and losses accompanying transformation. Sobchack offers an interesting critique of the concept of a "body-without-organs," which she describes as "a techno-body that has no sympathy for human suffering, cannot understand human pleasure, and since it has no conception of death, cannot possibly value life."[2] This critical perspective helps to distinguish between the usefulness of Deleuze and Guattari's thinking and the nihilism of Baudrillard's later writings in which there is no possibility of liberation or transgression. Deleuze and Guattari's thinking is not the same as Baudrillard's techno-fetishism, which, as Sobchack points out, obscures his anti-technological desires. A useful explanation and an introduction to the language of Deleuze and Guattari is provided by Steven Best and Doug Kellner: "The body-without-organs is not an organless body, but a body without 'organization,' a body that breaks free from its socially articulated, disciplined, semioticized, and subjectified state (as an 'organism'), to become disarticulated, dismantled, and deterritorialized, and hence able to be reconstituted in new ways."[3]

CRASH

The road in *Crash* is re-territorialized from a technology connecting in-between spaces to a place of desire itself. Film historian Peter Morris points out that "since the beginning of his career, Cronenberg has developed a visual dialectic between his characters and the space and architecture they occupy."[4] Morris argues that throughout Cronenberg's films the process of liberation is bound together with repression, that, for instance, free sexuality, because it is experienced within the repressive norms of the social, emerges along with the mutation of the body. This argument for an understanding of Cronenberg's films as engaging a necessarily unresolved dialectical process of liberation and repression counters the view of critics such as Robin Wood who describe Cronenberg's films in terms of a reactionary conservatism toward sexuality.[5] While operating

27 "Sex on the open road" in David Cronenberg's *Crash* (1996) (Copyright Alliance Communications Corporation, 1996)

within the limitations of mainstream conventions, Cronenberg's films are symptomatic of contradictory social anxieties toward technology and sexuality. That they do not offer clearly defined utopian alternatives reflects the critical limits of genre entertainment products and the highly ambivalent and contradictory desires and anxieties surrounding sexuality within Western media culture. Cronenberg's status as both commercial producer and individuated *auteur*, celebrated by fans and critics, makes his films particularly useful in the analysis of the limits and possibilities of contemporary media and technology. His films can help us understand how desire and identity function in complex and contradictory ways, expressing impulses of liberation *and* conservative fears over loss of social and bodily control.

   Crash can be understood as more than a simple affirmation of a loss of meaning on the part of the social and individual body, as is the case in some strains of Baudrillard-influenced postmodernist thinking. More useful is an approach which acknowledges a film's contradictory impulses rather than engaging reception either as critical affirmation or as expressions of angst over (simplistic) assumptions of the film's behavioral influence. Mainstream media attacks on the film reveal the tendency on the part of social institutions to discredit those cultural texts which reveal the complexities of the social production of desire.[6] The depiction of sex on the open road or at the site of a car crash is not what is pornographic in *Crash*, despite the shrill tones of the censorious and contrary to those critics who find the sex scenes to be overly mechanical and/or simply boring (**27**).[7] Rather, pornography is found in the invasive practices of the mass media in their reduction of private gesture to commodity within the mediascape and the routinization of expression "on the hour" as an extension of alienating labor. Indeed, Barbara Creed points out that while desire is central to *Crash*, within the film's austere self-enclosed world it is an experience co-extensive with contemporary mechanization and automation. Creed indicates:

> Cronenberg asks us to consider the nature of desire in the postindustrial postmodern age. Desire represents the opposite of the romantic ideal of truth, beauty and wholeness; the postmodern desiring subject yearns for an experience marked by crash culture—division, simulation, brutality, obscenity, perversity, death.[8]

Pornography, for Ballard, is a highly politicized form and it is true that he facetiously declared his book to be "the first pornographic novel based on technology."[9] Here, he is symptomizing alienation in the technologized mass commodity-scape.

Western culture eroticizes technology every day, no more so than in imagery of the car. *Crash* reveals these desires un-coopted by the commodity pretense of narrative convention. What is co-extensive with but outside of this movie frame is the recreational practice of gleeful car destruction at demolition derbies which take place throughout the summer in rural communities and small single-industry towns in North America. As Canadian writer Jane Farrow reports, the people in these communities are highly dependent on the car, yet their communities have been terribly devastated by the downsizing of automobile industries, such that "driving cars into one another might be the sanest possible response to post-industrial society."[10] The concept of "post-industrialism," popularized by Daniel Bell, assumes the rise of knowledge as commodity and the increased importance of the service sector over manufacturing.[11] It is also a discourse for the redemption of leisure and consumption through a fantasy of sanitation—the displacement of messy industry, "troublesome" unions, and the rise of individualism. The primacy of industrial development is no less significant in the contemporary era. It has, however, increasingly been relocated out of the sightlines of Western consumer society. The rhetoric of the information age, in turn, serves to negate the very materialist conditions which ground discourse. The state itself is not necessarily weakened but does function differently, as David Harvey explains in his critique of the neo-conservative championing of post-industrialism:

> It is called upon to regulate the activities of corporate capital in the national interest at the same time as it is forced, also in the national interest, to create a "good business climate" to act as an inducement to trans-national and global finance capital.[12]

This observation is important in situating the materialist context out of which *Crash* emerges, and allows us to understand the film as both a work of art and a manufactured product. The main character, Vaughan (Elias Koteas), is a photographer, a producer of images, but his images function as a consequence of a highly specific organization of production and consumption.

The eroticization of the car crash serves as transformative excess to the mechanization of high-speed human movement in service of the authoritarian demands of the industrial clock. According to Deleuze and Guattari, masochistic desire is not a passage through suffering for the sake of pleasure, it is the expression of desire itself, explicitly performed against social regimentation. In this way, the masochist is seeking not the destruction of the body but its necessary transformation in the context of the contemporary, described by J. G. Ballard in the introduction to his book:

> Thermonuclear weapons systems and soft drink commercials co-exist in an overlit realm ruled by advertising and pseudoevents, science and pornography. Over our lives preside the great twin leitmotifs of the twentieth century—sex and paranoia . . . Voyeurism, self-disgust, the infantile basis of our dreams and longings—these diseases of the psyche have now culminated in the most terrifying casualty of the century: the death of affect.[13]

Linda Ruth Williams points out that the film's re-creation of the James Dean car crash is a feminization of the car in order to "legitimize the collision of men," a displacement necessary within the film's homosocial context.[14] The bodies on film play as components of a single character or, better, of this cybernetic trajectory. They have transcended the instrumental function of the road, of narrative, and the morality of private sexuality. They collectively merge technology and sexuality to become "desiring machines," Deleuze and Guattari's term for bodily expression which has slipped free from the restraints of language, of subjectivity, and the problem of psychoanalysis which translates desire into fantasy or repression.[15] To invoke these thinkers is to engage the film in a way that is not tied to narrative convention and psychoanalytic regimentation. Film can serve the political purpose of deconstructing discursive and institutional structures if critical practice likewise creates space for the new by intervening in the solidification both of practices of representation and of the material institutions in which these practices take place.

If only the film were as transgressive as those who impose the label of pornography assume it to be. Roy Grundmann, writing in *Cineaste*, observes that penetration in the film is restricted to women:

> The anal and rear-entry sex, of which there is much in both the book and its film adaptation, is still perfectly compatible with a conventional male phallicism that flaunts its frontal assets while hiding its vulnerable behind . . . Cronenberg and Ballard keep their sphincters fortified.[16]

Cronenberg parodies this tight-assed characterization in *eXistenZ* (1999), a film which makes explicit the blurring of the body with media images. In that film, characters appear to enter into a virtual reality game world by allowing the technology to penetrate their body through a slippery opening at the base of the spine. In reply to the question of whether he has been equipped with a computer game "bio-port," a virginal boy-man confesses: "I would love to play your games. But I have this phobia about being penetrated surgically." Straight-boy fears of the sexual other come true when the newly installed port is infected and he is unable to perform. In fact, later scenes in the film, ostensibly within the computer game world environment, are photographically and narratively flat, suggesting one possible reading of the film as a parody of the conventions of the homosocial action movie and video game genre. This reading is prompted by Cronenberg's own reported frustrations in seeking major studio financing for a game-boy movie in which the lead performer/game designer was to be a woman: "Their own demographics tell them this kind of movie is going to be attractive to young men—because it's sci-fi and about games—and young men don't want the lead to be a girl. They want it to be them."[17] Yet, if a penis can rise erect out of a type-writer in *Naked Lunch* (1991), surely a dildo can emerge from the wreckage of *Crash*. The film's unwillingness to further develop themes of sexual difference and transgression as lived possibilities reflects the limits of expression within domi-nant media. While Cronenberg is an independent producer and director, and chooses *not* to live and work in Los Angeles, his films, however disruptive of genre conventions, are distributed within the mainstream media marketplace and must be understood as at least partially determined by these conditions even as they expand and call into question these limits.

    Crash articulates an urge to transcend alienation in the expression of desire at the limit of the flesh. The film is interesting precisely because it has it both ways, expressing a desirous yearning yet unable to transcend homosocial conven-tions. Transgression does not simply emerge with desire. What is offered in *Crash* is contained within the social regulation of gender and sexuality. Yet the film offers a Foucauldian emergence of the generative along with that which is prohibited in paternal law—we see repeated references to the crash fetishists' need to avoid the gaze of the police. Linda Ruth Williams observes:

> As male sex is foregrounded through the Ballard–Vaughan liaison, so the film shifts its interest from mainstream culture's banal feminization of cars as women to *Crash*-culture's masculinization of cars not as penis substitutes, but as male sexual arenas, not as tokens of virility, but as scarred extensions of damaged male flesh.[18]

In contrast, one far-fetched review charges the film with queer-bashing in the death of the character Vaughan.[19] While it is true that the film's problematic phallocentric sexual politics privileges the survival of the white heterosexual couple, a film should obviously not be assumed to be endorsing symptomatic cul-tural behavior simply through depiction. Likewise, neither the death nor the sex-uality of Vaughan should be simplified: his death is as much suicide as it is an accidental consequence of extreme edge play, and it is precisely the fluidity of his sexuality that is appealing to the film's other characters. Similarly, it is the tendency of behavioralist reductionism on the part of critics and more generally in society that is parodied in the crazed violent attack on the game designer at the opening of *eXistenZ*.

For the crash fetishists in the film, the best available porn is on a Swedish import video of car manufacturer crash tests: the repetition of back and forth crash impacts upon the bodies of collapsed cars and crash-test dummies. When the video player jams, Helen Remington, with increasing frustration, fumbles awkwardly for the remote control, saying "I'm sure we see this again in slow motion, closer I mean, in detail," until she finds the trigger point on the remote to release the caught image into an ejaculatory splendor of shattered glass. She breathes a sigh of relief and joins her fetish partners in mutual masturbation as they gaze intently at the flickering screen. The gaze directed toward these commodity-images displaces bodily contact. The characters sit alongside each other facing the television, each with one hand on the other's crotch. Interestingly, the images implode in destruction rather than remain as affirmations of commodity culture.

Our structures of communication propel human activity toward commodity fetishism, the fusing of identity with consumption. The Deleuzean response—useful to an understanding of the intersection in *Crash* of desire and violence—is the transformation of the body, the desiring machine, into a "body-without-organs," a line-of-flight, not a destination or state of identity, but a process of becoming. Deleuze and Guattari explain the "body-without-organs" not as a literal body but as a limit upon which are inscribed lines-of-flight: "The body without organs is not a dead body but a living body all the more alive and teeming once it has blown apart the organism and its organization . . . The full body without organs is a body populated by multiplicities."[20] This body emerges in the fusing of technological processes of mediation with a space of desire, collapsed together at the limit of metal and flesh. Whether one argues that "multiplicities" are reduced or expanded by the film's conclusion, what we are left with is the shattering of the conventions of narrative romance, as Fred Botting and Scott Wilson suggest:

> *Crash* offers only the relation of non-relation, an experience of redundancy in the face of endless work-sex-pleasure that unfolds on film in the absence of a *jouissance* that is always missed, that occurs elsewhere . . . in the missed instantaneousness of the crash."[21]

The gridlock of our urban highways is the morning-after hangover from the intoxicating dreams of progress, of exceeding limits, through technology. That dream of high-speed movement is entirely regimented within the straight-line system of routine and standardization. As Herbert Marcuse explained, social control is anchored to the linkage of pleasure with commodification: "Pleasure, thus adjusted, generates submission."[22] We can never go as fast as the technology allows, thus giving rise to alienation and aggression. We know, following Foucault, that the body is ground zero for the disciplinary structures of the city.[23] The car crash disrupts the instrumental and disciplinary movement of urban life between polarized zones of privacy. The bare flesh is exposed on the open road, just as the fast transience of sexuality performed in the cars of Cronenberg's movie suggests a rupture of the notion of intimacy situated in a fixed spatial and temporal relationship. If Marcuse is concerned with the way that liberation is constrained by the forces of production, forces which must be materially transformed in any movement toward social and political emancipation, Deleuze and Guattari offer a means of engaging desire beyond the frame of the social.

We consume space in our polluting back-and-forth automated movement. To disrupt or transform this process is to stop the ceaseless consumption of time, to re-territorialize the urban roadway, this space of mediation, into a place of desire, to recognize, following Walter Benjamin, the monuments of car culture, the privation of private space, as "ruins even before they have crumbled."[24] As intimacy becomes unbound from notions of the private sphere and is enacted upon and through the shattered glass of the car windshield (itself symbolic of the projection of voyeuristic desire toward the cinema screen), this instrumentalized space of the city is transformed in the performance of desire. Our introduction to the character of Ballard (James Spader) in *Crash* occurs in a film studio which, according to the published screenplay, is the set for a mini-van TV commercial. The scene begins with a dashboard and windshield being wheeled away from the perspective of the camera, as an assistant director is heard to ask: "Has anybody seen James Ballard? You know who I mean? The producer of this epic."[25] Ballard is then seen having to hurry toward orgasm with a female camera assistant among the tripods, film change bags, and mechanical gear of the camera department workroom. The scene makes explicit the linkage of work, commodity-image production, and casual sex.

We later learn, during Ballard and Catherine's verbal recounting of the workday and of each other's sexual experiences, that Ballard did not actually have an orgasm. Within this economy of the routinization of sex integrated into the daily labor of image production, the car crash is a liberation of sexual energy repressed by the linear organization of work, the Haussmann-like planning of roadways, and the buckle-up safety of seat-belt bondage. It is a release connected with death: the film's first crash-meeting of Ballard and Helen Remington (Holly Hunter) is marked by the death of the latter's husband when he is projected through the car windshield. The Ballard character, in characteristic deadpan, expresses a feeling of release following the accident: "After being bombarded endlessly by road-safety propaganda, it's almost a relief to have found myself in an actual accident." His thoughts are echoed by this review of the film:

> For J. G. Ballard, the novel *Crash* was a dystopian satire, a counter-blast to consumer safety advocate Ralph Nader. Ballard saw cars as the totem of American culture: aggressive, wasteful, violent, sexual, with a functional dimension. Naderism was an attempt to draw a veil over this reality, to pretend that seat-belts and crumple-zones and baby-seats would make safe this killing machine, domesticate it. But to Ballard, this was a lie, like the lie that the home itself is a safe place.[26]

Contrary to the moralistic media outrage which greeted the film, *Crash* does not offer itself as a realistic documentation of the near future; rather, it peels back the skin of the already present.

Ballard and Helen Remington have their first sexual encounter after the foreplay of sharing a crash experience, an event preceded cinematically by fetishized close-up shots of Ballard struggling with his seat belt and of Remington drawing in the smoke of her cigarette as they drive together, away from viewing the seductive lines of twisted metal of the previously wrecked car (body). Her leather-gloved hands slide over the steering wheel as he struggles to prolong control upon crash impact. She then suggests mutual relief in the nearby airport garage where they have to struggle with the barriers of steering wheel, car seat, and seat belt to press flesh against flesh.

The primary crash fetishist, Vaughan, drives a black 1963 Lincoln as a means of fulfilling his fantasy of driving a genuine celebrity crash(ed) car, as Ballard observes: "I take it that you see Kennedy's assassination as a special kind of car crash?" Vaughan *cruises* highway crash sites like a fetish addict haunting so many seedy backroom clubs, probing the ruins with his camera lens, as Roy Grundmann describes him: "Like an aroused teenager in a porn shop, he 'browses' these crash sites and comes in his pants at the site of mutilated bodies getting cut out of car wrecks by rescue workers."[27] After Vaughan's fatal crash, the metal body of his car is resurrected for the film's final crash orgasm, if ultimately unfulfilled due to the survival of the participants. The orgasm of crash impact is itself transcended by the performative value of the (celebrity) crash spectacle. When the fatal car crash of James Dean is re-created in the film it is staged as "a moment that would create a Hollywood legend"—making "real" that event of media history through a re-writing of the rules-of-the-road, of the hegemonic commodity value of the space of the city and the body in space, *and* through the creation of a new carnivalesque spectacle. The Dean reference further identifies what Grundmann describes as the North American "link between the sexual revolution and the car culture."[28] The disabled Gabrielle (Rosanna Arquette), bound in steel and black leather leg- and body-braces, can fondle a shiny new car in a dealer showroom, but when the sharp edge of her leg brace tears the expensive upholstery, the previously excited salesman becomes limp with despair. A reviewer of the film describes the transgression of rules along with a sense of hesitation toward its eroticization:

> Eventually everyone fucks everyone, although no one seems to be getting off. Staging a head-on collision between Eros and Civilization produces its own brand of performance anxiety . . . According to the rules that drive this particular fetish, anything short of self-destruction is just going through the motions. And in the end, the characters are in bondage to metaphor—which is, after all, the paradox of fetishism.[29]

Even as the police arrive and disperse the participants and spectators of the crash re-creation event, the film engages a rhizomatic assemblage, ceaselessly producing new networks of flight in the act of bodily contact, however fatal these may be. Jean-Luc Nancy describes bodily contact as the interruption of space, of the principle of spacing, in a philosophical move beyond the Heideggerian jargon of spatial authenticity. Nancy describes a spacing in-between the overlapping spheres of art and sensuality: "Touch *is* the interval and the heterogeneity of touch . . . the proximity of the distant, the approximation of the intimate."[30] Art gestures toward a destruction of unity, not a synaesthesia of that which is apprehended via cultural construction. The disciplined body likewise becomes a site of Deleuzean emancipation in the trajectory of desire out from under the catastrophe of history.

THE END OF VIOLENCE

The Nancyian move toward heterogeneity via touch is blockaded by the systems of technological mediation overdetermining the dominant culture of Wim Wenders' *The End of Violence*. In between human contact are the telephone, cellular phone, video phone, and e-mail, the gridlock of the so-called "information highway." A character in Wenders' film keeps asking: "Define violence?" Her fictional role in the film is as a stuntwoman, situating her own body in sites of physical danger for the sake of movie-made illusions of violence, illusions based on a double-displacement of the fictional body of the movie star and that of the body of the stunt double from the bodies in the space of the theater. The job requires knowing the limits of danger, and, after asking for a definition of violence in the opening shot, she turns her head toward the movie pyrotechnics and is burned on the face by the explosion. She asks her question once again, looking into the eye of the mass media storm, the viewer alienated by her pain. Her question draws attention to the violence of displacement. Later she is cast in a speaking role, but her personal and professional aspirations are disappointed when the production is prematurely stopped because it no longer fits the global-market strategy of the media conglomerate funding it.

Just as the spent metallic flesh of crashed car bodies is deposited beneath the elevated highways of *Crash*, it is beneath the concrete tangle of Los Angeles freeways in *The End of Violence* that the bullets of state-inscribed paranoia explode in the ground zero of human flesh. Like Haussmann's design of the wide boulevards of nineteenth-century Paris to facilitate state intervention in class-based revolt, the contemporary city structure serves the exigencies of the new global (communications) economy, a design which limits the organized resistance to the regime of, in David Harvey's words, "flexible accumulation."[31] For the grim-faced FBI boss in charge of setting up an electronic veil of surveillance cameras over the city, violence is clearly out there, down on the streets. He prophesies the "end of violence" through the amassing of visual data of the disenfranchised masses. The everyday is reduced to a stream of televisual images, as if the electronic compression of the video signal and its telephoto images "squeezes" away alternative possibilities for social discourse. Those who are visualized through this apparatus are presumed criminal. What, after all, are they doing on the streets of LA outside of their cars?

Violence here is the act of looking, whether the violence of bodily mutilation in the opening explosion for the sake of cinematic voyeurism, or in the invasiveness of the apparatus of surveillance upon the everyday (**28, 29, 30, 31**). It is the violence of human connection sterilized by mediating devices of electronic chatter. When the computer scientist employed to develop the surveillance system attempts to break the "silence" of state secrecy after witnessing through this electronic panopticon a murder conspiracy, he is executed by a high-powered FBI bullet while standing at the edge of a hill looking down on the smoggy city of Los Angeles. That he is doomed from the beginning to such a fate is signified by his disavowal of the automobile and his preference for walking up the hillside on the way to work. His stated expertise is in mapping the solar system, and the urban surveillance apparatus is housed in a giant observatory/observation tower. The film implies a loss of the collective desire necessary to a creative imagining of the heavens, with the gaze redirected from the sky down toward those on the ground below, no longer in the hope of discovery but resigned to the scrutiny of social decay. Likewise, in the final image of the film, we look down from a helicopter over an oceanside pier as the scientist's maid/lover is facing down the gaze of her FBI handlers. When she indicates that she is quitting her servitude to the state apparatus, they reach for the cold steel of their guns. The ending recalls the circular paranoia of an earlier detective film in which the main character becomes increasingly unable to properly see or control events as he becomes enmeshed in a web of conspiracy—Arthur Penn's post-Watergate *Night Moves* (1975), which ends with the main character, Harry Moseby (Gene Hackman), literally going around in circles, wounded and trapped alone in a boat called the *Point of View*. Penn's film suggests, as Tag Gallagher has suggested, that the solution to contemporary American malaise "lies in some kind of interior investigation."[32] In Wenders' film, identity outside of

28, 29, 30, 31
"The apparatus of
surveillance" in
Wim Wenders' *The
End of Violence* (1997)
(Copyright Road Movies
Filmproduktion, 1997)

the fixed regimentation of instrumental society, or beneath the city's surface images, is no longer possible, except for the film's marginalized immigrant laborers. In both films, layers of conspiracy extend like waves far beyond the individual.

The film's answer to the question "What is violence?" is that the foundation of violence is in the willful insulation of one human from another within the frame of the urban. As Wenders has explained in a recent interview: "More than any other city, LA has created images of violence, of violent conflict, and in the long run, those images that it keeps creating have influenced the way the city . . . functions."[33] Less well-known in the movie-made popular imagination is the significant presence of military defense contractors in and around Los Angeles. If *Crash* visualizes carnage on the concrete highway, the damaging space of the electronic highway is no less severe. To be sure, this scenario is not merely the dystopian nightmare of the modernist sensibility of the European *auteur*—the concrete infrastructure of Los Angeles is increasingly an electronic panopticon. With specific reference to the proliferation of private security firms in Los Angeles, Mike Davis, in *City of Quartz*, describes the merging of architecture and policing practices:

> Welcome to post-liberal Los Angeles, where the defense of luxury lifestyles is translated into a proliferation of new repressions in space and movement, undergirded by the ubiquitous "armed response" [signage on the manicured front lawns of the wealthy].[34]

Davis goes on to demonstrate that it is not only the citizenry who are alienated, but that alienation is a decisive strategy of the "few good men" of the LAPD.[35] In Wenders' film, the state security forces are anonymous, hiding behind an infrastructure of surveillance cameras, black sunglasses, and high-powered rifles, save for a well-intentioned but ineffective boyish cop who joined the force, inspired by movie-made crime thrillers. Davis notes, however, that the apparatus of surveillance, paranoia, and terror in real life LA far exceeds that of the movies— even if the movies are more likely to reference these phenomena than are news and public commentators.[36] It is with chilling glee that technocratic carpetbaggers describe the wired future-present:

It is a world where there will be nowhere to hide, nor anywhere to hide anything. There are already devices under development that will see through walls and strip-search suspects from a distance, looking under their clothes and inside their bodies. Individuals may be identified by their unique smells and tracked down, or "recognized" electronically, even before they have had time to complete a crime. And thanks to cheap digital video cameras and powerful new search algorithms, individuals will be tracked by computers. There will be no anonymity even in the once welcoming crowds.[37]

This celebration of technocratic representation is a culmination of nineteenth century uses of photography to make visual and indexical the prevailing cultural image of the criminal body for the purpose of social control.[38] The entanglement of the stuntwoman in the machinations of state paranoia serves here as a legacy of this disciplinary marking of the body. The fetish of digitalia is a culmination of the emergence of the era of mechanical reproduction which saw the transformation of spatial relations in determining the rhythms of daily life and the body.

In this city of near-absolute surveillance, anonymity still remains possible for the underclass of immigrant laborers and servants—their neighborhoods are more likely to be ghettoized than monitored. It is among the disenfranchised that the main character, Michael Max, hides when he becomes a target of the security apparatus, having received secret state documents via e-mail. The insidious plans for the vast surveillance network are transmitted to him through the supposedly anonymous system of electronic mail. The ironic overlap of silence and invisibility against the massive technological infrastructure of communication and control is evidenced in the scene in which Michael Max escapes FBI detection when accessing his e-mail account at a storefront service provider—he is invisible in the company of a Mexican laborer family. Shortly after his account is accessed, a gun-waving, suit-wearing band of FBI agents storm the store (which is a branch of Kinko's, a large North American chain providing office services twenty-four hours a day for the disenfranchised white-collar masses). Max and friends are allowed to leave the premises because they are assumed to be irrelevant within this white urban technological domain.

Michael Max, a film producer, or producer of consumable space, produces cinematic images of violence which explicitly play to mass paranoia toward the unknown Other. In his introductory voice-over he describes his entrance into the profession as concomitant with these fears: "When I was a kid movies scared the shit out of me, and then when I grew up I went into the movie business . . . [I] turned what you could call a basic fear of strangers into a multi-million dollar enterprise. After all, paranoia is our number one export, everybody needs an enemy." The Ballard character in *Crash* is similarly a producer of sexploitation films which, like those of the action thriller genre, are produced for consumption in the global media marketplace. The precondition of entrance into this marketplace typically means a disconnection from signifiers of distinctive local identity. Place is transformed into the generic codes of urban life as televisual commodity.

END OF THE CENTURY IMAGE-MAKING

Both Cronenberg and Wenders have produced work which directly engages the nature of late-twentieth-century image-making which, for Cronenberg, is problematized in the electronic surveillance form of *Videodrome* (1982) and the hallucinogenic, paranoid images of *Naked Lunch*. If Cronenberg's films provide critical insight into the instrumentalization of space, they function dialectically with Wenders' temporal concerns. For Wenders, the recurring theme is the nature of, and hoped-for auratic ideal of, the cinematic image—especially in those works which explicitly refer to image-making, from *Lightning Over Water* (1980) through to *Lisbon Story* (1994) and that other film of ends, *Until the End of the World* (1991). These cinematic *ends* should not be simplistically understood as reflecting a neo-conservative "end of history." Rather, Wenders articulates what Canadian communications thinker Harold Innis called a "Plea for Time."[39] This process is not a declaration of victory over the forces of history but a call for an understanding of community and tradition in the face of its erasure by our ever-mounting accumulation of information. In each of these films, there is the problem of an inability to complete the picture, to obtain an "end" in fulfillment of utopian desire, and, in *Until the End of the World*, images have a destructive power, as they depict the ruins of modernity covered over by the healing power of words. There is in the title an expressed desire for redemption through an affirmation of love and return to tradition which is co-extensive with a (however troubling) restoration of the father, even as the father is distant or absent.

The biological father is replaced by the cinematic. In *The End of Violence* Samuel Fuller plays the scientist's father: aged, incoherent, and surrounded by dusty books, banging away slowly on a manual typewriter. Robert Kolker and Peter Beicken in *The Films of Wim Wenders* describe the recurring paternal relationship in his films as follows:

> In a world without adequate images, a world whose *mise en scène* has been used up by television and advertising and movies without imagination, and where the filmmaker, orphaned and without place, wanders through yet another culture to find paternal nourishment, survival comes through cinematic oedipalization.[40]

It is a search for an idealized *heimat* in the face of our modernist dissolving of tradition, of our erasure of "home."

As a famous film producer and as a threat to state security, Michael Max emerges as hyper-identified within the state and media apparatus. He can only gain the promise of anonymity offered by the city by joining the army of servants disenfranchised from the system of power, raking the leaves on the vast green lawns of multi-millionaires—his former neighbors. These workers are represented as having bonds of empathy and affection which far exceed the disconnection and deceit among those who rule the system and set limits on its imagery. If, in this neo-pastoral idealization, Wenders can rightly be criticized for simplifying the lives of these workers, he does so in order to deconstruct the facile outside world of greed and paranoia. The film offers islands of poetry preserved against this sea of spectacle, whether among the Mexican workers or in the spoken-word performances in which several of the characters participate on a small open theatre stage, in humble contrast to the ego- and money-driven antics taking place on the movie-industry stage. While the latter is a space for exploitative genre fantasy, the former is a place of reflection grounded in the desires and suffering of the human body.

For Michael Max, it is outside of the hegemonic structure of mass communications that he learns empathy for and emotional attachment with the people around him, and begins to understand how his former self was implicated in the process of alienation which informs our systems of urban organization. His entrance into subaltern space is a "rhizomatic rupture of the system of instrumentalization." The "rhizome" is Deleuze and Guattari's organic conceptualization of the production of ceaseless connections between semiotic chains. It is a production of unconscious desires, not the reduction or interpretation of desire which is psychoanalysis. Following the spiraling metaphor here, Michael Max has, according to David Rodowick's interpretation of Deleuze, become Other in his embrace of community imagined outside the glare of the coercive state apparatus. As Rodowick explains:

> Power articulates itself as a socially mandated force that limits the body's range of dynamic affects; becoming other emerges from a countervailing desire to evade those limits, to find lines of flight wherein new potentialities for desire and identity can be expressed.[41]

The film concludes on one of the many piers which extend outward along the ocean shore of Los Angeles, free from the abstracting circulation of automobiles, and one of the few public spaces available for the underclass who come here to fish and to dream in the lapping waves despite the pollution of the water by nearby offshore oil rigs and despite the dark suited FBI agents circling toward yet another target of systematized paranoia.

Michael Max's identity is masked by his new found social position—a "mask" which becomes his new face. As Deleuze and Guattari point out, meaning is no longer attached to the fixedness of identity: "The signifier is always facialized. Faciality reigns materially over that whole constellation of significances and interpretations . . . The mask does not hide the face, it is the face . . . There is no subject, only collective assemblages of enunciation."[42] The subject of the gaze is, after all, formed not merely by its presence within the frame but through the operation of ideology in the process of framing, a process well understood by modernism. The gaze includes misrecognition. Thus, the city as apparatus of violence is countered by the persistence of spaces of alterity and practices of deinstrumentalization.

NOTES

1. J. G. Ballard, interview by Lynn Barber, *Penthouse*, September 1970, cited in V. Vale and Andrea Juno, eds, "J. G. Ballard," *Re/Search*, vol. 8, no. 9, 1984, p. 156.

2. Vivian Sobchack, "Beating the Meat/Surviving the Text, or How to Get Out of This Century Alive," in Paula A. Treichler, Lisa Cartwright, and Constance Penley, eds, *The Visible Woman: Imagining Technologies, Gender, and Science*, New York and London: New York University Press, 1998, p. 319.

3. Steven Best and Douglas Kellner, *Postmodern Theory: Critical Interrogations*, New York: Guilford Press, 1991, p. 90.

4. Peter Morris, *David Cronenberg: A Delicate Balance*, Toronto: ECW Press, 1994, p. 106.

5. Morris, *David Cronenberg*, p. 76. Of Cronenberg's *Shivers*, Robin Wood states: "The entire film is premised on and motivated by sexual disgust." Woods, "An Introduction to the American Horror Film," in Bill Nichols, ed., *Movies and Methods*, vol. 2, Berkeley, CA: University of California Press, 1985, p. 216.

6. Mark Kermode and Julian Petley, in an excellent account of British tabloid-like hysteria over the film, note that one British Board of Film Classification member was discredited in the press for the "atrocity" of being a single-parent. They also cite as an example of the very narrow-minded limits on morality in this passage from the *Daily Mail*, "the initially heterosexual characters lose their inhibitions [and] they experiment pleasurably with gay sex, lesbian sex, and *sex with cripples*." "Road Rage," *Sight and Sound*, June 1997, p. 16. In North America, media mogul Ted Turner attempted to block the release of the film through his distribution company Fine-Line Features because of his baffling fears of "copycat incidents." Brian D. Johnson, "Waiting for *Crash*," *Maclean's*, November 11 1996, p. 72.

7. Fred Botting and Scott Wilson explain that "boredom is the film's milieu." "Automatic Lover," *Screen*, vol. 39, no. 2, Summer 1998, p. 186. Canadian academics have been especially quick to dismiss the complexity of this film. Representative responses are Ramsay, cited below, and Bart Testa at www.film/queensu.ca/fsac/Crash.html. That some Canadian film scholars saw fit to post brief and largely negative or reactionary responses to the film on this scholarly association website reveals the challenge to cinematic form and pleasure offered in *Crash*. A much more nuanced and engaged response is provided by William Beard, *The Artist as Monster: The Cinema of David Cronenberg*, Toronto: University of Toronto Press, 2001.

8. Barbara Creed, "The *Crash* Debate: Anal Wounds, Metallic Kisses," *Screen*, vol. 39, no. 2, Summer 1998, p. 175.

9. J. G. Ballard, "Introduction to *Crash*," *Foundation*, 9, November 1975, reprinted in *Re/Search* 98.

10. Jane Farrow, "Crash," *This Magazine*, January–February 1997, p. 24.

11. Daniel Bell, *The Coming of Post-Industrial Society*, New York: Basic Books, 1976.

12. David Harvey, *The Condition of Postmodernity*, Cambridge, MA and Oxford, UK: Blackwell, 1990, p. 170.

13. J. G. Ballard, "Introduction to *Crash*," p. 96.

14. Linda Ruth Williams, "The Inside-out of Masculinity: David Cronenberg's Visceral Pleasures," in Michele Aaron, ed., *The Body's Perilous Pleasures: Dangerous Desires and Contemporary Culture*, Edinburgh: Edinburgh University Press, 1999, p. 44.

15. Gilles Deleuze and Félix Guattari, *Anti-Oedipus: Capitalism and Schizophrenia*, trans. Robert Hurley, Mark Seem, and Helen R. Lane, Minneapolis: University of Minnesota Press, 1983, p. 5.

16. Roy Grundmann, "Plight of the Crash Fest Mummies: David Cronenberg's *Crash*," *Cineaste*, 22, 4, Fall 1996, p. 27.

17. Chris Rodley, "Game Boy," *Sight and Sound*, April 1999, p. 10.

18. Linda Ruth Williams, "The Inside-out of Masculinity."

19. Christine Ramsay, "Dead Queers: One Legacy of the Trope of 'Mind Over Matter' in the films of David Cronenberg," *Canadian Journal of Film Studies*, 8, 1, Spring 1999, p. 54.

20. Gilles Deleuze and Félix Guattari, *A Thousand Plateaus: Capitalism and Schizophrenia*, trans. Brian Massumi, Minneapolis: University of Minnesota Press, 1987, p. 30.

21. Botting and Wilson, p. 191.

22. Herbert Marcuse, *One-Dimensional Man*, Boston: Beacon Press, 2nd edition, 1991, p. 75.

23. Michel Foucault, *Discipline and Punish: The Birth of the Prison*, trans. Alan Sheridan, New York: Vintage-Random House, 1979.

24. Walter Benjamin, "Paris, Capital of the Nineteenth Century," in Peter Demetz, ed., *Reflections*, trans. Edmund Jephcott, New York: Schocken Books, 1978, p. 162. I have taken some liberty with my citation of Benjamin which in *Reflections* reads as follows: "In the convulsions of the commodity economy we begin to recognize the monuments of the bourgeoisie as ruins even before they have crumbled."

25. David Cronenberg, *Crash*, London: Faber and Faber, 1996, p. 4.

26. Leslie Dick, "*Crash*," *Sight and Sound*, June 1997, p. 49.

27. Grundmann, p. 25.

28. Ibid., p. 25.

29. Brian D. Johnson, "Crash Test," *Take One*, Fall 1996, p. 8.

30. Jean-Luc Nancy, *The Muses*, trans. Peggy Kamuf, Stanford, CA: Stanford University Press, 1996, p. 17.

31. Harvey, p. 124.

32. Tag Gallagher, "*Night Moves*," *Sight and Sound*, Spring 1975. p. 87.

33. Scott Macaulay, "Crime Scene," *Filmmaker*, Fall 1997, p. 40.

34. Mike Davis, *City of Quartz: Excavating the Future in Los Angeles*, New York: Vintage-Random House, 1992, p. 224.

35. Davis, *City of Quartz*, p. 251.

36. Davis, *City of Quartz*, p. 252. Davis notes that police helicopter patrols over Los Angeles exceed those of the British army over Belfast.

37. "Technospy: Nowhere to Hide," *New Scientist*, 4, November 1995, p. 4, cited in Mike Davis, *Ecology of Fear: Los Angeles and the Imagination of Disaster*, New York: Metropolitan-Henry Holt, 1998, p. 368.

38. Tom Gunning, "Tracing the Individual Body: Photography, Detectives, and Early Cinema," in Leo Charney and Vanessa R. Schwartz, eds, *Cinema and the Invention of Modern Life*, Berkeley, CA: University of California Press, 1995, p. 20.

39. Innis made important links between systems of communication and the centralization of power, indicating that our contemporary obsession with the new reveals a spatial bias at the expense of an understanding of tradition, of continuity in time: "We must appraise civilization in relation to its territory and in relation to its duration. The character of the medium of communication tends to create a bias in civilization favourable to an over emphasis on the time concept or on the space concept and only at rare intervals are the biases offset by the influence of another medium and stability achieved." Harold A. Innis, *The Bias of Communication*, Toronto: University of Toronto Press, 1951, p. 64.

40. Robert Phillip Kolker and Peter Beicken, *The Films of Wim Wenders: Cinema as Vision and Desire*, Cambridge: Cambridge University Press, 1993, p. 89.

41. D. N. Rodowick, *Gilles Deleuze's Time Machine*, Durham, NC, and London: Duke University Press, 1997, p. 155.

42. Rodowick, *Gilles Deleuze's Time Machine*, pp. 115, 130.

CODA

THE CITY REBORN: CINEMA AT THE TURN OF THE CENTURY

JOHN ORR

The concept of the cinematic city suggests for us an objective material world, the narrative or documentary framed against the agora of human densities, asphalt in summer heat. Yet we know this is often a *trompe l'oeil*. In *Blade Runner* (1982), Animoid Row on the Warner back lot, the same thoroughfare that had once been Main Street in *The Big Sleep* (1946), seems more real to the viewing eye than Ridley Scott's takeover of LA's Bradley Building as the chic detritus of future worlds. We cannot say that the studio back lot is designed and the city building is real, because the latter was also designed as the expression of a form with a future, both living and lived-in. In the course of time, with neglect or decay, any great building can end up as chic detritus and that is surely one of the poignant visual moments of Scott's film. Harlem, built as a pricey extension of Manhattan for a class of bourgeois customers who did not exist in large enough numbers to fill it, became at the turn of the twentieth century something else. Many of its sumptuous apartments were subdivided for families of poor migrants providing cheap labor. Most of those families were black. A century later it has remained a badge of ethnic identity in the city, a Dutch name with an African-American character, a city within a city. Officially part of Manhattan, it is usually seen at the north end of Central Park, as being *apart* from Manhattan, a chasm whose essence is captured, quite brilliantly, by Spike Lee in *Jungle Fever* (1991).

The designed world of the cinematic city thus refracts the designed world of the living city, and often adds its own signatures. This has been one of the great challenges of location shooting of the past thirty years or more. It isolates the urban segment and transforms it into a scene.[1] For *Blow-up* (1966), Antonioni took over Marion Park in South London, had it spruced up, then had its tree-trunks painted gray and its grass greener to make it change identity at different stages of the film. In *Do the Right Thing* (1989), Spike Lee took over two blocks in Brooklyn's Bedford-Stuyvesant, his security guards moving out local drug dealers for the duration of the shoot while store-fronts and buildings were painted red in order to connote summer heat. In *Cyclo* (1995), Tran Anh Hung got authorization to build a two-story house on a gap site in the Cholon district of Saigon, aka Ho Chi Minh City, only to burn it down to the ground in the final sequence of the film, a conflagration that is Poet's nemesis, the doomed figure of Tony Leung engulfed in apocalyptic flames.[2] In *Nil by Mouth* (1997), the most architectural of the London films of the 1990s, Gary Oldman uses an uninhabited council estate in South London for its concrete walkways and endless corridors to chart the restless search of Charlie-Creed Miles for his next fix. As a narrative that is in part a memory film, *Nil by Mouth* brings back to life the recently disused and discredited—the modernist high-rise become instant slum, deserted by most of its dwellers, and then closed down. The film thus reinstates the moribund dwelling-place as live *mise en scène*, evoking once more its transient conquest of nature by concrete. The sequence of its use transforms it cinematically into an image of living death.

In a way, the cinematic city always imitates urban life. City dwellers not only live in a world planned for them by designers, builders, and architects, they also create their own life-worlds within, saturated in the symbolic, which is drenched and varied.[3] The metropolis is thus never the sum of its physical parts but an accretion of living tissue, of both humdrum activities (work, commuting, shopping, eating, and sleeping) and public spectacle (the festivals, celebrations, riots, and demonstrations which define its flowing history). A film is both representation of that living tissue and an integral element within it. It not only records and documents the symbolic. It is itself symbolic. Thus, technically, film is always a two-fold meditation on the ground and the nature of its own being. In the contemporary city, the density of the nature of being, social and symbolic, refracts itself in narrative and iconic density. This is neatly illustrated by the Warsaw apartment block Kieślowski uses in his *Dekalog* series (1988). In the 1980s it was a modern but modest building for professionals a few minutes walk from the city center. In Kieślowski's ten narratives it comes to have a filmic identity which goes far beyond its actual one.[4] For the duration of the *Dekalog* shoot the flat-dwellers continue with their own lives, though getting increasingly tired, as Kieslowki admitted, of obtrusive film shoots featuring fictional characters on their patch. For their building gets taken over as a character in a film series so that it wears a double identity—an actual one which is always symbolic, and a symbolic one grounded in the actual where it becomes both more and less than what it is in everyday life.

What sparks the revival of the cinematic city in time present? There is no one factor but many prevailing ones which surprise, which enrich, and which in their scope now encompass the globe. Let us take nine world cities and nine films each set in one of them: New York, London, Birmingham, Paris, Copenhagen, Hong Kong, Ho Chi Minh City, Buenos Aires, Toronto. The films are as follows: *Jungle Fever*, *Naked*, *Felicia's Journey*, *J'ai pas sommeil*, *Pusher*, *Fallen Angels*, *Cyclo*, *Happy Together*, and *Crash*. Taken together these films probe and challenge. They unsettle the viewer. They invoke our curiosity not through the prurient or the sensational, but through their vision of what in our everyday lives we often wish to ignore. Above all, they are not politically correct in any devalued sense of the term, paying token homage, as Hollywood sometimes does, to something it neither believes nor understands. The films all share a discomforting vision of the cruel or the unjust that has no obvious solution. They vary in their affirmative structures of feeling. For all present us with iconic figures moving through high densities of metropolitan life, who remain, in so many different ways, solitary, and forlorn. Often anti-heroic, these figures are fated to be free, but city life has a circularity of its own which can bring them all back to a destructive point of origin. This, above all, is the *fabula* of the cinematic city.

We can start with Claire Denis' *J'ai pas sommeil* (*I Can't Sleep*, 1994) since, in Anglophone culture, it is the most neglected of the nine films.[5] Based on an actual case of the serial killing of aging women in Paris, it stands at the epicenter of so many themes here. Like Atom Egoyan's *Felicia's Journey* (1999), it inverts the conventions of the Hollywood serial killing genre and touches base with its great European predecessor, Fritz Lang's *M* (1931). Like Wong Kar-wai's *Happy Together* (1997), it follows the incomer into the foreign city and explores the contingencies of a gay relationship without sentimentality. Like Neil Jordan's *The*

Crying Game (1992), it probes the lure and risk of gay transvestitism. Like *Jungle Fever*, it confronts the city tensions of racial difference and interracial passion. Like *Naked* (1993) and *Fallen Angels* (1998), it charts the phenomenology of the transient dwelling-place. Like his counterpart in *Pusher* (1996), its central male figure is doomed by a criminality that seems acquired through place and propinquity, drift and perversity, and that is clearly no second skin. Like Kowloon in the films of Wong Kar-wai, Montmartre here is both a place of migrants and a place of transient contacts leading nowhere in particular. We can pair other films in similar ways. *Crash* (1996) and *Felicia's Journey* see the car as a source of serial destruction. *Naked* and *Felicia's Journey* project the incomer as heroic victim of the English city. *Cyclo* and *Pusher* chart the wafer-thin but vital difference between criminal and gangster in the world of street risk. *Cyclo* and *Naked* have apocalyptic overtones normally found in the futuristic city of science fiction but here retro-fitted into the living city of the present with disturbing consequences. Finally, *Crash* and *Fallen Angels* are symphonies of spatial disconnection that show us living closely beside each other but never with each other. The former cannot escape from the world of the car while the latter never enters it.

Spatial disconnection is in fact a key theme running through the *fabula* of the new cinematic city. The recent digital feature by Mike Figgis, *Time Code 2000*, runs four parallel stories time-coded onto a screen with a four way split, each narrative filmed simultaneously in a single take on a Friday afternoon in 1999.[6] A mobile psychodrama of vacant media people in Hollywood, it has strong echoes of Altman's *Short Cuts* (1993) and *The Player* (1992). Yet its stylistic ingenuity lies in making the stories overlap as characters swap frames by moving from one screen into another and as the hand-held cameras at times practically converge, invading each other's filmic space. Thus the characters and their stories are conceded by overlapping, time-coded spaces but the mode of filming the narrative and of viewing the film on a screen split into four segments suggests a disconnection both plastic and psychological at the same time, dislocation as both a psychic and a technical predicament. One thing is for sure. The digital use of cinematic space here calls into question the clichéd sign-posting of the postmodern as the pure site of pastiche or nostalgia, or as a triumph of popular over art cinema.

Similarly, Denis' film is neither highbrow nor popular, nor is it concerned with pastiche or nostalgia. It is concerned, urgently, with the psychic and plastic disconnections of the living moment and if we wish to save the concept of the "postmodern," forge it as intellectual force field, and not retain it as a cardboard effigy, we have to push it in that direction or invent an analogous term. Lyotard, for example, has recently viewed the literary postmodern against the grain as a complex fable of solitude about modernity's fate.[7] Equally, the cinema at its most daring fabulates the fate of modernity in the city through its negative dialectic, through its denial of any rhetoric of the organic life-world and through its polyphonic vision of disconnection. Here solitude so conceived is both social and psychic condition and often rendered through a *mise en scène* of free indirect subjectivity.[8] We see the city through the eyes of the figure in the city—David Thewlis in London's *Naked*—but the camera is also fixed on the seeing figure placed in the urban scene as interstitial, as intersecting matrix of configuration and event. The lens, we might say, is focused on the figure as a form of magnificent obsession. This double-register is an indexical challenge to film form and to its constant reinsertion. This phenomenology of the peripatetic that results, of the lone figure moving through a volatile cityscape where speed of solitary movement is matched by speed of collective rotation, is a vision altered through a skewed point of view of the *coeval disconnection* that affects us all.[9] So many things happen at once that we are both a part of them and apart from them, torn and turned around by imploding ubiquities. There is no reclusive garret, no alienation, no hiding place. We are among those from whom and from which we are detached. We experience simultaneously a multitude of events that are unrelated. In Kieślowski's *Three Colors: Red* (1994), young Geneva city dwellers find their lives to be governed by the diktat of the telephone as a source of fragmented and discontinuous connection, only for one of them, Irène Jacob, to find out that Jean-Louis Trintignant, retired judge on the edge of the city, has set up his own system of illicit bugging, a renegade nerve center of sonic surveillance. Thus it is that she confronts the hidden voyeur of her own intimacies in a fractured gesture of love.

We may call the cinematic fable of the contemporary city *hyper-modern* if we wish to indicate a number of vital things.[10] The first is the implosive nature of communication. We now have more ways of communicating with each other than ever before, which move with greater speed than ever before but, as *Red* shows us, the power of the telephone disconnects as much as it connects. Of course, the speed of connection and disconnection is referenced in mainstream Hollywood movies but they have specific agendas of closure that undermine the vision. In Stone's *Wall Street* (1987), they are rampant but still play second fiddle to an old-fashioned, at times sentimental, melodrama, when Charlie Sheen learns a moral lesson about greed. In romantic comedy, by contrast, closure is a form of magical enchantment. *One Fine Day* (Michael Hoffman, 1996) lives up to its title by showing us the speed synchronizations of Manhattan life for hyperactive professionals. Architect Michelle Pfeiffer and journalist George Clooney are single parents fated to meet through their respective kids, and they fretfully negotiate mutual childcare to save their day from disaster—which, against all odds, they finally do, and fall in love at the same time.

This then is the fairytale of the speed city for late-night video viewing. But the cinematic vision of disconnection is something much tougher and more disturbing. There are no magical resolutions. In *J'ai pas sommeil*, Denis shows us the intersecting Parisian lives of two different icons of otherness, the criticized gay Camille (Richard Courcet) from Martinique, the tough disoriented Daiga (Katerina Kolubeva) from Lithuania. They are binary opposites from east and west of the sophisticate's favorite world city—one black male, the other white female, one Francophone, the other speaking no French—criss-crossing without obvious issue as Denis uses deft parallel montage in a stylistic echo of *M* to match its disturbing theme. Both central figures are tough and tender in alternating ways. Their lives intersect in the same hotel yet they are separate. Camille beats up his white lover then adores his young nephew. Drunk, Daiga dances affectionately with Line Renaud as the older woman reminisces about men, yet earlier she has rammed the car of the theater director who betrayed her acting ambitions. Camille and his white lover are the serial killers sought by the police at the start of the movie, but Denis does not reveal this until halfway through, and then casually as if plot revelation is like the act of murder itself, a necessary surplus, an adjunct to daily life for the transgressing lovers, an ancillary ritual of desire.

Absence of motive here is intentional, and the lack of affect links Denis' film to the city movies of Kieślowski and Wong Kar-wai. The event supersedes the motive. The look supersedes the spoken word. How can that be? How can it work, that is to say, as credible narrative? The answer lies in another facet of the city equation, the chance encounter. From the outside, they are strangers. Yet Camille and Daiga are aware of each other as their paths intersect, and here Denis is superb in displaying their bodily chemistry. Daiga's curiosity about the gay Caribbean mirrors our own and reverses the gender conventions of watching. Denis shows crude instances of male harassment of Daiga in street and cinema but then she becomes a casual pursuer of Camille and her curiosity becomes a form of desire. She suspects him of being the killer the police seek yet makes no judgment. Desire, in her case, is purely for the fleeting proximity of the Other's body, an erotic moment Denis renders superbly in a wordless café scene between the two of them. Desire as the fleeting proximity of the Other's body: a central trope for the cinematic city.

We can link the predicament here with Wong Kar-wai's gay Hong Kong couple adrift in Buenos Aires where the presence of the *known* other threatens to cancel out the capacity of the stranger for adventure in the foreign city. *Happy Together* is an ironic title precisely because contingency-in-isolation is a source of misery. The lovers who are no longer lovers are neither strictly tourists nor migrants, unsure about the length of their stay and taking up odd jobs and hustling in order to survive. In the foreign city on "the other side of the globe," Leslie Cheung and Tony Leung cannot bear to live either with or without each other. Unlike Paris, the promised city where Daiga is betrayed, Buenos Aires is not a promised city in the mythic sense that San Francisco might be for the disoriented lovers. It is the site of an indeterminate existence where the Southern part of the continent lacks the aura of its Northern counterpart. The Southern hemisphere is not the Northern hemisphere. Argentina is not the United States, and since there is no American Dream there is no betrayal by it either. There is simply a series of disconnected episodes by which the lovers try to impose meaning on an open-ended adventure reeking of *ennui.* Yet the visual image is anything but indeterminate. The seedier sections of Buenos Aires, to which the filmmakers seem naturally to gravitate, are given a visual force equivalent to Kowloon in their Hong Kong movies.[11]

The most affirmative of the key city films of the last decade or so is, strangely enough, *Jungle Fever*, often overlooked by critics enraptured by Lee's equally powerful *Do the Right Thing*.[12] The unease felt by many viewers and critics when watching this film is the racial cross-over in passion, a divide boldly broached by Cassavetes in *Shadows* (1959) but studiously avoided, for example, in the New York films of Allen and Scorsese. The tensions of racial divide here are countered by disparities of class. Lee, who grew up in the Bensonhurst section of Brooklyn, where part of the action is set, proves himself a sharp observer of both African-American and Italian-American lifestyles and an expert director of both black and Italian actors. Here the central relationship is between a middle class black architect (Wesley Snipes) and a working class temping secretary (Annabella Sciorra) who is appointed to his office. The issue of race makes salient a form of identity and difference that also appears in *Naked*—the pairing of characters matching identical trajectories of fate to non-identical natures. Sciorra leaves the shy, self-effacing neighborhood boy Paulie (John Turturro) for the sensuous, talented, and self-assertive Snipes. Yet Turturro then falls, on the rebound, for the only black woman in his neighborhood. The personalities of Snipes and Turturro are as alike as chalk and cheese, yet both opt for interracial intimacy—erotic curiosity about the racial other that generates conflict within their own families. Within his family, the ambition of Snipes contrasts with the social descent of his brother, a thieving crack-head out on the street and robbing his own parents to feed his habit. This fraternal pairing is echoed in Denis' film where Camille, the hustler, is contrasted with brother Richard, the house decorator, striving against the stigma of race to make an honest franc, and also struggling, like Snipes, to keep his family together.

Yet this is not the naturalistic narrative of misfiring intimacies we associate with Allen, though Lee does share the same comic powers of observation. Snipes' architect is called Flipper Purify and this fabulist naming, in which he inherits with some irony the "purifying" mantle of his clergyman father (Ossie Davis), recalls the idiom of Ralph Ellison's novel *Invisible Man* (1952). Flipper differs from Ellison's unnamed narrator in being highly visible in a changed world but equally frustrated in his ambitions by the structures of white power. Moreover, Lee uses Flipper's family as a hyper-modern device to compress a whole range of social potentialities into a single spectrum. The devout fundamentalist father, the narrow, diligent mother, the sophisticated light-skinned wife, and Gator, the conniving addicted brother (Samuel Jackson), embody much more than "character." They are living attributes of different aspects of life in the city that, pressed hopelessly together, explode. Thus the preacher-father's murder of the crack-head brother is a hyper-event, echoing in real life the murder of Marvin Gaye by his own clergyman father, and echoing here a vast array of differences within black American life topographically compressed into the space of Harlem itself and which the term "ghetto" cannot hope to encompass. As Snipes heads off from his parents' elaborate middle class apartment to the crack emporium nicknamed "Taj Mahal" where Gator is hanging out, the scene changes from family neighborhood to desolate wasteland populated by hookers and hustlers. Yet city anonymity is no alternative to neighborhood either. Snipes, thrown out of his own house by his unforgiving spouse, rents with Sciorra a desolate Manhattan apartment to which as a couple they fail to give any identity. The apartment as site of interracial passion that might be permanence to the "jungle fever" is an illusion. It remains a non-place through which they fleetingly pass before returning to their separate neighborhoods. Here Lee plays on "jungle" in its double sense, where the delirium of racial desire is fused with the rhythms of city, the rhythms here not of Harlem or Brooklyn but of the common meeting-point, Manhattan. Yet the metaphor takes hold. The fever subsides at the point where freedom becomes empty because disconnection is too great.

Audience unease with Lee's hyper-modern strategy is compounded by the nuances of pigmentation the film engages. This is not a film for anxious liberals seeking release through movie stereotypes of streetwise African-Americans talking cool and telling it how it is (**32**). The film shows that racial difference confounds us all and takes its urgency from that very predicament and has its own ironies. In choosing to have an affair, Snipes cheats on his wife with an Italian-American woman who appears darker in skin tone than she does. Tight-lipped liberal aversion to the talking through of racial difference is also counter-manded in a series of bluesy improvisations which are by turn witty, abrasive, therapeutic, and relentless. It is an acting out of something that remains a puzzle to its social actors even when they are pretending to themselves and to others that it does not. The film plays and replays that ragged ambiguity. For Lee, curiosity about the racial other is both affirmative and destructive, a breeding-ground of contradictions. In the life of the city where things move so quickly and so fleetingly, it can be enhancing or lethal.

The talking-out in *Jungle Fever*, though distinctly African-American, is also

32 Spike Lee's *Jungle Fever* (1991) (Copyright Universal Pictures, 1991)

part of a wider idiom within the city films of much Anglophone culture. Lee's fellow New Yorkers—Allen, Scorsese, and Cassavetes—most obviously come to mind, but in British cinema one encounters it too in the London films of Loach, Leigh, and Oldman. The "talk-out" influence of Lee and Scorsese on a younger generation of European filmmakers is equally apparent in other city movies that have made a recent impact—*La Haine* (1995), *Trainspotting* (1996), and *Pusher.* It invokes a performative aesthetic where the spoken word is itself a symbolic take upon the rhythms of the city life-world. The sound of the voice matches the pulse of movement. It hyper-ventilates in a ritual of ceaseless mimicry but, of course, is also an integral part of movement itself. Just as Gilles Deleuze stresses that in moving pictures there can be no separation of image and object, so the voice is integral to the audio-visual image *in perpetuum mobile.*[13] At the same time, there is a diametrical opposite, the aesthetic of ellipsis where in the films of Kieślowski, Egoyan, Denis, and Wong Kar-wai the word is used sparingly or indirectly, either in voice-over or in disembodied form on screens, radios, and telephones. It is as if in the cinematic city language is pushed to extremes in opposite directions and evacuates the middle ground of natural speech. The spoken word is everywhere or nowhere. Normal talk ceases to exist.

In *Naked*, the Word is certainly everywhere. Everyone talks but none more so than Johnny (David Thewlis) who can only rarely stop talking. The figure of the displaced rogue male recalls Travis Bickle in *Taxi Driver* (1976), but there are two key differences. Bickle is a psychopath who cannot articulate his rage and tries to replace the reality of a city he regards as a biblical Sodom with a deranged fantasy world of his own making. Johnny is articulate to a fault but incessant speculation runs away with him. He is smart enough to know the world he lives in is beyond his control but rejects, proactively, every aspect of it. He is thus a sociopath in one specific sense. He is reflexive enough to repudiate the social fabric of which he is a part, but his repudiation is addictive, unstoppable, and has a life of its own. Thus he disrespects—"disses"—everyone he knows and everyone he meets. Yet he cannot bear to leave the social stage that is street and city encounter. Repudiation must be endlessly repeated even if it brings in its wake danger and injury, which inevitably it does. Like the new generation of rogue males adrift in the city, he is also a misogynist, but this itself is a key symptom for the male sociopath. Generalized hatred of the social crystallizes around the figure of the sexual Other and brings in its wake a sado-masochist trap sprung out of the remnants of conscience, where he expects to be punished, gratuitously, for his own cruelty and is.

The disconnections of male and female are as stark here as in any recent film. Like Spike Lee, Mike Leigh uses doubling effects of identity and difference throughout his film. Whereas Lee invokes common destiny but different natures, Johnny's doubles are socially different versions of the same. His ex-girlfriend's posh landlord, Jeremy, acts out ceremonies of sexual degradation with the hapless Sophie (Katrin Cartlidge) which echo his own earlier in the picture. At night he encounters his Glaswegian double, quasi-criminal and fellow driver Archie (Ewen Bremner) as he waits for his feisty girl Maggie (Susan Vidler) in order to show male contempt. But Archie's contempt is mindless, not willful and reflexive, and Johnny watches the fractious encounter between the disconnected couple with his own disdain, only to realize, as their raised voices drift off, the chasm of city solitude which lies beyond all words.

In *Naked*, the different forms of misogyny are all a function of that solitude, but the single women in the film all suffer from the same plight. The expressionist tropes Leigh uses here—"Woman in Window," "Café Girl"—are the nameless faces that Thewlis meets and tries, without success, to seduce, falling back on that disdain for all things human that issues from disconnection. Leigh's London is in that respect not only a place where the homeless drift, but also a homeless place. The interior spaces of the film belong to no one in the film: the empty postmodern office block watched over by the night security guard, the featureless café waitressed by Gina McKee, the flat she borrows from two gays on extended holiday, are all placeless abodes like the rented house in which Louise and Sophie live and where Johnny crashes out, exploiting both of them from below just as Jeremy, their public school landlord, exploits them from above.

One key layer in the renewal of the cinematic city is thus the revelation of the *sociopathic*. We have already found it in *J'ai pas sommeil* where the serial killings are a form of anti-social rite. We see it too in the male dysfunctioning of *Nil by Mouth* where the unspoken insecurities of the working class male made socially redundant, find expression in the city's culture of risk, in the raw circulation of narcotics and violence as twinned addictions forming their own vicious circle. In *Fallen Angels*, Wong Kar-wai twins the narratives of two contrasting Hong Kong sociopaths who see themselves as part of the city's fabric and act out contrasting rituals of violation. Leon Lei is a professional hitman, meticulous in preparation, and kills without emotion. Takeshi Kanishero is a petty thief who takes over other people's businesses at night and enjoys terrorizing passers-by into becoming unlikely customers. The absurd thief is the deadpan killer's comic double. Their parallel lives circulate and pulsate as part of the city's amoral energy and, though they know nothing of each other, Wong glosses the irony of plot through vagaries of love. Michele Reis switches from her unrequited love for the hitman after he dies to an instant passion for the vaudeville sociopath who sweeps her away on his motorbike (**33**).

In *Crash*, Cronenberg glosses a different form of amoral circulation where sociopathic addiction twins the risk of the car crash with the erotic excitement it portends. The city here, Toronto, is a place of arterial routes and connections with no boundaries, no dividing line of city and suburb, city and country. The conurbation is literally meta-physical. The ritual event that defines the car is

Are we still partners?

33 Leon Lai and Michele Reis in Wong Kar-wai's *Fallen Angels* (1997) (Copyright Kino International, 1995)

also climactic, the destructive crash damaging flesh and metal alike, the orgasm of copulating car couples celebrating twinned forms of bodily motions moving with the car and each other at the same time. The sociopathic trope here is the banality of Eros and death. Choice of partner and car are both mechanical, until all the permutations are exhausted. If the prime mover of all this, Vaughan (Elias Koteas), is psychopathic in his death wish, it is because he has a utopian longing to expire in mid-crash. He wants to *die* like this while his (interchangeable) bourgeois friends and lovers simply want to *live* like this. They see no end to their studied perversion of the social, and they continue to be its living, but maimed, creatures.

The sociopathic city, therefore, is the habitus of those who see no alternative to perverse praxis and see no need of one. The reflexive car sociopaths of *Crash* are enthralled by their staged simulation of James Dean's fatal 1955 accident. The street sociopath of *Naked* catches an unlikely security guard off guard late at night by spouting at him from Revelations. In *Pusher*, the world of drugs also exudes a local knowledge that sustains and convulses all pushers in their brief delusions of grandeur. To know is to be smart, to be street-wise, to clinch the Big Deal. The deal, however, is prey to the vagaries of risk. Refin's film takes the form of a cine-diary, a week in the life of Frank (Kim Bodnia) in the streets, bars, and brothels of Copenhagen's Vesterbro district. Shot in the style of Dogme 95, it does what Dogme has to date studiously avoided. It insinuates its moving camera into the living tissue of the contemporary city. Though this is the land of Kierkegaard, this Diary of a Pusher is no Diary of a Seducer. There are no meditations on Eros, Faith, and the Existential Angst of Wrong Decisions. Yet this is precisely a film about wrong decisions. Somehow its visceral patterns externalize the angst of the impossible risk and the power of the false. It is written into the body language of its hapless hero and the terseness of talk without meditation. The chain of circularity is endless. He terrorizes and is terrorized, lends and borrows, betrays and is betrayed. Money and drugs are the only sources of credit in the sociopathic city and Frank, predictably, ends up without either. Betrayed by his dumb buddy and later by his hooker girlfriend, he is hounded by his gangster creditors into a void of non-being. He is still there on the city streets, ready for action, but his image is that of a ghost. Street wisdom is worthless but he knows no other world than this. It is a sorry predicament but the paradox is clear. This and its kindred pathologies in all the films we have looked at, and many more besides, have reinvigorated the cinematic city of recent years.

NOTES

1. Richard Sennett, *The Conscience of the Eye: The Design and Life of Cities*, London: Faber and Faber, 1993, pp. 159–63.
2. Tony Rayns, "Here and Now," *Sight and Sound*, April 1995, pp. 18–20.
3. Henri Lefebvre *The Production of Space*, Oxford: Blackwell, 1991, pp. 28–42. For the relationship of speed, space, and time in the contemporary city, see Barbara Adam, *Timewatch*, Oxford: Polity Press, 1995, pp. 107–23; Leon Kreitzman, *The 24 Hour Society*, London: Profile Books, 1999, pp. 136–51.

4. Darius Stok, ed., *Kieślowski on Kieślowski*, London: Faber and Faber, 1993, pp. 161–72.

5. Indeed, its scandalous lack of UK distribution ranks high among the recent atrocities of film commerce.

6. Jonathan Romney, "Time Code," *Sight and Sound*, August 2000, pp. 16–17.

7. Jean-Francois Lyotard, *Postmodern Fables*, trans. Georges van den Abbeele, Minneapolis: University of Minnesota Press, 1997, pp. 100–101.

8. Pier Paolo Pasolini, "The Cinema of Poetry," in *Heretical Empiricism*, Bloomington, IN: Indiana University Press, 1988, pp. 176–81. See also John Orr, *Contemporary Cinema*, Edinburgh: Edinburgh University Press, 1998, pp. 1–15.

9. John Orr, *The Art and Politics of Film*, Edinburgh: Edinburgh University Press, 2000, pp. 14–20.

10. For the use and meaning of the term "hyper-modern," see Mark Auge, *The War of Dreams*, London: Pluto Press, 1999, pp. 23–5; Paul Virilio, *Blue Skies*, London: Verso, 1995, pp. 48–61; Orr, *The Art and Politics of Film*, pp. 1–25.

11. See Chris Doyle's "To the End of the World," *Sight and Sound*, May 1997, pp. 14–17.

12. For an overall view of Lee's work, see Geoff Andrew, *Stranger than Paradise: Maverick Filmmakers in Recent American Cinema*, London: Prion Books, 1998, pp. 199–232.

13. Gilles Deleuze, *Cinema 2: The Time-Image*, London: Athlone Press, 1989, pp. 128–9.

LIST OF CONTRIBUTORS

Jude Davies is Senior Lecturer in American Studies at King Alfred's College Winchester, England. He is joint author of *Gender, Ethnicity and Sexuality in Contemporary American Film* (Keele University Press, 1998) and sole author of *Diana, A Cultural History: Gender, Race, Nation and the People's Princess* (Palgrave, 2001), as well as of numerous articles on US film and television, popular music, and the work of Theodore Dreiser.

Tony Fitzmaurice is College Lecturer at the Center for Film Studies/UCD School of Film, University College Dublin where he specializes in postwar American cinema and European—particularly Italian—modernist cinema. A graduate of UCD in English and in Film Studies, he previously taught at the National College of Art and Design, Dublin. He is the co-editor (with Mark Shiel) of *Cinema and the City: Film and Urban Societies in a Global Context* (Blackwell, 2001), and has published articles on Hollywood in the 1970s and on Irish and international contemporary art.

Matthew Gandy teaches geography and urban studies at University College London. He has also taught at the University of Sussex and has been a visiting scholar at UCLA and Columbia University. His most recent book is *Concrete and Clay: Reworking Nature in New York City* (MIT Press, 2002) which is an interdisciplinary account of the environmental history and changing landscape of New

York City. In addition to his research on urban and environmental history he has also published articles on the depiction of landscape in postwar European film.

Martin Gaughan was formerly Subject Leader in the History and Theory of Art at the University of Wales Institute, Cardiff, and previously taught at the universities of Leeds and East Anglia. His doctoral research was on Berlin Dada and Constructivism. He has published chapters on various aspects of German visual culture, most recently in *Crisis and the Arts: The History of Dada* (vol. 3, 1997), and "A Problem for Visual Representation in Germany in the 1920s" in *Work and the Image* (vol. 2, 2000). He has also co-edited volume 7 of *Crisis and the Arts: The History of Dada*, to be published in 2002. Forthcoming publications include a chapter on Berlin and Zurich Dada for the Open University, and a book on the relationship between technology and visual culture in Germany, 1907–37, due out in 2003.

Paul Gormley is Lecturer in Film and Media Studies in the School of Innovation and Cultural Studies at the University of East London. His research interests include contemporary film and film theory, and cultural theory. He has published articles on contemporary film in various publications including *Angelaki: A Theoretical Journal of the Humanities* and Chillfish.com.

Peter Jelavich is Professor of History at the Johns Hopkins University. He is the author of *Munich and Theatrical Modernism: Politics, Playwriting, and Performance, 1890–1914* (1985), *Berlin Cabaret* (1993), and the forthcoming *Berlin Alexanderplatz: Radio, Film, and the Death of Weimar Culture*. He currently is undertaking a study of censorship of the arts in Germany from 1890 to the present.

Jessie Labov is a doctoral candidate in the Department of Comparative Literature at New York University, where she is about to defend her dissertation, "Reinventing Central Europe from the West: *Cross-Currents* and the Dissident Intellectual in the 1980s." Her article on the politics of pseudonyms and blacklisting in US cinema, "Smithee in *The Twilight Zone*: *The People v John Landis* et al. and Other Trials of Authorship," appears in the volume *Directed by Allan*

Smithee (University of Minnesota Press, 2001). She has also written on Polish film and censorship during the Cold War, and the transatlantic reception of Andrzej Wajda and Jerzy Andrzejewski.

Paula J. Massood is Assistant Professor of Film Studies in the Film Department of Brooklyn College, City University of New York. Her articles on African-American film have appeared in *Cinema Journal*, *African-American Review*, and *Cineaste*. Her book, *Cities in Black: Visualizing African-American Urban Experiences in Film*, is forthcoming from Temple University Press.

Tyrus Miller is Associate Professor of Literature at the University of California at Santa Cruz, where he also coordinates the research cluster in Modernist and Avant Garde Studies. He is author of *Late Modernism: Politics, Fiction, and the Arts Between the World Wars* (University of California Press, 1999) and is completing a manuscript entitled *Resonances of the Readymade: Finding and Delay in Avant Garde Aesthetics*. For 2001–2003, he is Director of the University of California Study Center in Budapest, Hungary.

John Orr is Emeritus Professor of Sociology at the University of Edinburgh. Among his recent publications are *The Art and Politics of Film*, *Contemporary Cinema*, and *Post-Cinema and Modernity*, a film reader co-edited with Olga Taxidou. He is currently co-editing a book with Èlzbieta Ostrowska on Andrjez Wajda for Wallflower Press and researching in the areas of film theory and contemporary film.

Mark Shiel is Lecturer in Film Studies at the University of Leicester, where he specializes in American cinema, politics, and urban history. He is a graduate of Trinity College Dublin and completed his PhD, 'Radical Agendas and the Politics of Space in American Cinema, 1968–1974', at the British Film Institute in London in 1999. He is co-editor (with Tony Fitzmaurice) of *Cinema and the City: Film and Urban Societies in a Global Context* (Blackwell, 2001), has published a number of articles on the cinema–city relationship with regard to Dublin, Paris, Los Angeles, and New York, and is currently writing a book, *Italian Neorealism: Introduction to an Urban Cinema*, for publication with Wallflower Press in 2003.

Allan Siegel is a filmmaker and teacher. He was a founding member of the film production and distribution collective, Newsreel, and a co-director of Third World Newsreel. His films have been exhibited extensively at the major international film festivals and on television both in the United States and Europe. Both in New York and Chicago, he has taught in a wide range of academic and non-institutional environments, and continues to be actively engaged in issues of media education. Currently, he is an Adjunct Associate Professor in the Department of Film, Video, and New Media at the School of the Art Institute of Chicago. Among his present projects is the screen adaptation of the novel *Bait* by the celebrated Yugoslavian writer David Albahari.

David Sorfa is Lecturer in Screen Studies at Liverpool John Moores University, having previously lectured in film at Middlesex University, the International Study Center (Queen's University, Canada) and the Universities of Brighton and Sussex. He completed his MA in Literary Studies at the University of Cape Town, is currently finishing his PhD on Jan Švankmajer, Franz Kafka, and the Brothers Quay at the University of Kent at Canterbury, and will publish a monograph on Jan Švankmajer with Creation Books in 2003.

Carsten Strathausen is an Assistant Professor at the German and Russian Studies Department at the University of Missouri (Columbia). He has published numerous articles on literary and film history and on media theory. His book *The Look of Things: Poetry and Vision around 1900* is forthcoming from the University of North Carolina Press. He is currently working on a book-length manuscript entitled *Digital Photography and the Rhetoric of Seeing*.

Darrell Varga has a PhD in Social and Political Thought from York University, Toronto, and is completing a book on Spatial Theory and Canadian Film.

INDEX